BARRON'S

IELTS®

PRACTICE EXAMS

Third Edition

Lin Lougheed
Ed.D., Teachers College
Columbia University

IELTS® is a registered trademark of University of Cambridge ESOL, the British Council, and IDP Education Australia, which neither sponsor nor endorse this publication.

AUDIO AND AUDIOSCRIPTS

The MP3 files and audioscripts for all listening segments can be found online at
http://barronsbooks.com/tp/ielts/audio/

All inquiries should be addressed to:
Barron's Educational Series, Inc.
250 Wireless Boulevard
Hauppauge, New York 11788
www.barronseduc.com

Library of Congress Control Number: 2016939616

ISBN: 978-1-4380-7635-5 (Book with MP3 CD)

PRINTED IN THE UNITED STATES OF AMERICA
9 8 7 6 5 4 3 2

10%
POST-CONSUMER
WASTE
Paper contains a minimum
of 10% post-consumer
waste (PCW). Paper used
in this book was derived
from certified, sustainable
forestlands.

Contents

Introduction

WHAT IS IELTS?

The IELTS (International English Language Testing System) measures your English language proficiency for either academic or professional purposes. The Academic Module is for those planning to attend a university where English is the spoken language. The General Training Module is for those planning to live or work in an English-speaking country. The test is divided into four sections; each section tests a different language skill—Listening, Reading, Writing, and Speaking. The Listening and Speaking sections are the same for the Academic and General Training Modules, but the Reading and Writing sections differ.

TIP

Audioscripts for the Listening section of each test can be found on pages 421–457. If you do not have access to the MP3 files on the enclosed disk, please refer to the audioscripts when prompted to listen to an audio passage.

HOW TO USE THIS BOOK

This book contains six complete Academic Module tests and six Reading and Writing sections for the General Training Module.

The IELTS has four sections: Listening, Reading, Writing, and Speaking. The listening and speaking sections are identical for both Academic and General Training test takers. Therefore, those two sections are not repeated in the General Training part of this book. Students who are studying for the General Training module should use the Listening and Speaking sections of the Academic Module tests, and turn to the General Training part of this book for the Reading and Writing sections.

You can take each complete practice test, or you can focus on any specific section you wish. To take a complete test, Academic Module students can follow the sections of a test in the order they appear in the book. General Training Module students can do the following: Turn to Practice Test 1 in the Academic Module part of this book and complete the Listening section. Then turn to Practice Test 1 in the General Training part and complete the Reading and Writing sections. Return to the Academic Module and complete the Speaking section of the practice test. Repeat this process for each test.

Use these charts to find the sections you wish to study.

Academic Module

Practice Test	Listening Pages	Reading Pages	Writing Pages	Speaking Pages
1	16–20	24–32	38–40	41–42
2	58–62	66–75	82	83
3	98–102	106–116	122	123
4	138–142	146–156	162–163	164
5	180–184	188–196	202–204	205
6	220–224	228–236	242–243	244–245

General Training Module

Practice Test	Listening Pages	Reading Pages	Writing Pages	Speaking Pages
1	16–20	262–272	278	41–42
2	58–62	290–300	306	83
3	98–102	318–330	336	123
4	138–142	346–356	362	164
5	180–184	372–382	388	205
6	220–224	400–410	416	244–245

You can improve your language and test-taking skills by studying these additional IELTS books published by Barron's:

Barron's IELTS
Essential Words for IELTS
IELTS Strategies and Tips
Writing for the IELTS

USING THE ANSWER EXPLANATIONS

At the end of each test, you will find the Answer Explanations. By studying these explanatory answers, you will learn why your answer choice was correct or why it was wrong.

Of course, in the Writing and Speaking sections, there are many possible answers. In the Answer Explanations for the Writing section, you are shown a model answer that would receive a high band score.

The model answers for the Writing section demonstrate elements found in a high band score, including:

- addressing all parts of the task
- fluent cohesion of ideas with appropriate use of reference and logical connectors
- appropriate paragraphing with clear main ideas and adequate support
- accurate use of a wide range of vocabulary, idiomatic usage, and sense of lexical collocation
- fluent use of a wide variety of grammatical structures with a predominance of compound and complex sentences
- no personal references except in personal letters or personal opinion tasks

In the Answer Explanations for the Speaking section, you are shown a sample of the type of answers that would successfully complete the task. However, these are only models. During the actual IELTS Speaking section, an examiner will guide you through a conversation. It will be a normal conversation, not a scripted performance.

The Answer Explanations for the Speaking section demonstrate elements found in a high band score, such as:

- appropriate use of a variety of vocabulary
- use of a variety of well-connected sentence structures with consistent accuracy
- ability to discuss a variety of topics fluently and develop the topics well
- natural and accurate use of idioms

TIP

American English vs. British English **This book uses American English spelling, pronunciation style, and vocabulary. There are footnotes if British spelling or grammar differ from American. You will not be penalized if you use American spelling when you write your answers on the IELTS.**

When you answer the questions in the Speaking section of the IELTS, you will also be scored on your pronunciation and ability to speak clearly. To listen to and read transcripts of a sample IELTS speaking test, visit the IELTS.org website:

http://www.ielts.org/test_takers_information/test_sample/speaking_sample.aspx

IELTS STUDY CONTRACT

You must make a commitment to study English. Sign a contract with yourself. A contract is a promise. You should not break a contract, not even a contract with yourself.

- Print your name on the blank on the first line of the contract.
- On lines 5–8, write the amount of time you will spend each week studying English. Think about how much time you can study English every day and every week. Make your schedule realistic.

IELTS STUDY CONTRACT

I, _____ , promise to study for IELTS. I will begin my study with *Barron's IELTS*, and I will also study English on my own.

I understand that to improve my English I need to spend time using English.

I promise to study English _____ a week.

I will spend _____ hours a week listening to English.

I will spend _____ hours a week writing English.

I will spend _____ hours a week speaking English.

I will spend _____ hours a week reading English.

This is a contract with myself. I promise to fulfill the terms of this contract.

_____   _____
Signed   Date

- Sign your name and date the contract on the last line.
- At the end of each week, add up your hours. Did you meet the requirements of your contract?

SELF-STUDY ACTIVITIES

Here are some ways you can study English on your own. Check the ones you plan to try. Add some of your own ideas.

Internet-Based Self-Study Activities

LISTENING

☐ Podcasts on the Internet
☐ News websites: ABC, BBC, CBS, CNN, NBC
☐ Movies and TV shows in English
☐ YouTube
☐ Ted.com
☐ _____
☐ _____

SPEAKING

☐ Use Skype to talk to English speakers
☐ _____
☐ _____

WRITING

☐ Write e-mails to website contacts
☐ Write a blog
☐ Leave comments on blogs
☐ Post messages in a chat room
☐ Use Facebook and Twitter
☐ _____
☐ _____

READING

☐ Read news and magazine articles online
☐ Do web research on topics that interest you
☐ Follow blogs that interest you
☐ _____
☐ _____

Other Self-Study Activities

LISTENING

☐ Listen to CNN and BBC on the radio or on TV
☐ Watch movies and TV shows in English
☐ Listen to music in English
☐ _____
☐ _____

SPEAKING

☐ Describe what you see and what you do out loud
☐ Practice speaking with a conversation buddy
☐ Sing or recite song lyrics
☐ _____
☐ _____

WRITING

☐ Write a daily journal
☐ Write letters to an English speaker
☐ Make lists of the things you see every day
☐ Write descriptions of your family and friends
☐ _____
☐ _____

READING

☐ Read newspapers and magazines in English
☐ Read books in English
☐ Read song lyrics
☐ _____
☐ _____

Examples of Self-Study Activities

Whether you read an article in a newspaper or on a website, you can use that article in a variety of ways to practice reading, writing, speaking, and listening in English.

- Read about it.
- Make notes about it.
- Paraphrase, summarize, or write comments about it.
- Give a talk or presentation about it.
- Record or make a video of your presentation.
- Listen to or watch what you recorded. Write down your presentation.
- Find and correct your mistakes.
- Do it all again.

PLAN A TRIP

Go to *www.cntraveler.com*

 Choose a city, choose a hotel, go to that hotel's website, and choose a room. Then choose some sites to visit (*reading*). Write a report about the city (*writing*). Tell why you want to go there. Describe the hotel and the room you will reserve. Tell what sites you plan to visit and when. Where will you eat? How will you get around?

Now write a letter to someone recommending this place (*writing*). Imagine you have to give a lecture on your planned trip. Make a video of yourself talking about this place (*speaking*). Then watch the video and write down what you said (*listening*). Correct any mistakes you made and record the presentation again. Then choose another city, and do this again.

SHOP FOR AN ELECTRONIC PRODUCT

Go to *www.cnet.com*

 Choose an electronic product and read about it (*reading*). Write a report about the product (*writing*). Tell why you want to buy one. Describe its features.

Now write a letter to someone recommending this product (*writing*). Imagine you have to give a talk about this product. Make a video of yourself talking about this product (*speaking*). Then watch the video and write down what you said (*listening*). Correct any mistakes you made and record the presentation again. Then choose another product and do this again.

DISCUSS A BOOK OR CD

Go to *www.amazon.com*

 Choose a book or CD or any product. Read the product's description and reviews (*reading*). Write a report about the product (*writing*). Tell why you want to buy one or why it is interesting to you. Describe its features.

Now write a letter to someone recommending this product (*writing*). Pretend you have to give a talk about this product. Make a video of yourself talking about this product (*speaking*). Then watch the video and write down what you said (*listening*). Correct any mistakes you made and record the presentation again. Then choose another product and do this again.

DISCUSS ANY SUBJECT

Go to *https://simple.wikipedia.org/wiki/Main_Page*

 This website is written in simple English. Pick any subject and read the entry (*reading*).

Write a short essay about the topic (*writing*). Give a presentation about it. Record the presentation (*speaking*). Then watch the video and write down what you said (*listening*). Correct any mistakes you made and record the presentation again. Then choose another topic and do this again.

DISCUSS ANY EVENT

Go to *http://news.google.com*

 Google News has a variety of links. Pick one event and read the articles about it (*reading*).

Write a short essay about the event (*writing*). Give a presentation about it. Record the presentation (*speaking*). Then watch the video and write down what you said (*listening*). Correct any mistakes you made and record the presentation again. Then choose another event and do this again.

REPORT THE NEWS

Listen to an English language news report on the radio or watch a news program on TV (*listening*). Take notes as you listen. Write a summary of what you heard (*writing*).

Pretend you are a news reporter. Use the information from your notes to report the news. Record the presentation (*speaking*). Then watch the video and write down what you said (*listening*). Correct any mistakes you made and record the presentation again. Then listen to another news program and do this again.

EXPRESS AN OPINION

Read a letter to the editor in the newspaper (*reading*). Write a letter in response in which you say whether you agree with the opinion expressed in the first letter. Explain why (*writing*).

Pretend you have to give a talk explaining your opinion. Record yourself giving the talk (*speaking*). Then watch the video and write down what you said (*listening*). Correct any mistakes you made and record the presentation again. Then read another letter to the editor and do this again.

REVIEW A BOOK OR MOVIE

Read a book (*reading*). Think about your opinion of the book. What did you like about it? What didn't you like about it? Who would you recommend it to and why? Pretend you are a book reviewer for a newspaper. Write a review of the book with your opinion and recommendations (*writing*).

Give an oral presentation about the book. Explain what the book is about and what your opinion is. Record yourself giving the presentation (*speaking*). Then watch the video and write down what you said (*listening*). Correct any mistakes you made and record the presentation again. Then read another book and do this again.

You can do this same activity after watching a movie (*listening*).

SUMMARIZE A TV SHOW

Watch a TV show in English (*listening*). Take notes as you listen. After watching, write a summary of the show (*writing*).

Use your notes to give an oral summary of the show. Explain the characters, setting, and plot. Record yourself speaking (*speaking*). Then watch the video and write down what you said (*listening*). Correct any mistakes you made and record the presentation again. Then watch another TV show and do this again.

LISTEN TO A LECTURE

Listen to an academic or other type of lecture on the Internet. Go to any of the following or similar sites and look for lectures on topics that are of interest to you:

http://lecturefox.com

http://podcasts.ox.ac.uk

http://freevideolectures.com

http://www.ted.com/talks

Listen to a lecture and take notes as you listen. Listen again to check and add to your notes (*listening*). Use your notes to write a summary of the lecture (*writing*).

Pretend you have to give a lecture on the same subject. Use your notes to give your lecture (*speaking*). Record yourself as you lecture. Then watch the video and write down what you said. Correct any mistakes you made and record the lecture again. Then listen to another lecture and do this again.

WHERE CAN I FIND EXTRA HELP?

Visit the Learning Center on Dr. Lin Lougheed's website to view sample essays

www.lougheed.com

For test tips and new vocabulary words, follow Dr. Lin Lougheed on Twitter @LinLougheed.

Want your essays posted to Facebook for feedback from others? Post them directly.

http://www.facebook.com/EssayTOEFL.IELTS/
or search on Facebook for "**IELTS and TOEFL Essay Writing.**"

PART 1
Academic Module

**NOTE TO GENERAL TRAINING
MODULE TEST TAKERS**

If you are studying for the General Training Module Test, you will take the
Listening and Speaking sections in the Academic Module Practice Tests.
The Listening and Speaking sections are the same for all test takers.
See the charts on pages 1–2 for page numbers.

Academic Module

PRACTICE TEST 1

IELTS Listening Answer Sheet

No.	Answer	✓	✗		No.	Answer	✓	✗
1		1			21		21	
2		2			22		22	
3		3			23		23	
4		4			24		24	
5		5			25		25	
6		6			26		26	
7		7			27		27	
8		8			28		28	
9		9			29		29	
10		10			30		30	
11		11			31		31	
12		12			32		32	
13		13			33		33	
14		14			34		34	
15		15			35		35	
16		16			36		36	
17		17			37		37	
18		18			38		38	
19		19			39		39	
20		20			40		40	

Listening Total

ACADEMIC MODULE TEST 1

Candidate Name _____

International English Language Testing System

LISTENING

Time: Approx. 30 minutes

INSTRUCTIONS TO CANDIDATES

Do not open this booklet until you are told to do so.

Write your name in the space at the top of this page.

You should answer all questions.

All the recordings will be played ONCE only.

Write all your answers on the Question Paper.

At the end of the test, you will be given ten minutes to transfer your answers to an Answer Sheet.

Do not remove this booklet from the examination room.

INFORMATION FOR CANDIDATES

There are **40** questions on this question paper.

The test is divided as follows:

Section 1	Questions 1–10
Section 2	Questions 11–20
Section 3	Questions 21–30
Section 4	Questions 31–40

Track 2

SECTION 1

Questions 1–4

Complete the schedule below.
*Write **NO MORE THAN THREE WORDS** for each answer.*

TIP
If you do not have access to the MP3 files on the enclosed disk, please refer to the audioscripts starting on page 421 when prompted to listen to an audio passage.

Example

........Globetrotters...... Language School

Class Schedule

Chinese
Level: Advanced
Days: **1** .... evenings

Japanese
Level: **2** ....
Days: Tuesday and Thursday mornings

Level: **3** ....
Days: Monday, Wednesday, and Friday mornings

French
Level: Intermediate
Days: Friday **4** ....

Questions 5–8

Complete the information below.
*Write **NO MORE THAN ONE NUMBER** for each answer.*

Tuition Information

One week	**5** $.............................
Four weeks	**6** $.............................
Six weeks	**7** $.............................
Twelve weeks	**8** $.............................

Questions 9 and 10

Complete the sentences below.
*Write **NO MORE THAN THREE WORDS** for each answer.*

9 Students can register for a class by visiting ....

10 .... is in charge of student registration.

SECTION 2

Questions 11–15

Label the map below.
*Write the correct letter, **A–I**, next to **Questions 11–15**.*

City Shopping District

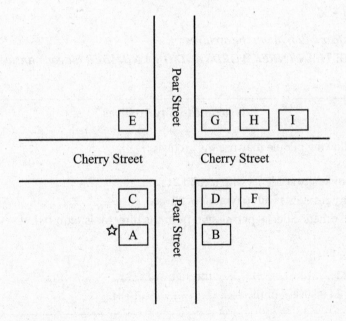

11 Harbor[1] View Bookstore ....

12 Pear Café ....

13 Souvenir Store ....

14 Art Gallery ....

15 Harbor Park ....

---

[1]British: harbour

Questions 16–20

Complete the sentences below.
Write **NO MORE THAN ONE WORD OR A NUMBER** *for each answer.*

Harbor Park

16 The park was built in ....

17 A .... stands in the center[2] of the park.

18 Take the path through the ....

19 In the middle of the garden is a ....

20 A .... takes you down to the harbor and a view of the boats.

(Track 4) **SECTION 3**

Questions 21–24

Complete the information about the archives.
Write **NO MORE THAN THREE WORDS AND/OR A NUMBER** *for each answer.*

Welcome to City Archives

The following people may use the archives:

- University students with a valid **21** ....
- City residents with payment of **22** ....
- All others: Special permission from the director is required.

Hours:
Days: **23** .... through ....
Hours: **24** 9:30 A.M. until .... P.M.

---

[2]British: centre

Questions 25–30

What can be found on each floor[1] of the archives building?
*Write the correct letter, **A–G**, next to **Questions 25–30**.*

> **CITY ARCHIVES**
>
> **A** nineteenth-century documents
> **B** maps
> **C** personal papers
> **D** photographs
> **E** books about the city
> **F** newspapers
> **G** information about the woolen[2] mill

Floor of the building

25 basement   ....

26 ground floor   ....

27 second floor   ....

28 third floor   ....

29 fourth floor   ....

30 fifth floor   ....

Track 5

SECTION 4

Questions 31–33

Complete the notes below.
*Write **NO MORE THAN TWO WORDS** for each answer.*

	Historical Uses of Wind Power
Ancient China	Windmills were used to **31** ....
Ancient Persia	Farmers used wind power to **32** ....
The Netherlands	People used windmills to **33** ....

---

[1]In the United States, the ground floor is considered the first floor; the next floor up is the second floor, and so on.

[2]British: woollen

Questions 34–40

Complete the chart[1] below.
*Write **NO MORE THAN TWO WORDS** for each answer.*

Wind Power

Advantages	Disadvantages
Unlike oil and coal, wind power does not cause **34**	The cost of the initial investment is high.
There are limited supplies of oil and coal, but wind is a **35**	The **37** .... of the wind is not constant.
It **36** .... to generate electricity with the wind.	Wind turbines are usually located far from **38** ....
Wind turbines do not take up much land.	Wind turbines may spoil **39** ....
	Wind turbines are as **40** .... as a high-speed car.

> **Take ten minutes to transfer your answers onto the Answer Sheet on page 13.**

---

[1]British: table

ANSWER SHEET
Academic Module
Practice Test 1

IELTS Reading Answer Sheet

	✓ 1 ✗
1	
2	2
3	3
4	4
5	5
6	6
7	7
8	8
9	9
10	10
11	11
12	12
13	13
14	14
15	15
16	16
17	17
18	18
19	19
20	20

	✓ 21 ✗
21	
22	22
23	23
24	24
25	25
26	26
27	27
28	28
29	29
30	30
31	31
32	32
33	33
34	34
35	35
36	36
37	37
38	38
39	39
40	40
Reading Total	

ACADEMIC MODULE TEST 1

Candidate Name _____

International English Language Testing System

ACADEMIC READING

Time: 1 hour

INSTRUCTIONS TO CANDIDATES

Do not open this booklet until you are told to do so.

Write your name in the space at the top of this page.

Start at the beginning of the test and work through it.

You should answer all questions.

If you cannot do a particular question, leave it and go on to the next. You can return to it later.

All answers must be written on the Answer Sheet.

Do not remove this booklet from the examination room.

INFORMATION FOR CANDIDATES

There are **40** questions on this question paper.

The test is divided as follows:

Reading Passage 1	Questions 1–13
Reading Passage 2	Questions 14–26
Reading Passage 3	Questions 27–40

Reading Passage 1

*You should spend about 20 minutes on **Questions 1–13**, which are based on Reading Passage 1 below.*

Odonata

Odonata is the order of insects that includes dragonflies and damselflies. To the human eye, their shining colors[1] and delicate-looking wings make them beautiful creatures to behold. In the natural world, however, they are fearsome predators. Dragonflies and damselflies get their name from the powerful serrated jaws they use to tear apart their prey. The word *odonata* means "toothed jaw."

Dragonflies and damselflies are often confused with each other because they are very similar. Close observation reveals the differences between them. The most obvious difference is the way they hold their wings while at rest. Dragonflies hold their wings out to the side while damselflies fold their wings back. Dragonflies have very large eyes that seem to cover the entire face because they are so close together that they touch each other. Damselflies' eyes are smaller, and there is a space between them. Dragonflies are larger and stronger animals than damselflies and fly longer distances. Thus, they can be found in woods and fields away from the water. Damselflies are not such strong fliers and are most often seen around the edges of ponds and streams since they do not normally fly far from the water.

The largest odonata living today are the Hawaiian endemic dragonfly and the Central American damselfly, each of these species having a wingspan of 19 centimeters. The smallest is the libellulid dragonfly, native to east Asia, with a wingspan of just 20 millimeters. Fossils have been discovered that prove that dragonflies have been in existence for over 300 million years. The largest dragonfly fossil ever found belongs to the now-extinct *meganeura monyi*, which lived 300 million years ago and had a wingspan of 75 centimeters. This giant was a fearsome predator indeed, which feasted on small amphibians as well as on other insects.

Dragonflies and damselflies both lay their eggs on or just below the surface of the water in a pond or stream. Some species lay their eggs on the stem of an aquatic plant. The babies emerge from the eggs in the form of nymphs. They live underwater, breathing through gills and preying upon water insects, tadpoles, small fish, and even other nymphs. They hunt by hiding in the shadows at the bottom of a pond or stream, waiting for prey animals to swim by. They have a special lip that they can extend far forward in order to grab their prey when it comes close. Depending on the species, they live this way for several months or even several years. As the nymph grows, it sheds its skin several times. Finally, it leaves the water and sheds its skin one last time. The adult emerges, ready to live the next few weeks or months on land and in the air. The adults do not live for more than four months, and many species live as adults for only a few weeks.

---

[1]British: colours

The exceptional visual abilities and flying skills of dragonflies and damselflies make them very adept hunters. Their special eyes give them a nearly 360-degree field of vision, and they can detect even the smallest movement or flash of light caused by other flying insects. They have two sets of wings that can move independently of each other. This gives them great maneuverability[1] in the air, which is important to these creatures because they catch their prey while flying. They can hover, make sharp turns, and fly backward. Some species of dragonflies can fly 60 kilometers an hour or more. Their prey consists of flying insects such as mosquitoes, deerflies, smaller dragonflies, and butterflies and moths. One species of dragonfly takes spiders out of their webs.

Bloodthirsty predators that they are, dragonflies and damselflies are prey for other animals in their turn. The nymphs are eaten by fish, frogs, toads, and other aquatic creatures. In the adult stage, they are hunted by birds, frogs, and larger dragonflies and damselflies. They might also be caught in a spider's web. What goes around comes around.

Questions 1–6

Which of the facts below are true of dragonflies, and which are true of damselflies, according to the information in the passage? On lines 1–6 on your answer sheet, write:

A	**if it is a fact about dragonflies only**
B	**if it is a fact about damselflies only**
C	**if it is a fact about both dragonflies and damselflies**

1 They have sawlike jaws.

2 They hold their wings on their backs while resting.

3 Their eyes have a gap between them.

4 They can be seen in fields at a distance from ponds and streams.

5 The largest species has a wingspan of 19 centimeters.

6 The largest fossil has a wingspan of 75 centimeters.

---

[1]British: manoeuvrability

Questions 7–13

*Complete the notes about the life cycle of odonata below. Choose your answers from the box below and write the correct letter, **A–K**, on lines 7–13 on your answer sheet.*

A	in the air
B	with their lips
C	tadpoles
D	fliers
E	near the water's surface
F	nymphs
G	at the bottom of a pond
H	months or years
I	weeks or months
J	swimmers
K	with their wings

The eggs are laid **7** .... The young dragonflies and damselflies, called **8** ...., live underwater for a few **9** ....
They eat small water animals, catching their food **10** .... When they are almost fully grown, they leave the water. The adults live for only a few **11** .... They are skillful[1] **12** .... and catch their prey **13** ....

Reading Passage 2

*You should spend about 20 minutes on **Questions 14–26**, which are based on Reading Passage 2 below.*

History of Fire Fighting and Prevention

More than two thousand years ago, Roman emperor Augustus organized[2] a group of watchmen whose job was mainly to look out for fires and sound an alarm in the event of one. For many centuries that followed, fire equipment was limited to buckets of water that got passed from person to person. The ax[3] was later found to be a useful tool both for removing fuel in large fires and for opening holes to allow smoke and flames to escape from burning buildings. Watchmen also learned to create firebreaks with long hooked poles and ropes in order to pull down structures that provided fuel for a fire. In 1066, in order to reduce the risk of

---
[1]British: skilful
[2]British: organised
[3]British: axe

fire in thatched-roof houses, King William the Conqueror made a ruling: Citizens had to extinguish their cooking fires at night. His term *couvre-feu*, meaning "cover fire," is the origin of the modern day term *curfew*, which no longer carries a literal translation.

The event that had the largest influence in the history of fire fighting was the Great Fire of London in 1666. The devastating blaze originated at the King's Bakery near the London Bridge. At the onset, Lord Mayor Bludworth showed little concern for the fire, assuming it would extinguish itself before he could organize a group of men to attend to it. However, the summer of 1666 had been uncharacteristically hot and dry, and the wooden houses nearby caught fire quickly. Within a short time, the wind had carried the fire across the city, burning down over 300 houses in its path. Although the procedure of pulling down buildings to prevent a fire from spreading was standard in Britain, the mayor grew concerned over the cost it would involve to rebuild the city and ordered that the surrounding structures be left intact. By the time the king ordered the destruction of buildings in the fire's path, the fire was too large to control. It was not until the Duke of York ordered the Paper House to be destroyed in order to create a crucial firebreak that the London fire finally began to lose its fuel.

When it became clear that four-fifths of the city had been destroyed by the fire, drastic measures were taken in London to create a system of organized fire prevention. At the hands of architects such as Christopher Wren, most of London was rebuilt using stone and brick, materials that were far less flammable than wood and straw. Because of the long history of fires in London, those who could afford to build new homes and businesses began to seek insurance for their properties. As insurance became a profitable business, companies soon realized[1] the monetary benefits of hiring men to extinguish fires. In the early years of insurance companies, all insured properties were marked with an insurance company's name or logo. If a fire broke out and a building did not contain the insurance mark, the fire brigades were called away and the building was left to burn.

The British insurance companies were largely responsible for employing people to develop new technology for extinguishing fires. The first fire engines were simple tubs on wheels that were pulled to the location of the fire, with water being supplied by a bucket brigade. Eventually, a hand pump was designed to push the water out of the tub into a hose with a nozzle. The pump allowed for a steady stream of water to shoot through a hose directly at the fire source. Before long, companies began to utilize water pipes made from hollowed tree trunks that were built under the roadway. By digging down into the road, firemen could insert a hole into the tree-trunk pipe and access the water to feed into the pump.

Fire fighting became a competitive business, as companies fought to be the first to arrive at a scene to access the water pipes. After a series of fires destroyed parts of London, fire-fighting companies were forced to reconsider their intentions. By the eighteenth century, fire brigades began to join forces, and in 1833 the Sun Insurance Company along with ten other London companies created the London Fire Engine

---

[1]British: realised

Establishment. In 1865, the government became involved, bringing standards to both fire prevention and fire fighting and establishing London's Metropolitan Fire Brigade. Though the firemen were well paid, they were constantly on duty and thus obliged to call their fire station home for both themselves and their families.

New technology for fighting fires continued to develop in both Europe and the New World. Leather hoses with couplings that joined the lengths together were hand-sewn in the Netherlands and used until the late 1800s, when rubber hoses became available. The technology for steam engine fire trucks was available in Britain and America in 1829, but most brigades were hesitant to use them until the 1850s. It was the public that eventually forced the brigades into putting the more efficient equipment to use. In the early 1900s, when the internal-combustion engine was developed, the trucks became motorized.[1] This was a timely advancement in fire-fighting history, as World War I put added pressure on brigades throughout the world.

Questions 14–20

Complete the chart below.
*Use **NO MORE THAN THREE WORDS** from the text for each answer. Write your answers on lines 14–20 on your answer sheet.*

Cause	Effect
Men used poles and ropes to pull down buildings near a fire.	The fire did not have 14 ....
Thatched-roof houses burn down easily. At the time of the Great Fire of London, the weather was 16	The King ordered people to 15 .... their fires nightly. The fire spread quickly.
The Mayor of London thought it would be too expensive to 17	He told people not to pull down buildings in the fire's path.
The Great Fire destroyed most of London.	People built new buildings out of 18 ....
There had been many 19 .... in London over time.	People started to buy insurance to protect their homes.
Insurance companies did not want to pay for rebuilding clients' houses destroyed by fire.	Insurance companies hired men to 20 ....

---

[1]British: motorised

Questions 21–23

*Choose the correct letters, **A–C**, and write them on lines 21–23 on your answer sheet.*

21 The first fire engines

   A carried water to the site of the fire.

   B used hand pumps.

   C had very long hoses.

22 In 1865,

   A London was destroyed by a series of fires.

   B fire brigades began to join forces.

   C the Metropolitan Fire Brigade was established.

23 Firemen who worked for the Metropolitan Fire Brigade

   A earned low salaries.

   B lived at the fire station.

   C were not allowed to marry.

Questions 24–26

Do the following statements agree with the information in the reading passage? On lines 24–26 on your answer sheet, write:

YES	*if the statement agrees with the views of the writer.*
NO	*if the statement contradicts the views of the writer.*
NOT GIVEN	*if it is impossible to say what the writer thinks about this.*

24 Leather hoses for fire fighting were made by machine.

25 Steam engine fire trucks were used until the early 1900s.

26 Fires caused a great deal of damage in London during World War I.

Reading Passage 3

*You should spend about 20 minutes on **Questions 27–40**, which are based on Reading Passage 3 below.*

The Luddites

The term *Luddite* is used to refer to a person who is opposed to new technology. The word derives from the name Ned Ludd, a man who may or may not have actually existed. The original Luddites were textile workers in early nineteenth-century England who protested changes brought on by the industrial revolution. These weavers made lace and stockings by hand, carrying out their craft independently in their homes according to traditional methods. In the 1800s, automated power looms and stocking frames were introduced, radically changing the traditional work system. Weavers' work was moved from individual homes to factories; individuals could not afford to buy the new machines for themselves. The new machines were not difficult to run. They could be operated by unskilled workers and turned out an inferior product, but they produced large quantities cheaply, which was the aim of the new factory owners. The makers of finely crafted, hand-made textiles could not compete with the new machines. Instead of continuing their tradition as skilled, independent workers, they would have to go to work in factories for low wages.

The industrial revolution was happening everywhere. In the textile-producing towns of England, workers focused on the new weaving machines as the source of their troubles. The height of Luddite activity occurred in the years 1811–1812. Groups of men, often in disguise, would arrive at a factory and make demands for higher wages and better working conditions. If these demands were not met, the group retaliated by smashing the factory machines. These groups often claimed that they were working under the command of General Ned Ludd, and thus came to be called Luddites.

Who was Ned Ludd? Rumors[1] about this mysterious person abounded. He came to be associated with that traditional champion of the poor, Robin Hood. The original Luddite activity was centered[2] around Nottingham, and many said that Ned Ludd hid out in nearby Sherwood Forest, just as the legendary Robin Hood had. According to another tradition, Ned Ludd was a weaver who had accidentally broken two stocking frames, and from that, came to be the one blamed any time an expensive piece of weaving equipment was damaged. Whoever Ned Ludd may or may not have been, riots protesting the new factories were carried out in his name throughout England's textile-producing region.

---

[1]British: rumours
[2]British: centred

Workers' families suffered as wages fell and food prices rose. There were food riots in several towns, and Luddite activity spread. In the winter of 1812, the Frame-Breaking Act was passed, making the destruction of factory equipment a crime punishable by death. The government sent thousands of troops into areas affected by the riots. In the spring of that year, several factory owners were killed during Luddite riots, and a number of textile workers died as well. Following one of the largest incidents, when rioters set fire to a mill in Westhoughton, four rioters, including a young boy, were executed. In another incident that spring, a group of over a thousand workers attacked a mill in Lancashire with sticks and rocks. When they were beaten back by armed guards protecting the mill, they moved to the mill owner's house and burned it down. The wave of violence resulted in a crackdown by the government. Suspected Luddites were arrested and imprisoned, and many of them were hanged.

By the summer of 1812, Luddite activity had begun to die down, although there continued to be sporadic incidents over the next several years. In 1816, a bad harvest and economic downturn led to a small revival of rioting. In June of that year, workers attacked two mills, smashing equipment and causing thousands of dollars worth of damage. Government troops were brought in to stop the violence. In the end, six of the rioters were executed for their participation. However, rioting never again reached the levels it had in 1811 and 1812.

The Luddites were short-lived, but they left an impressive mark. They were responsible for destroying close to one thousand weaving machines during the height of their activity in 1811–1812, as well as burning down several factories. Beyond the physical damage, however, they left their mark in people's minds. The famed English novelist Charlotte Brontë set her novel *Shirley* in Yorkshire at the time of the riots. This novel is still widely read today. In our present time of rapid technological change, people who are concerned about the pace of technological advance often call themselves Neo-Luddites. Although the responses to it may differ, concern about the changes brought on by technology continues.

Questions 27–32

Match each cause in List A with its effect in List B. Write the correct letter, A–J, on lines 27–32 on your answer sheet. There are more effects in List B than you will need, so you will not use them all.

List A Causes		List B Effects	
27	The new weaving machines were expensive to buy.	A	Troops were sent into the area.
28	The new weaving machines were easy to operate.	B	Weavers stopped working at home and went to work in factories.
29	Workers' demands for better pay and conditions were not met.	C	Rioters often wore disguises.
30	Rioting spread to many towns.	D	Workers destroyed factory equipment.
31	A law was passed against destroying factory equipment.	E	Many rioters were hanged.
32	Economic conditions worsened in 1816.	F	Charlotte Brontë wrote a novel about the Luddites.
		G	Prices went up, and salaries went down.
		H	Factory owners did not need to hire skilled weavers.
		I	Luddite rioting started again.
		J	People compared Ned Ludd to Robin Hood.

Questions 33–40

Do the following statements agree with the information given in the passage? On lines 33–40 on your answer sheet, write:

YES	*if the statement agrees with the views of the writer.*
NO	*if the statement contradicts the views of the writer.*
NOT GIVEN	*if it is impossible to say what the writer thinks about this.*

33 A Luddite is a person who resists new technology.

34 Before the nineteenth century, weavers made lace by hand.

35 Factory owners as well as workers died as a result of Luddite rioting.

36 The Luddite movement did not spread beyond England.

37 Nobody knows for certain who Ned Ludd was.

38 Worker protests during the economic downturn of 1816 were nonviolent.

39 Luddite activity lasted for many years.

40 Neo-Luddites do not use computers.

Writing Answer Sheet

TASK 1

_____
_____
_____
_____
_____
_____
_____
_____
_____
_____
_____
_____
_____
_____
_____
_____
_____
_____
_____
_____
_____
_____

ANSWER SHEET
Academic Module
Practice Test 1

-2-

ANSWER SHEET
Academic Module
Practice Test 1

-3-

TASK 2

ANSWER SHEET
Academic Module
Practice Test 1

-4-

ACADEMIC MODULE TEST 1

Candidate Name _____

International English Language Testing System

ACADEMIC WRITING

Time: 1 hour

INSTRUCTIONS TO CANDIDATES

Do not open this booklet until you are told to do so.

Write your name in the space at the top of this page.

All answers must be written on the separate answer booklet provided.

Do not remove this booklet from the examination room.

INFORMATION FOR CANDIDATES

There are **2** tasks on this question paper.

You must do **both** tasks.

Underlength answers will be penalized.[1]

---

[1]British: penalised

Writing Task 1

You should spend about 20 minutes on this task.

> *The following diagrams show how a pellet stove and a pellet boiler work to heat a house.*
>
> *Summarize[1] the information by selecting and reporting the main features, and make comparisons where relevant.*

Pellet Stove

Exhaust Duct
(extruding from rear panel)

hot air

Combustion Fan

Wood Pellets

Fuel Hopper

hot air

Controls

Combustion
Chamber

Ash Pan

Fuel Feed

---

[1]British: Summarise

Pellet Boiler

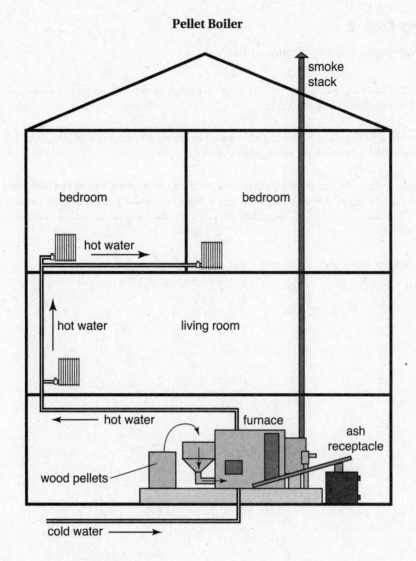

Write at least 150 words.

Writing Task 2

You should spend about 40 minutes on this task.

> *Write about the following topic:*
>
> *Everybody should be allowed admission to university or college programs[1] regardless of their level of academic ability.*
>
> *To what extent do you agree or disagree with this statement? Give reasons for your answer and include any relevant examples from your own knowledge or experience.*

Write at least 250 words.

---

[1]British: programmes

SPEAKING

Examiner questions:

Part 1

Neighborhood

Describe the neighborhood[1] where you live.

What do you like about living there?

What do you dislike about your neighborhood?

What kind of neighborhood would you like to live in?

Walking

Do you like walking? Why or why not?

Are there places you can walk near your house?

Do people in your country like walking? Why or why not?

What other kinds of exercise do you enjoy?

Part 2

You will have one to two minutes to talk about this topic.

You will have one minute to prepare what you are going to say.

Describe a friend who is important to you.

You should say:

The name of your friend

When and where you met this friend

What kinds of things you and this friend like to do together and explain why this friend is important to you

---

[1]British: neighbourhood

Part 3

Making Friends

Is it easier to make friends when we're young or when we're older? Why?

Where do people typically make friends?

Why do you think certain friendships last a lifetime?

Friends versus Family

What do friends provide that family cannot?

Are friends ever more important than family?

Do you spend more time with your friends or with your family? Why?

Friends and Time

What impact has technology (computers, cell phones, the Internet, etc.) had on your friendships?

How do friendships change as we age?

ANSWER KEY
Practice Test 1

Listening

1. Wednesday and Friday
2. intermediate
3. beginning
4. mornings
5. $125
6. $410
7. $575
8. $1,050
9. the school office
10. Mr. Lindsay
11. A
12. C
13. F
14. H
15. I
16. 1876
17. statue
18. woods
19. fountain
20. staircase
21. identification card/ID/ university ID card
22. (an) annual fee
23. Tuesday; Sunday
24. 8:30
25. D
26. A
27. F
28. B
29. G
30. C
31. pump water
32. grind grain
33. drain lakes/move water
34. pollution
35. renewable resource
36. costs less
37. strength
38. cities
39. the scenery
40. noisy

Reading

1. C
2. B
3. B
4. A
5. C
6. A
7. E
8. F
9. H
10. B
11. I
12. D
13. A
14. fuel
15. extinguish
16. hot and dry
17. rebuild the city
18. stone and brick
19. fires
20. extinguish fires
21. A
22. C
23. B
24. No
25. Yes
26. Not Given
27. B
28. H
29. D
30. A
31. E
32. I
33. True
34. True
35. True
36. Not Given
37. True
38. False
39. False
40. Not Given

ACADEMIC MODULE—PRACTICE TEST 1

Listening

1. *Wednesday and Friday* evenings is when the advanced Chinese class meets, and the man can't take that class because he works evenings.

2. *intermediate.* This is the level of the Japanese class that meets Tuesday and Thursday mornings.

3. *beginning.* This is the level of the Japanese class that meets Monday, Wednesday, and Friday mornings.

4. *mornings.* The intermediate French class meets on Friday mornings.

5. *$125* is the cost if the student pays one week at a time.

6. *$410* is the cost of four weeks of classes.

7. *$575* is the cost for a six-week class.

8. *$1,050* is the cost of twelve weeks of classes.

9. *the school office.* "What you'll need to do is to visit the school office today or tomorrow."

10. *Mr. Lindsay.* "When you arrive, ask for Mr. Lindsay. He is in charge of student registration."

11. **(A)** The tour begins at the bookstore, marked with a star.

12. **(C)** The café is the next building up from the bookstore.

13. **(F)** On the corner is the clothing store, and the souvenir store is next to that.

14. **(H)** The art gallery is one building down from the corner and across the street from the souvenir store.

15. **(I)** Harbor Park is next to the art gallery.

16. *1876.* The speaker says, "Captain Jones designed the park himself, and it was built in 1876."

17. *statue.* The speaker says, "Exactly in the center of the park a statue of Captain Jones was erected, and it's still standing there today."

18. *woods.* The speaker says, "you can follow the path that goes through the woods just behind."

19. *fountain.* The speaker says, "It will lead you to a lovely garden, in the middle of which is a fountain."

20. *staircase.* The speaker says, "There, you'll find a wooden staircase, which will take you down to the harbor."

21. *identification card/ID/university ID card.* The librarian says, "All you need to do is show your university identification card . . . ."

22. *(an) annual fee.* The librarian says, "City residents pay an annual fee . . . ."

23. *Tuesday; Sunday.* The librarian says, "So you can come any day, Tuesday through Sunday . . . ."

24. *8:30.* The librarian says, we're open from nine thirty in the morning until eight thirty in the evening.

25. **(D)** The librarian says, "Yes, we store all the photographs in the basement."

26. **(A)** The librarian says, "Now, if you're interested in seeing documents from the nineteenth century, those are here on the ground floor."

27. **(F)** The librarian says, "No, all the newspapers from the earliest ones, in the eighteenth century, up to the current time, are on the second floor."

28. **(B)** The student mentions the room devoted to maps, and the librarian remarks that the room is on the third floor.

29. **(G)** The student asks, "What's this on the fourth floor—Ogden's Woolen Mill?"

30. **(C)** The librarian says, "The personal papers would be on the fifth floor, where we keep all the personal papers of famous residents of our city."

31. *pump water.* The speaker says, "In ancient China, farmers used a rudimentary sort of windmill to pump water."

32. *grind grain.* The speaker says, "In Persia, for example, farmers used wind-powered mills to grind their grain."

33. *drain lakes/move water.* The speaker says, "During the Middle Ages in the Netherlands, people went back to the ancient idea of using the power of the wind to move water. They used windmills to drain lakes, thereby creating more land for farming."

34. *pollution.* The speaker says, "Wind power, on the other hand, is clean. It causes no pollution . . . ."

35. *renewable resource.* The speaker says, "Another great advantage of wind power is that it's a renewable resource. Oil and coal reserves are limited, but we'll never run out of wind."

36. *costs less.* The speaker says, "Using the wind to generate electricity costs less, much less, than running other types of generators."

37. *strength.* The speaker says, "Wind doesn't blow at a constant strength."

38. *cities.* The speaker says, "Wind turbines usually have to be located in rural areas . . . . Their distance from cities, where the most electricity is needed, is another issue."

39. *the scenery.* The speaker says, "Rural residents often feel that the beautiful local scenery is spoiled by the sight of the wind turbines."

40. *noisy.* The speaker says, "In fact, one wind turbine can produce as much noise as a car traveling at highway speeds."

Reading

PASSAGE 1

1. **(C)** Paragraph 1: "Dragonflies and damselflies get their name from the powerful serrated jaws they use to tear apart their prey."

2. **(B)** Paragraph 2: "Dragonflies hold their wings out to the side while damselflies fold their wings back."

3. **(B)** Paragraph 2: "Damselflies' eyes are smaller, and there is a space between them."

4. **(A)** Paragraph 2: "Dragonflies are larger and stronger animals than damselflies and fly longer distances. Thus, they can be found in woods and fields away from the water."

5. **(C)** Paragraph 3: "The largest odonata living today are the Hawaiian endemic dragonfly and the Central American damselfly, each of these species having a wingspan of 19 centimeters."

6. **(A)** Paragraph 3: "The largest dragonfly fossil ever found belongs to the now-extinct *meganeura monyi*, which lived 300 million years ago and had a wingspan of 75 centimeters."

7. **(E)** Paragraph 4: "Dragonflies and damselflies both lay their eggs on or just below the surface of the water in a pond or stream."

8. **(F)** Paragraph 4: "The babies emerge from the eggs in the form of nymphs."

9. **(H)** Paragraph 4: "Depending on the species, they live this way for several months or even several years."

10. **(B)** Paragraph 4: "They have a special lip that they can extend far forward in order to grab their prey when it comes close."

11. **(I)** Paragraph 4: "The adults do not live for more than four months, and many species live as adults for only a few weeks."

12. **(D)** Paragraph 5: "They have two sets of wings that can move independently of each other. This gives them great maneuverability in the air . . . . They can hover, make sharp turns, and fly backward."

13. **(A)** Paragraph 5: "they catch their prey while flying."

PASSAGE 2

14. *fuel.* Paragraph 1: "Watchmen also learned to create firebreaks with long hooked poles and ropes in order to pull down structures that provided fuel for a fire."

15. *extinguish.* Paragraph 1: "In 1066, in order to reduce the risk of fire in thatched-roof houses, King William the Conqueror made a ruling: Citizens had to extinguish their cooking fires at night."

16. *hot and dry.* Paragraph 2: "However, the summer of 1666 had been uncharacteristically hot and dry . . . ."

17. *rebuild the city.* Paragraph 2: "the mayor grew concerned over the cost it would involve to rebuild the city and ordered that the surrounding structures be left intact."

18. *stone and brick.* Paragraph 3: "most of London was rebuilt using stone and brick, materials that were far less flammable than wood and straw."

19. *fires.* Paragraph 3: "Because of the long history of fires in London, those who could afford to build new homes and businesses began to seek insurance for their properties."

20. *extinguish fires.* Paragraph 3: "As insurance became a profitable business, companies soon realized the monetary benefits of hiring men to extinguish fires."

21. **(A)** Paragraph 4: "The first fire engines were simple tubs on wheels that were pulled to the location of the fire . . . ." Choice (B) is incorrect because hand pumps were added "eventually," that is, later. Choice (C) is incorrect because water was "supplied by a bucket brigade."

22. **(C)** Paragraph 5: "In 1865, the government became involved, ... establishing London's Metropolitan Fire Brigade. Choice (A) is mentioned in the same paragraph but not as something that occurred in 1865. Choice (B) is mentioned as something that happened in the eighteenth century or earlier.

23. **(B)** Paragraph 5: "Though the firemen were well paid, they were constantly on duty and thus obliged to call their fire station home . . . ." Choice (A) is incorrect because the paragraph mentions that firemen were well paid. Choice (C) is incorrect because the paragraph mentions firemen's families.

24. *No.* Paragraph 6: "Leather hoses with couplings that joined the lengths together were hand-sewn in the Netherlands . . . ."

25. *Yes.* Paragraph 6 explains that steam engine fire trucks were used from about the 1850s until the early 1900s, when the trucks became motorized.

26. *Not Given.* World War I is mentioned, but its particular effect on London is not.

PASSAGE 3

27. **(B)** Paragraph 1: "Weavers' work was moved from individual homes to factories; individuals could not afford to buy the new machines for themselves."

28. **(H)** Paragraph 1: "The new machines were not difficult to run. They could be operated by unskilled workers . . . ."

29. **(D)** Paragraph 2: "If these demands were not met, the group retaliated by smashing the factory machines."

30. **(A)** Paragraph 4: "Luddite activity spread . . . . The government sent thousands of troops into areas affected by the riots."

31. **(E)** Paragraph 4: "the Frame-Breaking Act was passed, making the destruction of factory equipment a crime punishable by death." Paragraphs 4 and 5 mention several incidents where rioters were imprisoned or executed.

32. **(I)** Paragraph 5: "In 1816, a bad harvest and economic downturn led to a small revival of rioting."

33. *True.* Opening sentence: "The term *Luddite* is used to refer to a person who is opposed to new technology."

34. *True.* Paragraph 1: "These weavers made lace and stockings by hand . . . . In the 1800s, automated power looms and stocking frames were introduced . . . ."

35. *True.* Paragraph 4: "In the spring of that year, several factory owners were killed during Luddite riots, and a number of textile workers died as well."

36. *Not Given.* The article describes Luddite activity in England but does not mention whether it occurred in other countries.

37. *True.* Paragraph 3 discusses possible explanations of who Ned Ludd was and implies that none of them is accepted as fact.

38. *False.* Paragraph 5: "In 1816, a bad harvest and economic downturn led to a small revival of rioting."

39. *False.* According to Paragraphs 2 and 5, most Luddite activity occurred in the years 1811 and 1812.

40. *Not Given.* Paragraph 6 describes Neo-Luddites as people concerned about technological advances but does not give any specifics about their activities.

Writing

These are models. Your answers will vary. See page 2 in the Introduction to see the criteria for scoring.

WRITING TASK 1

The diagrams show the components of a wood pellet stove and a wood pellet boiler and how they are used to heat a house. When a wood pellet stove is used, first the wood pellets are fed into the fuel hopper. Then the pellets move through the fuel feed and into the combustion chamber, where they are burned. As they burn, the ashes drop into the ash pan below. The hot air from the burning rises to the combustion fan. It is blown out into the room by the fan. Smoke from the fire exits through the exhaust duct.

When a wood pellet boiler is used, the pellets are also fed into a hopper. From there, they move into the furnace, where they are burned. The ashes go into the ash receptacle and the smoke goes up the smoke stack. Cold water moves into the furnace, where it is heated by the burning pellets. The heated water moves into radiators, which heat each room of the house.

The major difference between the two systems is that the stove heats with hot air and the boiler heats with water.

WRITING TASK 2

I agree that everybody, no matter what his or her level of academic ability, should be admitted to university programs. In the first place, everyone has the right to an education and no one can take this away. Also, people are generally attracted to educational programs that fit their interests and abilities. Finally, there are different university programs designed to fit different kinds of students.

Everybody has the right to an education, and this includes education beyond high school. Some people choose to go to a university while others choose some other form of training. No matter what form of education a person chooses, no one else has the right to make that choice for him or her.

People tend to choose educational programs that fit their interests and abilities. They do not need someone else to tell them what they can and cannot do. If a person is interested in studying law, for example, it is probably because he or she feels it is something he or she likes and will do well at. Also, when students are interested in their program of study, they are motivated to work hard, even when some of the assignments are difficult for them.

There are all different kinds of university programs. There are programs that suit different interests, goals, and abilities. Because of this, there is no reason to deny a university education to anyone. There is something for everyone who wants it at the university level.

Everyone has the right to an education, including a university education if that is what he or she chooses. It should not be denied to anyone.

Speaking

These are models. Your answers will vary. See page 2 in the Introduction to see the criteria for scoring.

PART 1

Describe the neighborhood where you live.
The neighborhood I live in is right outside of the city. It's almost like living in the city, except that it has houses instead of apartment buildings. The houses are small with small yards. People in the neighborhood really like to garden, so there are a lot of flowers and nice plants. It's very pretty. We are near a bus stop, so it's easy to get to the city. There are a few small stores that sell food and newspapers and things like that.

What do you like about living there?
What I like about my neighborhood is that it's close to the city. It's very easy to get to work. Also, it's not very expensive. I can afford to live there and not spend all my money on rent.

What do you dislike about your neighborhood?
My neighborhood is in a boring area. If I want to do something interesting like go to a movie or a concert or if I want to shop at good stores, I have to go to the city. It's quiet, so it's a good place to relax, but it's not a good place to have fun.

What kind of neighborhood would you like to live in?
When I start making more money, I'm going to move into the city. I would like to live in a city neighborhood that's full of activity. I'd like to live near restaurants and stores and clubs. I'd like to live in a place where I can walk out my front door and be right in the middle of everything.

Do you like walking? Why or why not?
I don't dislike walking, but I can't say that I particularly like it. I walk to the bus stop every day, and I often walk to the store because it's nearby. I walk to get places, but I never walk for fun. I don't think it's an interesting thing to do.

Are there places you can walk near your house?
There's a nice park not far from my house. It has pretty gardens and some walking trails through the woods. A lot of my neighbors go there to take walks. It's also easy to walk around my neighborhood because there are sidewalks everywhere.

Do people in your country like walking? Why or why not?
Walking is popular in my country. A lot of people walk for their health. In fact, there are walking clubs. Often, early in the mornings you can see groups of people walking around the neighborhood together. These are the walking clubs. They walk together every morning, I think.

What other kinds of exercise do you enjoy?

I never walk for exercise, but I enjoy bike riding. I often ride my bike on weekends. I go wherever I can find bike trails. There are a lot of them near where I live. When the weather is bad, I go to the gym and use the exercise machines there. I really like doing that. I like to play soccer, too. I play it with my friends every week.

PART 2

My friend's name is Bob. We've known each other most of our lives. We met in preschool when we were around four or five years old, and we've been friends ever since. We like to do a lot of things together. When we were little kids, we played a lot of different kinds of games together. In high school, we used to study together, but we don't do that anymore because Bob isn't studying business administration like I am. He's studying law. We're both busy with school and work, but we still get together often. It's easy because we're still living in the same city. We play soccer with some other friends at least once a week, and we go to soccer games together. When the weather's nice, we go to the beach or hang out in the park. We talk about things we're doing now, and these days we also talk a lot about the future, the things we hope to do after we finish school. Bob is an important friend because we've known each other all our lives. We grew up together. I guess you could say we know just about everything about each other. I know if I ever needed serious help or if I needed money or any kind of support, Bob would help me. And I would help him if he needed it. He's the kind of friend you can always count on. I think we'll always be friends, all our lives. I hope so.

PART 3

Is it easier to make friends when we're young or when we're older? Why?

I think it's easier to make friends when we're young. Young people are more open. Also, when you're young, you're in school. You're surrounded by lots of other people who want to make friends. When you're older you have to pay more attention to taking care of your family, so you have less time to make new friends.

Where do people typically make friends?

I think people make most of their friends at school. Sometimes kids also make friends in their neighborhood. It depends on what kind of neighborhood they live in, if there are a lot of kids and if they play together or not. Adults sometimes make friends at work, or they might join some kind of club and make friends that way. Sometimes parents make friends with the parents of their children's friends.

Why do you think certain friendships last a lifetime?

Sometimes you really connect with another person. I think this is especially true with friends you make early on in life, when you're still a child. Then you experience growing up together and going through the important stages of life together. When you share important things like that, like graduating from school, getting your first job, getting married, all those things, then you form a deep connection with the person who saw you go through those things and supported you.

What do friends provide that family cannot?

One thing a friend can provide is someone to share interests with. Probably not everyone in your family likes the same things you do, so then you look for friends who enjoy what you enjoy. For example, if you like to play tennis or see certain movies or anything like that, your relatives may not enjoy these things but your friends may. Friends can also share different points of view with you. They may see the world differently than people in your family do, so you can learn different ways of thinking. Friends can also help you if you have a misunderstanding with someone in your family. They can give you lots of support.

Are friends ever more important than family?

Friends can be very important if you are away from your family for any reason. If your family isn't there, your friends are. Sometimes friends can understand things about you that your family doesn't, so that's important too. But usually, I think, the people in your family are the most important people in your life. They are the ones who will always be there for you, no matter what.

Do you spend more time with your friends or with your family? Why?

At this time in my life, I spend more time with my friends. That's because I am living in a different city away from my family. Also, I'm still young. I like to go out and enjoy myself with my friends. I think when I get older I will spend more time with my family.

What impact has technology (computers, cell phones, the Internet, etc.), had on your friendships?

I think technology has made it easier to have friends. I can post something on the Internet and all my friends instantly know about it. Communication is very easy. My friends can always know where I am and what I'm doing. If I need to talk with someone, I can call anyone anytime on my cell phone, or send an e-mail. It's all so easy and fast.

How do friendships change as we age?

When we're younger, our friendships are about doing things together. Children play together, and teenagers and young adults like to go places together, to the movies or cafés, things like that. When people get married and start their own families, maybe their friendships are about helping each other. They help with the children, or they talk about problems and try to find solutions. So their friendships are more about talking and less about doing.

Academic Module

PRACTICE TEST 2

ANSWER SHEET
Academic Module
Practice Test 2

IELTS Listening Answer Sheet

1		✓ 1 ✗
2		2
3		3
4		4
5		5
6		6
7		7
8		8
9		9
10		10
11		11
12		12
13		13
14		14
15		15
16		16
17		17
18		18
19		19
20		20

21		✓ 21 ✗
22		22
23		23
24		24
25		25
26		26
27		27
28		28
29		29
30		30
31		31
32		32
33		33
34		34
35		35
36		36
37		37
38		38
39		39
40		40
	Listening Total	

ACADEMIC MODULE TEST 2

Candidate Name _____

International English Language Testing System

LISTENING

Time: Approx. 30 minutes

INSTRUCTIONS TO CANDIDATES

Do not open this booklet until you are told to do so.

Write your name in the space at the top of this page.

You should answer all questions.

All the recordings will be played ONCE only.

Write all your answers on the Question Paper.

At the end of the test, you will be given ten minutes to transfer your answers to an Answer Sheet.

Do not remove this booklet from the examination room.

INFORMATION FOR CANDIDATES

There are **40** questions on this question paper.

The test is divided as follows:

Section 1	Questions 1–10
Section 2	Questions 11–20
Section 3	Questions 21–30
Section 4	Questions 31–40

SECTION 1

TIP

If you do not have access to the MP3 files on the enclosed disk, please refer to the audioscripts starting on page 421 when prompted to listen to an audio passage.

Questions 1–5

Complete the chart[1] below.
*Write **NO MORE THAN TWO WORDS** for each answer.*

Example	Plainfield Community Center[2]	
Classes and Activities		
Days	**Class/Activity**	**Age Group**
Wednesday, Saturday	1	children, teens
2	Tennis	3 ....
Tuesday, Thursday	4	children, teens, adults
Friday	Book club	5 ....

Questions 6–10

Complete the notes below.
*Write **NO MORE THAN THREE WORDS AND/OR A NUMBER** for each answer.*

Membership fees **6** $ .... (individual)

7 $ .... (family)

Located at 107 **8** .... Street

Parking is located **9** ....

The Center is closed on **10** ....

---

[1]British: table
[2]British: Centre

SECTION 2

Questions 11–15

Choose **FIVE** letters, **A–J**.
Which **FIVE** things should hikers take on the hiking trip?

A   sleeping bag
B   tent
C   food
D   dishes
E   hiking boots
F   backpack
G   walking poles
H   maps
I   jacket
J   first-aid kit

Questions 16–20

Complete the sentences below.
Write **NO MORE THAN TWO WORDS** for each answer.

Safety Rules for Hiking
Always stay ahead of the **16** ....
Stop and wait at any **17** ....
Don't try to climb **18** ....
Don't **19** .... wild animals.
Always carry **20** .... with you.

SECTION 3

Questions 21–24

Choose **FOUR** letters, **A–G**.
Which **FOUR** of the following are required of student teachers?

A   weekly journal
B   sample lesson plans
C   meetings with other student teachers
D   observing other teachers
E   evaluation from supervising teacher
F   portfolio
G   final exam

Question 25

Choose the correct letter, **A, B,** or **C.**

25   Who has to sign the agreement form?

   A   the student teacher
   B   the supervising teacher
   C   the advisor

Questions 26–30

Complete the schedule below.
Write **NO MORE THAN THREE WORDS** for each answer.

First week	**26** .... due
Fourth week	**27** .... meeting
Seventh week	**28** ....
Fourteenth week	**29** .... due
Fifteenth week	**30** ....

SECTION 4

Questions 31–35

*Choose the correct letter, **A**, **B**, or **C**.*

31 Retailers place popular items

    A in the back of the store.

    B near the front entrance.

    C at the end of the aisle.

32 Carpet patterns are used to

    A help shoppers feel comfortable.

    B appeal to shoppers' decorative sense.

    C encourage shoppers to walk in certain directions.

33 Retailers can keep customers in the store longer by

    A providing places to sit.

    B keeping the doors closed.

    C lowering the prices.

34 Music is used in stores to

    A entertain customers.

    B slow customers down.

    C make customers shop faster.

35 The scent of vanilla has been used in

    A ice cream shops.

    B bakeries.

    C clothing stores.

Questions 36–40

Complete the chart about the effects of color.[1]

Write **NO MORE THAN TWO WORDS** for each answer.

Color	Effect
Purple	encourages people to 36 ....
Orange	makes restaurant customers 37 ....
Blue	conveys a sense of 38 ....
Bright colors	appeal to 39 ....
Soft colors	appeal to 40 ....

Take ten minutes to transfer your answers onto the Answer Sheet on page 55.

[1]British: colour

ANSWER SHEET
Academic Module
Practice Test 2

IELTS Reading Answer Sheet

		✓ ✗
1		▭ 1 ▭
2		▭ 2 ▭
3		▭ 3 ▭
4		▭ 4 ▭
5		▭ 5 ▭
6		▭ 6 ▭
7		▭ 7 ▭
8		▭ 8 ▭
9		▭ 9 ▭
10		▭ 10 ▭
11		▭ 11 ▭
12		▭ 12 ▭
13		▭ 13 ▭
14		▭ 14 ▭
15		▭ 15 ▭
16		▭ 16 ▭
17		▭ 17 ▭
18		▭ 18 ▭
19		▭ 19 ▭
20		▭ 20 ▭

		✓ ✗
21		▭ 21 ▭
22		▭ 22 ▭
23		▭ 23 ▭
24		▭ 24 ▭
25		▭ 25 ▭
26		▭ 26 ▭
27		▭ 27 ▭
28		▭ 28 ▭
29		▭ 29 ▭
30		▭ 30 ▭
31		▭ 31 ▭
32		▭ 32 ▭
33		▭ 33 ▭
34		▭ 34 ▭
35		▭ 35 ▭
36		▭ 36 ▭
37		▭ 37 ▭
38		▭ 38 ▭
39		▭ 39 ▭
40		▭ 40 ▭
	Reading Total	

ACADEMIC MODULE TEST 2

Candidate Name _____

International English Language Testing System

ACADEMIC READING

Time: 1 hour

INSTRUCTIONS TO CANDIDATES

Do not open this booklet until you are told to do so.

Write your name in the space at the top of this page.

Start at the beginning of the test and work through it.

You should answer all questions.

If you cannot do a particular question, leave it and go on to the next. You can return to it later.

All answers must be written on the Answer Sheet.

Do not remove this booklet from the examination room.

INFORMATION FOR CANDIDATES

There are **40** questions on this question paper.

The test is divided as follows:

Reading Passage 1	Questions 1–13
Reading Passage 2	Questions 14–26
Reading Passage 3	Questions 27–40

Reading Passage 1

*You should spend about 20 minutes on **Questions 1–13**, which are based on Reading Passage 1 below.*

The Vikings' Wayfaring Ways

Perhaps best known as fierce warriors, the Vikings were also the most far-ranging of peoples. In fact, the term *Viking*, in Old Norse, means "to go on an expedition." From the late 700s until the eleventh century, Viking explorers journeyed from their native Norway, Denmark, and Sweden to many distant lands. They traveled[1] as far west as Newfoundland in present-day Canada, and as far east as Baghdad.

Those from Norway sailed west to the British Isles, and eventually across the Atlantic Ocean. During their first expedition, in 793, a force of Viking warriors sacked the famed abbey at Lindisfarne, on England's northeast coast. In the 800s, groups of raiders went on to occupy the Shetland Islands, north of the British Isles and west of Norway, and the Orkney Islands off northern Scotland.

By 870, the Vikings were settling Iceland. In 980, an Icelandic assembly found a man named Eric "the Red" Ericson guilty of murder and sent him into exile. Eric the Red responded by sailing to a large island to the west, which he called "Greenland." An Icelandic saga mentions that people would be attracted to go to Greenland if it had a favorable[2] name. Around 998, Eric the Red's son, Leif "the Lucky" Ericson, and a small Viking fleet sailed west to North America. There they established the first European settlement in the New World, called "Vinland."

Vikings from Denmark, meanwhile, ravaged large swaths of England and France. In 866, a Viking "Great Army" landed in England, occupying much of the country's north and east. They forced the English king to acknowledge their control of much of England under the so-called Danelaw. To the west, they conquered coastal portions of Ireland, and in 841 founded Dublin, today a major Irish city, but originally a Viking fort. The Vikings remained a major power in Ireland until the early eleventh century.

To the south, the Vikings conquered France, moving swiftly up rivers in long boats, powered by oar and sail. From 845 to 886, they surged up the Seine to attack Paris three times. To stop the raids, French King Charles III the Simple in 911 offered the Viking chief Rollo territories in northwest France, called Normandy, after the Normans or "Northmen." There they set up a powerful kingdom and, in 1066, under William, Duke of Normandy, defeated King Harold at the battle of Hastings in England.

Farther south, in 844, the Vikings had raided Portugal and Spain, then largely controlled by Arab Moors. A fleet of 100 Viking ships seized Lisbon and boldly sailed up the Guadalquivir River to occupy Seville. However, the Moors dealt

---

[1]British: travelled
[2]British: favourable

them a rare defeat. The Moors catapulted flaming projectiles onto the Viking vessels, forcing a retreat.

Still other Vikings sailed much farther, to raid Morocco, then to the eastern Mediterranean and beyond. Many of these Vikings enlisted with the military forces of the Byzantine Empire, the Greek-speaking successors to the Roman Empire. Vikings made up the Byzantine Emperor's elite Varangian Guard. In 902, hundreds of Varangians served as marines during a Byzantine naval assault on the island of Crete. Varangians battled Arab forces in Syria in 955, and even fought in Jerusalem. So many men left Scandinavia for the Byzantine Empire that, to stem the outflow, Sweden passed a law denying inherited property to anyone serving under the Byzantines.

The Vikings of Sweden, meanwhile, were moving out of Scandinavia to the east and south. They journeyed through the Baltic Sea, then built inland trading posts in Germany and Poland. In time, they struck out across Central and Eastern Europe, down the Vistula River in Poland, and the Dnieper, Volga, and Don Rivers in Russia. Their vessel of choice was the "knar," a cargo ship with a deep draft and wide hull. Viking merchants on horseback penetrated far into the Asian heartland, trading with towns on the Caspian and Black seas.

The most significant settlements were in Russia and Ukraine. In 862, Vikings settled in the town of Novgorod, in northwestern Russia. It became the capital of a country called Rus, after the Finnish name for the Swedes. Rus came from the word *Rutosi*, meaning "rowers." Rus formed the foundation of Russia, as the Russian and Viking leaders of Rus intermarried, converted to Christianity, and steadily expanded their territory. And after lucrative trade relations were established with the Byzantines and with Muslim lands, the Rus moved their capital southward to Kiev, later the capital of Ukraine.

Another important Viking market town was Bulgar, on the Volga River. There, merchants peddled honey, wax, amber, and steel swords. The Viking's most common commodity may have been skins: they dealt in horse, beaver, rabbit, mink, ermine, and sable skins. They also traded hazelnuts, fish, cattle, and falcons. Another commodity was slaves, many of them Slavs from Eastern Europe. The merchants eagerly exchanged their goods for Arab silver coins. In Sweden, archeologists[1] have excavated about 100,000 such coins, minted in such distant cities as Cairo and Tashkent.

Like their Danish and Norwegian relatives, the Swedish Vikings traveled to the most exotic realms. They took part in the Silk Road trade with India and China. Archeological evidence shows that Viking traders even traveled by camel caravan to Baghdad.

Given the wide-ranging travel of the Vikings, it is fitting the Anglo-Saxons gave them the nickname "Færgenga"—"Far Going."

---

[1]British: archaeologists

Questions 1–5

Answer the questions below.
Choose **ONE NUMBER ONLY** *from the text for each answer.*
Write your answers on lines 1–5 on your answer sheet.

1 When did Viking warriors raid an abbey on the coast of England?

2 When was Eric the Red convicted of a crime?

3 When did Vikings establish a fort in Ireland?

4 When was a Viking chief granted lands by a king of France?

5 When did Viking warriors defeat an English king?

Questions 6–13

Complete the summary using the list of words, **A–O**, *below. Write the correct letter,* **A–O**, *on lines 6–13 on your answer sheet.*

A warriors	**E** trade with	**H** settled in	**L** a parade
B an attack	**F** conquered	**I** ship	**M** archeologists
C capital	**G** burning objects	**J** oars	**N** silver coins
D explorers		**K** market	**O** horse

The people known as Vikings were given this name because they were
6 .... · Groups of Vikings from Norway traveled west to Britain,
Iceland, and beyond. They were the first Europeans who 7 .... North
America. Groups from Denmark 8 .... large areas of England and
France. Other groups of Vikings raided areas of Portugal and Spain. The Moors of
Seville, Spain, drove the Vikings away by throwing 9 .... at them.
Large numbers of Vikings left Scandinavia for the Byzantine Empire, and many of these
joined the Byzantine military. At one point, they took part in 10 .... on
the Greek island of Crete. Groups of Swedish Vikings crossed the Baltic Sea to explore
the lands beyond. They traveled down Russian rivers, then journeyed deep into Asia
by 11 .... · After settling in northwest Russia, they expanded their
territories toward the south. Kiev, Ukraine, eventually became the Vikings' territorial
12 .... · The Vikings also had an important 13 .... in
the town of Bulgar on the Volga River.

Reading Passage 2

*You should spend about 20 minutes on **Questions 14–26**, which are based on Reading Passage 2 below.*

Dyslexia

Dyslexia, also referred to as "specific reading disability," predominantly affects a person's ability to read and write. Dyslexics have difficulty connecting visual symbols (i.e., letters) with their corresponding sounds. Many people who suffer from dyslexia also have trouble with enunciation, organization,[1] and short-term memory. Dyslexia is the most common learning disability in children. It is not related to intellectual ability, vision, or access to education. Approximately 5–10 percent of school-age children in North America suffer from the condition, with each case varying in severity. Children are generally diagnosed with dyslexia during the elementary school years when they are learning how to read and spell.

Determining the definite cause of dyslexia is a difficult task since studies of the morphology of the brain are generally conducted in an autopsy. One hypothesis suggests that dyslexic children suffer from "strabismus," the tendency of the eyes to focus on two different points. When reading, for example, one eye focuses on the beginning of the word and the other focuses on the end. This theory could explain why dyslexics have difficulty reading. Many dyslexic children read letters and words backwards, often mistaking a *b* for a *d* or reading *was* instead of *saw*. These reversals are normal for children under the age of six, but indicate a problem if they persist beyond the early elementary grades. Neurological research points to tiny flaws in the dyslexic brain called ectopias and microgyria. These flaws alter the structure of the cortex, the area of the brain that is responsible for connecting visual and audio processing. Genetic research, often in the form of twins studies, shows that dyslexia may be passed on in families.

Though most children are not diagnosed with dyslexia until they enter the school system, there are some early signs of the disability. Toddlers who talk much later than average, have difficulty learning new words, or do not understand the concept of rhyming may develop other dyslexic symptoms. As children begin school, teachers are trained to look for warning signs, such as an inability to recognize[2] letters or spaces between words on a page or difficulty following instructions given with more than one command at a time. Properly screening children for dyslexia is important since other factors can limit reading abilities, including vision or hearing impairment, anxiety, or other neurological problems.

Dyslexia is a type of learning disorder that can often be compensated for with therapy and motivational techniques. Phonological training, which involves iden-

---

[1]British: organisation
[2]British: recognise

tifying and separating sound patterns, is the most common form of therapy used in the school system. Depending on the severity of the disorder, dyslexic children are pulled from regular classroom activities in order to work one-on-one with a language specialist. Studies have shown that activity in the right temporoparietal cortex tends to increase after sufficient phonological training. Improvements in visual focus can sometimes be achieved when students are given an eye patch to wear while they learn to read. Encouraging children to use many senses while reading also has proven benefits. Some teachers find that having students listen to a book on tape before reading the text can help with information processing as well.

Though it is properly classified as a learning disability, dyslexia is commonly mistaken for a behavioral[1] disorder. Dyslexic children often exhibit behavior that seems abnormal but is caused by frustration at their own inability to perform at the same level as their peers. Some studies show that attention deficit disorder co-occurs with dyslexia in up to 50 percent of cases. In general, behavioral problems decline as dyslexic students are diagnosed and begin to receive treatment.

Other learning disabilities are neurologically linked to dyslexia, including dyscalculia, dysgraphia, and dyspraxia. People who suffer from dyscalculia can usually perform difficult mathematical tasks, but have trouble with formulas or basic addition and subtraction. Dysgraphia prevents people from writing in an organized manner. Dyspraxia impedes the performance of routine tasks that involve balance and fine motor skills.

The earlier children are diagnosed with dyslexia, the more likely they are to overcome their disabilities and progress to adult reading levels. Many studies show that children who are diagnosed after grade three have a much lower chance of eliminating the symptoms of dyslexia. Some dyslexics, especially those who are not diagnosed as children, naturally develop their own coping mechanisms such as an increased visual memory. In some instances, dyslexics develop keen spatial and visual abilities that prepare them for very specialized[2] careers.

---

[1]British: behavioural
[2]British: specialised

Questions 14–20

Do the following statements agree with the information in the reading passage? On lines 14–20 on your answer sheet write:

YES	*if the statement agrees with the views of the writer*
NO	*if the statement disagrees with the views of the writer*
NOT GIVEN	*if there is no information on this in the passage*

14   Dyslexia is a disorder related to intelligence.

15   Dyslexia is usually diagnosed during a child's first years of school.

16   People with dyslexia often read in reverse.

17   Children with dyslexia learn to speak at a younger than average age.

18   Scientists are looking for a drug treatment for dyslexia.

19   Dyslexia in children is often accompanied by behavioral problems.

20   People with dysgraphia have difficulty with math.

Questions 21–23

Which of the following are signs of dyslexia mentioned in the passage? Choose THREE answers from the list below and write the correct letters, **A–F**, on lines 21–23 on your answer sheet.

A   learning to talk at a later than normal age
B   trouble with new vocabulary
C   leaving big spaces between words
D   problems following directions
E   difficulty turning the pages of a book
F   inability to give commands

Questions 24–26

Which of the following are treatments for dyslexia mentioned in the passage? Choose THREE answers from the list below and write the correct letter, **A–F**, on lines 24–26 on your answer sheet.

A   using special computers
B   learning to identify sounds
C   wearing eyeglasses
D   attending a special school
E   covering one eye while reading
F   listening to tapes

Reading Passage 3

*You should spend about 20 minutes on **Questions 27–40**, which are based on Reading Passage 3 below.*

Catastrophe Theory

A

In the late eighteenth and early nineteenth centuries, the popular theory among Earth scientists was that a number of major catastrophes had taken place over a relatively short period of time to give Earth its shape. French geologist Baron Georges Cuvier introduced this idea, which was later coined the "catastrophe theory." Proponents of the catastrophe theory used fossilized[1] creatures and the faunal changes in rock strata to support their beliefs that major events such as volcanoes had occurred on a worldwide scale. The catastrophe theory was used to support the notion that Earth's history was not a relatively long one.

B

In response to the catastrophe theory, a handful of Earth scientists searched for explanations that would provide a better scientific basis for Earth's geology. James Hutton, the father of geology, is best known for his gradualist theory, a paradigm that became known as "uniformitarianism." Hutton published *Theory of the Earth* in 1795, after which many other geologists including Charles Lyell, adopted the idea that small changes on Earth occurred over a large expanse of time. Uniformitarians rejected the idea that cataclysmic events could shape the Earth so quickly, and instead proposed the theory that the key to the present is the past. The term *deep time* was used to describe the span in which gradual geological processes occurred, especially the formation of sedimentary rock. Charles Darwin later based his work on the idea, by developing his theory of evolution.

C

The majority of paleontologists[2] and geologists adopted the gradualist theory of Earth's history for more than 100 years. In 1980, a discovery in Italy gave scientists a reason to reconsider the discarded theories of catastrophism. Geologist Walter Alvarez discovered a clay layer in the K-T boundary that intrigued him. The K-T boundary refers to the layer of Earth between the Cretaceous and Tertiary periods. The geologist with the help of his father Luis Alvarez, a prominent physicist, analyzed the clay for heavy metals. After careful examination, the clay was found to contain high levels of iridium. Samples taken from the K-T boundary in other parts of the world were examined, with the same findings.

---

[1]British: fossilised
[2]British: palaeontologists

D

The Alvarez group wrote a historic paper that applied the catastrophe theory to their discovery. According to their hypothesis, the iridium in the K-T boundary was caused by an asteroid or a comet that hit Earth near the end of the Cretaceous period, over 65 million years ago. They also proposed that the impact would have raised enough dust to block the sun and cool Earth, which in turn would have prevented photosynthesis. This chain reaction would have led to the extinction of plants and animals. The main reason that the Alvarez theory took hold so quickly in both the world of science and the public realm, was that it could account for the extinction of the dinosaurs at the end of the Cretaceous period. The acceptance of this theory was widespread, even before the discovery in 1990 of a 180-kilometer[1] crater in Mexico's Yucatan Peninsula, a potential piece of evidence of the asteroid impact.

E

Events that have occurred on Earth in the last 100 years or more have proved to geologists that not all processes are gradual. Major rivers have flooded areas in a matter of days, and volcanoes have erupted, causing mass devastation. The eruption of Mount St. Helens was proof of how a catastrophe could easily change the Earth's landscape. Modern research on fossils even supports the theory of a marine catastrophe, not unlike the legends and stories among many peoples of great floods. Some scientists believe that animal remains found within the layers of sedimentary rock may have been casualties of such a flood. Sedimentary rock is made up of layers such as sandstone and limestone and is created by water movement. In addition, some scientists propose that the glacial ice sheet that once spread out across North America melted catastrophically rather than having a slow glacial retreat. Deep erosion up to 100 meters wide was discovered along the bottom of some of the Great Lakes. Within the gullies, layers of periodic sediment point to catastrophic melting.

F

Though there is little debate that catastrophic events caused the mass extinction of several of Earth's species, namely the dinosaurs, geologists still question whether asteroids, volcanoes, or other natural disasters were the cause. The idea that the moon was formed as a result of catastrophic events is a related field of study and one that has been debated for decades.

---

[1]British: kilometre

Questions 27–32

*Complete the notes using the list of words, **A–L**, below.*
*Write the correct letter, **A–L**, on lines 27–32 on your answer sheet.*

A	short
B	small
C	Charles Darwin
D	long
E	definite
F	disasters
G	James Hutton
H	mysterious
I	Walter Alvarez
J	evolution
K	Georges Cuvier
L	layers

Catastrophe Theory

First introduced by **27** ....

Proposes that major **28** .... have given Earth its shape.

Supports the idea that the Earth has a **29** .... history.

Gradualist Theory

First introduced by **30** ....

Proposes that many **31** .... changes in the shape of the

Earth happened over a **32** .... period of time.

Questions 33–39

*The passage has six paragraphs, **A–F**. Which paragraph mentions the following information?*

*Write the correct letter, **A–F**, on lines 33–39 on your answer sheet. You may use any paragraph more than once.*

33 proof that not all changes on Earth have occurred gradually

34 a theory explaining the presence of iridium beneath Earth's surface

35 publication of a book about the gradualist theory

36 discovery of a large crater that could have been caused by an asteroid

37 evidence of the occurrence of a large flood in Earth's past

38 recurrence of interest in the catastrophe theory

39 ideas about how quickly ice age glaciers disappeared

Question 40

*Choose the correct letter, **A, B, or C**, and write it on line 40 on your answer sheet.*

40 Most scientists now agree that

    A the gradualist theory is correct.

    B catastrophic events occur regularly on the moon.

    C a major catastrophe caused the dinosaurs to disappear.

ANSWER SHEET
Academic Module
Practice Test 2

Writing Answer Sheet

TASK 1

_____

_____

_____

_____

_____

_____

_____

_____

_____

_____

_____

_____

_____

_____

_____

_____

_____

_____

-2-

-3-

TASK 2

_____
_____
_____
_____
_____
_____
_____
_____
_____
_____
_____
_____
_____
_____
_____
_____
_____
_____
_____

ACADEMIC MODULE TEST 2

ANSWER SHEET
Academic Module
Practice Test 2

-4-

ACADEMIC MODULE TEST 2

Candidate Name _____

International English Language Testing System

ACADEMIC WRITING

Time: 1 hour

INSTRUCTIONS TO CANDIDATES

Do not open this booklet until you are told to do so.

Write your name in the space at the top of this page.

All answers must be written on the separate answer booklet provided.

Do not remove this booklet from the examination room.

INFORMATION FOR CANDIDATES

There are **2** tasks on this question paper.

You must do **both** tasks.

Underlength answers will be penalized.[1]

---

[1]British: penalised

Writing Task 1

You should spend about 20 minutes on this task.

> The graph below shows the percentage of urban/suburban and rural households in a certain country that had Internet access between 2011 and 2016.
>
> Summarize[1] the information by selecting and reporting the main features, and make comparisons where relevant.

Household Internet Access

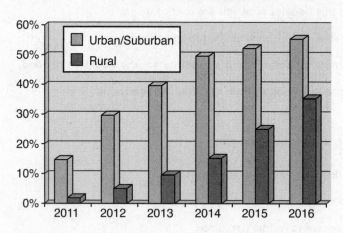

Write at least 150 words.

Writing Task 2

You should spend about 40 minutes on this task.

> *Write about the following topic:*
>
> *Because of the busy pace of modern life, many children spend most of their time indoors and have little exposure to the natural world.*
>
> *Discuss the effects lack of experience with and understanding of nature can have on children as they grow up. Give reasons for your answer and include any relevant examples from your own knowledge or experience.*

Write at least 250 words.

---

[1]British: Summarise

SPEAKING

Examiner questions:

Part 1

Leisure

When and how much leisure time do you generally have in a week?

Who do you generally spend your leisure time with?

What are some activities you enjoy in your leisure time?

What do you like about these activities?

Music

What kinds of music do you like listening to?

Have you learned to play a musical instrument? Why or why not?

Tell me about any traditional music in your country.

Do you think that traditional music will be popular in the future? Why or why not?

Part 2

You will have one to two minutes to talk about this topic.

You will have one minute to prepare what you are going to say.

> **Describe a movie that you saw recently.**
>
> **You should say:**
>
> > The title of the movie and what it was about
> >
> > When and where you saw it
> >
> > Who you saw it with and explain why you enjoyed/didn't enjoy seeing this movie

Part 3

Movie Habits

What types of movies are popular in your culture? Why do you think people like these types of movies?

Why do people often prefer to go to movie theaters rather than watch movies on their TV or computer?

Movies Past and Future

How are movies different now than they were in the past?

What impact has technology had on the film industry?

ANSWER KEY
Practice Test 2

Listening

1. tutoring sessions
2. Sunday
3. teens, adults
4. Yoga
5. adults
6. 75
7. 225
8. Eliot
9. across the street/in a garage
10. Monday
11. A
12. D
13. E
14. F
15. I
16. sweep/rear leader
17. intersection
18. rocks
19. feed
20. water
21. A
22. B
23. D
24. F
25. B
26. term paper topic
27. first evaluation
28. student teacher conference
29. term paper
30. semester review
31. A
32. C
33. A
34. B
35. C
36. spend money
37. leave faster
38. security
39. younger people/ younger clientele
40. older people/older clientele

Reading

1. 793
2. 980
3. 841
4. 911
5. 1066
6. D
7. H
8. F
9. G
10. B
11. O
12. C
13. K
14. No
15. Yes
16. Yes
17. No
18. Not Given
19. Yes
20. No
21. A
22. B
23. D
24. B
25. E
26. F
27. K
28. F
29. A
30. G
31. B
32. D
33. E
34. D
35. B
36. D
37. E
38. C
39. E
40. C

ACADEMIC MODULE—PRACTICE TEST 2

Listening

1. *tutoring sessions.* The man says, "during the school year, we have tutoring sessions for children and teens, in all subjects."

2. *Sunday.* The man says, "We have tennis lessons on Sunday mornings for teens and Sunday afternoons for adults."

3. *teens, adults.* The man says, "We have tennis lessons on Sunday mornings for teens and Sunday afternoons for adults."

4. *Yoga.* The man says, "Our yoga classes take place on Tuesday and Thursday evenings . . . there's one class for younger children, one for teens, and one for adults."

5. *adults.* The man says, "actually, that book club is for adults only."

6. *75.* The man says, "The yearly fee is seventy-five dollars for individuals and two hundred twenty-five dollars for families."

7. *225.* The man says, "The yearly fee is seventy-five dollars for individuals and two hundred twenty-five dollars for families."

8. *Eliot.* The man says, "It's at 107 Eliot Street."

9. *across the street/in a garage.* The man says, "You can park just across the street. There's a garage there."

10. *Monday.* The man says, "but don't come on Monday because we're closed . . . ."

11. **(A)** The speaker says, "First, you'll need a warm and comfortable sleeping bag."

12. **(D)** The speaker says, "We've found, though, that it's more efficient for each person to bring his or her own dishes . . . ."

13. **(E)** The speaker says, "Perhaps the most important item to put on your list is a comfortable pair of hiking boots."

14. **(F)** The speaker says, "a backpack is necessary for carrying your equipment."

15. **(I)** The speaker says, "And don't forget to bring a warm jacket."

16. *sweep/rear leader.* The speakers says, "At the end of the line will be the rear leader, or sweep. It's important to always stay ahead of this person while we're on the trail."

17. *intersection.* The speaker says, "When you come to any intersection of trails, stop and wait for the rest of the group to catch up."

18. *rocks.* The speaker says, "Don't be tempted to go off on your own and try to climb some rocks."

19. *feed.* The speaker says, "we'll encounter some large wild animals along the way. The last thing you want to do is try to feed any of them."

20. *water.* The speaker says, "you must always be sure to carry an adequate supply of water with you."

21. **(A)** The advisor says, "I require all my students to keep a journal about their teaching experience."

22. **(B)** The advisor says, "Another thing I'll want from you is a few sample lesson plans."

23. **(D)** The advisor says, "You will, however, have to observe some of the other teachers in the school, besides the teacher you'll be working with."

24. **(F)** The advisor says, "I'll base it on several things. One is your required portfolio . . . ."

25. **(B)** The student teacher asks about the person who will sign the agreement form, and the advisor explains that it is the supervising teacher. Choices (A) and (C) are the speakers.

26. *term paper topic.* The advisor says, "You should let me know your term paper topic by the end of the first week of the semester."

27. *first evaluation.* The advisor explains, "during the fourth week of the semester, we'll have our first evaluation meeting to discuss my observations."

28. *student teacher conference.* The student mentions the student teacher conference, and the advisor says, "The conference takes place, let me check, yes, the seventh week of the semester."

29. *term paper.* The advisor says, "The term paper is due by the end of the fourteenth week of the semester."

30. *semester review.* The advisor explains, "Then during the fifteenth and final week, we'll get together one last time for a semester review."

31. **(A)** The speaker says, "For example, a common practice among retailers is to place the store's best-selling merchandise near the back of the store." Choices (B) and (C) are mentioned in the talk but not as places where popular items are placed.

32. **(C)** The speaker says, "Carpets are also used to direct customers through particular areas of the store." Choices (A) and (B) are mentioned as reasons for having carpets, but not as reasons for the patterns on carpets.

33. **(A)** The speaker says, "One way to do this is to provide comfortable seating throughout the store, but not too close to the doors." Choice (B) is confused with the suggestion of putting seating "not too close to the doors." Choice (C) is plausible but is not mentioned.

34. **(B)** The speaker says, "Music . . . can slow the customers' pace through the store . . . ." Choice (A) is wrong because the speaker says it is not the reason for music. Choice (C) is the opposite of what the speaker says.

35. **(C)** The speaker says, "For example, the scent of vanilla has been used to increase sales in clothing stores." Choice (A) is associated with the scent of vanilla but is not mentioned. Choice (B) is mentioned with the scent of baking bread, not vanilla.

36. *spend money.* The speaker says, "People shopping in an environment where light purple is the predominating color seem to spend money more . . . ."

37. *leave faster.* The speaker says, "Orange . . . encourages customers to leave faster."

38. *security.* The speaker says, "Blue . . . gives customers a sense of security . . . ."

39. *younger people/younger clientele.* The speaker says, "Stores that cater to a younger clientele should use bold, bright colors, which tend to be attractive to younger people."

40. *older people/older clientele.* The speaker says, "Stores that are interested in attracting an older clientele will have more success with soft, subtle colors . . . ."

Reading

PASSAGE 1

1. *793*. Paragraph 2: "During their first expedition, in 793, a force of Viking warriors sacked the famed abbey at Lindisfarne, on England's northeast coast."

2. *980*. Paragraph 3: "In 980, an Icelandic assembly found a man named Eric 'the Red' Ericson guilty of murder and sent him into exile."

3. *841*. Paragraph 4: "To the west, they conquered coastal portions of Ireland, and in 841 founded Dublin, today a major Irish city, but originally a Viking fort."

4. *911*. Paragraph 5: "French King Charles III the Simple in 911 offered the Viking chief Rollo territories in northwest France, called Normandy, after the Normans or 'Northmen . . . .'"

5. *1066*. Paragraph 5: "in 1066, under William, Duke of Normandy [they], defeated King Harold at the battle of Hastings in England."

6. **(D)** Paragraph 1: "In fact, the term *Viking*, in Old Norse, means 'to go on an expedition.'"

7. **(H)** Paragraph 3: "There they established the first European settlement in the New World, called 'Vinland.'"

8. **(F)** Paragraph 4: "Vikings from Denmark, meanwhile, ravaged large swaths of England and France."

9. **(G)** Paragraph 6: "The Moors catapulted flaming projectiles onto the Viking vessels, forcing a retreat."

10. **(B)** Paragraph 7: "In 902, hundreds of Varangians served as marines during a Byzantine naval assault on the island of Crete."

11. **(O)** Paragraph 8: "Viking merchants on horseback penetrated far into the Asian heartland, trading with towns on the Caspian and Black seas."

12. **(C)** Paragraph 9: "the Rus moved their capital southward to Kiev, later the capital of Ukraine."

13. **(K)** Paragraph 10: "Another important Viking market town was Bulgar, on the Volga River."

PASSAGE 2

14. *No*. Paragraph 1: "It is not related to intellectual ability . . . ."

15. *Yes*. Paragraph 1: "Children are generally diagnosed with dyslexia during the elementary school years when they are learning how to read and spell."

16. *Yes*. Paragraph 2: "Many dyslexic children read letters and words backwards. . . ."

17. *No*. Paragraph 3: "Toddlers who talk much later than average . . . may develop other dyslexic symptoms."

18. *Not Given*. There is no mention of drug treatment for dyslexia.

19. *Yes*. Paragraph 5: "Dyslexic children often exhibit behavior that seems abnormal but is caused by frustration at their own inability to perform at the same level as their peers."

20. *No.* Paragraph 6 explains that dysgraphia describes difficulty with writing; difficulty with math is called dyscalculia.

21. **(A)** Paragraph 3: "Toddlers who talk much later than average . . . may develop other dyslexic symptoms."

22. **(B)** Paragraph 3: "have difficulty learning new words . . . ."

23. **(D)** Paragraph 3: "As children begin school, teachers are trained to look for warning signs, such as an inability to recognize letters or spaces between words on a page or difficulty following instructions given with more than one command at a time."

24. **(B)** Paragraph 4: "Phonological training, which involves identifying and separating sound patterns, is the most common form of therapy . . . ."

25. **(E)** Paragraph 4: "Improvements in visual focus can sometimes be achieved when students are given an eye patch to wear while they learn to read."

26. **(F)** Paragraph 4: "Some teachers find that having students listen to a book on tape before reading the text can help with information processing as well."

PASSAGE 3

27. **(K)** Paragraph A: "French geologist Baron Georges Cuvier introduced this idea . . . ."

28. **(F)** Paragraph A: "the popular theory among Earth scientists was that a number of major catastrophes had taken place over a relatively short period of time to give Earth its shape."

29. **(A)** Paragraph A: "The catastrophe theory was used to support the notion that the Earth's history was not a relatively long one."

30. **(G)** Paragraph B: "James Hutton, the father of geology, is best known for his gradualist theory, ..."

31. **(B)** Paragraph B: "the idea that small changes on Earth occurred over a large expanse of time."

32. **(D)** Paragraph B: "the idea that small changes on Earth occurred over a large expanse of time."

33. **(E)** The topic sentence for paragraph E is "Events that have occurred on Earth in the last 100 years or more have proved to geologists that not all processes are gradual."

34. **(D)** "According to their hypothesis, the iridium in the K-T boundary was caused by an asteroid or a comet that hit Earth . . . ."

35. **(B)** "Hutton published *Theory of the Earth* in 1795 . . . ."

36. **(D)** "the discovery in 1990 of a 180-kilometer crater in Mexico's Yucatan Peninsula, a potential piece of evidence of the asteroid impact."

37. **(E)** "Some scientists believe that animal remains found within the layers of sedimentary rock may have been casualties of the flood."

38. **(C)** "In 1980, a discovery in Italy gave scientists a reason to reconsider the discarded theories of catastrophism."

39. **(E)** "In addition, some scientists propose that the glacial sheet that once spread out across North America melted catastrophically rather than having a slow glacial retreat."

40. **(C)** Paragraph F: "Though there is little debate that catastrophic events caused the mass extinction of several of Earth's species, namely the dinosaurs . . . ." Choice (A) is incorrect because paragraph E discusses evidence that this theory is not correct. Choice (B) is confused with the debate over whether the moon was formed through a series of catastrophic events.

Writing

These are models. Your answers will vary. See page 2 in the Introduction to see the criteria for scoring.

WRITING TASK 1

The bar graph provides data on Internet access in both urban/suburban and rural areas of a certain country between the years 2011 and 2016. During this time, household Internet access increased dramatically in both areas.

In 2011, only 15 percent of homes in urban/suburban areas had Internet access, while less than 5 percent of rural homes had it. By the following year, Internet access in urban/suburban homes had doubled to 30 percent, while in rural homes it had increased slightly, to around 5 percent.

Over the next few years, Internet access continued to increase in both areas. Then, between 2014 and 2016, the percentage of urban/suburban homes with Internet access remained steady, at close to 50 percent. Meanwhile, the percentage of rural homes with Internet access continued growing and reached 35 percent by 2016.

While the percentage of households with Internet access increased in both areas during the years shown on the graph, the percentage in urban/suburban areas remained higher than the percentage in rural areas.

WRITING TASK 2

Modern children are busy with school, computers, television, and other indoor activities and therefore spend little time outdoors in nature. Because of this, they often end up with no knowledge or understanding of the natural world. In my opinion, this is a serious problem. Children need to understand and appreciate nature, not only for their own good but for the good of the planet as a whole.

Spending time outdoors in nature is important for children's development. Most people will agree that children need to be physically active, and the best way to achieve this is to allow them to spend a good part of each day playing outdoors in the fresh air and sunshine. Exploring the outdoors also gives children the chance to develop their curiosity and increase their knowledge of the natural world around them. When children don't have the chance to play freely outdoors, it has a negative effect on their physical health and limits their knowledge of the world. They may even learn to fear things that are part of nature because they don't understand them.

Children who haven't developed an appreciation of the natural world will have a hard time understanding the importance of protecting the environment. It will be difficult for them to realize how the trash they throw away could end up harming an ocean bird, for example. It will be hard for them to understand that keeping the planet healthy for plants and animals also means keeping it healthy for humans.

Children need to spend a lot of time outdoors interacting with the natural world. It keeps them healthy and it helps them learn to keep our planet healthy. It is important for the future of everyone.

Speaking

These are models. Your answers will vary. See page 2 in the Introduction to see the criteria for scoring.

PART 1

When and how much leisure time do you generally have in a week?
I have a normal work schedule, nine to five, Monday through Friday, so my leisure time is in the evenings and on the weekends.

Who do you generally spend your leisure time with?
I spend my evenings at home with my family. I rarely see other people during the week. On weekends we might get together as a family with other families that have children the same age as ours. Sometimes on weekends I have the chance to spend time with my own friends, without my family.

What are some activities you enjoy in your leisure time?
Sometimes I just like to sit and relax because I'm so tired after work. I also enjoy talking with my family and playing games with my children. On weekends we often enjoy going to the movies together. We also spend time at the park if the weather is nice.

What do you like about these activities?
For me, leisure time is important because it's my time to relax and be with my family. I like playing games with my children because it gives me the chance to know them better and also to teach or guide them. Also, it's fun. I enjoy my children. After we've seen a movie together, we always talk about it. It's nice to share things like this with my family. It's interesting to hear what my children think about and how they understand things.

What kinds of music do you like listening to?
I listen to music to relax, so I generally like slow, quiet music. I often listen to classical music, and I like romantic music, too.

Have you learned to play a musical instrument? Why or why not?
When I was a child, I took piano lessons for about a year. I wasn't very good at it, though, so I wasn't motivated to continue or to try another instrument. I just don't think I have musical talent. But I like listening to other people play music.

Tell me about any traditional music in your country.

We mostly hear traditional music on holidays or at special festivals. It's played with guitar and some other string instruments. Some of the songs are very pretty. I like it, but I don't get the chance to hear it much since it's just for special occasions. There are some traditional dances that go with the music, but hardly anyone knows them anymore.

Do you think that traditional music will be popular in the future? Why or why not?

These days our traditional music is played only by certain musicians who specialize in it. Not many people know how to play it or know the songs. Children learn a few of the songs in school, but that's all. It's very nice music, but it isn't commonly played or listened to now, so I think in the future it will be even less common. Unfortunately, it may soon die out. I think in the near future there won't be anyone left who knows how to play our traditional music.

PART 2

I recently saw a movie called *The Secret Garden*. It takes place more than 100 years ago. It's about a lonely little girl who is an orphan. She goes to live with an elderly relative in a big house in the country. There she discovers a garden that no one is allowed to enter. The movie is about how she discovers the secret history of the garden, and how she makes some friends in the process and isn't lonely anymore. I saw the movie with my husband and children a few weeks ago. We saw it at the movie theater that's near our house, where we often go to see movies. I really enjoyed this movie. It's a nice story for children. It shows them some sad things in life—loneliness and loss, and some good things as well—friendship and gardens. It's a little bit scary but not too scary, and the ending is very happy. The characters seem very real, and the actors are very good. The movie didn't rely on special effects or fast action or loud music to hold children's attention. Rather, it was a well-done movie with a good story. My children enjoyed it too and it gave us a lot to talk about afterward.

PART 3

What types of movies are popular in your culture? Why do you think people like these types of movies?

Action movies are very popular in my culture. People like to see movies with lots of excitement, car chases, people in danger, things like that. These movies are very exciting. I guess people like the feeling of excitement. Romance movies are very popular too. They make you feel good in a different way from action movies, but in all they make you feel good. Usually you feel very happy after watching a romance movie. I think that's why people like them.

Why do people often prefer to go to movie theaters rather than watch movies on their TV or computer?

I think when people go to see a movie in a theater it's because they want to get out of the house and be with their friends. It's a social thing. Usually when you make a plan to see a movie with a friend, you invite a group of friends, and you go to a café together before the movie, or you might go to a restaurant for dinner after the movie. When you watch a movie at home, it's because you want to see the movie. When you watch a movie at a theater, it's because you want a social event.

How are movies different now than they were in the past?

I think movies now have a lot more depth to them than they did in the past. There are more movies that show the development of the characters and there are more movies that focus on feelings. Of course there are many movies that are just superficial entertainment, too. But I think now we have more artistic movies than we had in the past. We also have more variety in movies. There are so many more different kinds of movies now than there were in the past.

What impact has technology had on the film industry?

Technology has had a big impact on movies. Action movies have so many more interesting special effects than they used to, so they are more exciting and more interesting. There are a lot of animated movies now because of computer animation. Movie makers can be a lot more creative now than they used to be because of technology.

Academic Module

PRACTICE TEST 3

ANSWER SHEET
Academic Module
Practice Test 3

IELTS Listening Answer Sheet

	✓ 1 ✗		✓ 21 ✗
1		21	
2	▭ 2 ▭	22	▭ 22 ▭
3	▭ 3 ▭	23	▭ 23 ▭
4	▭ 4 ▭	24	▭ 24 ▭
5	▭ 5 ▭	25	▭ 25 ▭
6	▭ 6 ▭	26	▭ 26 ▭
7	▭ 7 ▭	27	▭ 27 ▭
8	▭ 8 ▭	28	▭ 28 ▭
9	▭ 9 ▭	29	▭ 29 ▭
10	▭ 10 ▭	30	▭ 30 ▭
11	▭ 11 ▭	31	▭ 31 ▭
12	▭ 12 ▭	32	▭ 32 ▭
13	▭ 13 ▭	33	▭ 33 ▭
14	▭ 14 ▭	34	▭ 34 ▭
15	▭ 15 ▭	35	▭ 35 ▭
16	▭ 16 ▭	36	▭ 36 ▭
17	▭ 17 ▭	37	▭ 37 ▭
18	▭ 18 ▭	38	▭ 38 ▭
19	▭ 19 ▭	39	▭ 39 ▭
20	▭ 20 ▭	40	▭ 40 ▭

Listening Total

ACADEMIC MODULE TEST 3

Candidate Name _____

International English Language Testing System

LISTENING

Time: Approx. 30 minutes

INSTRUCTIONS TO CANDIDATES

Do not open this booklet until you are told to do so.

Write your name in the space at the top of this page.

You should answer all questions.

All the recordings will be played ONCE only.

Write all your answers on the Question Paper.

At the end of the test, you will be given ten minutes to transfer your answers to an Answer Sheet.

Do not remove this booklet from the examination room.

INFORMATION FOR CANDIDATES

There are **40** questions on this question paper.

The test is divided as follows:

Section 1	Questions 1–10
Section 2	Questions 11–20
Section 3	Questions 21–30
Section 4	Questions 31–40

Track
10

TIP

If you do not
have access
to the MP3
files on the
enclosed
disk, please
refer to the
audioscripts
starting on
page 421 when
prompted to
listen to an
audio passage.

SECTION 1

Questions 1–4

Complete the form below.

*Write **NO MORE THAN TWO WORDS AND/OR A NUMBER** for each answer.*

Example	Grandview Hotel

Reservation Form

Arrival date: **1** .... 13th. Number of nights: 2....

Number of guests: **2** ....

Guest name: Roxanne **3** ....

Credit card number **4** ....

Questions 5–7

*Choose **THREE** letters, A–G.*

*Which **THREE** places will the caller visit?*

A art museum
B science museum
C shopping mall
D monument
E post office
F restaurant
G park

Questions 8–10

*Choose the correct letter, **A**, **B**, or **C**.*

8 When will the caller arrive at the airport?

    A In the morning

    B In the afternoon

    C At night

9 How will the caller get to the hotel?

    A Subway

    B Bus

    C Taxi

10 What time does the hotel front desk close?

    A 10:00

    B 12:00

    C 2:00

SECTION 2

Questions 11 and 12

Complete the information below.
*Write **ONE NUMBER** for each answer.*

City Tours
Fare Information

Adult All-Day Pass: **11** $ ....

Children ages 5–12 All-Day Pass: **12** $ ....

Children under age 5: Free

Questions 13–15

Label the map below.
*Write **NO MORE THAN TWO WORDS** for each answer.*

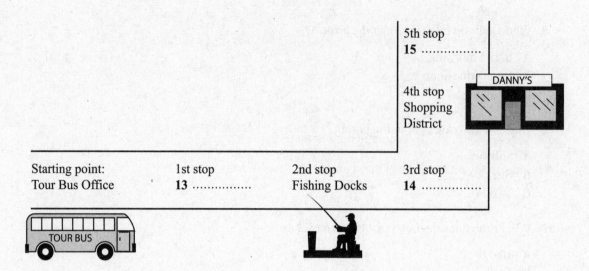

Questions 16–20

Complete the chart[1] below.
*Write **NO MORE THAN ONE WORD** for each answer.*

Place	Activity
First stop	Enjoy the **16**............................... of the bay
Second stop	Look at the **17**...............................
Third stop	**18**............................... fish.
Fourth stop	Purchase **19**...............................
Fifth stop	Visit the **20**...............................

---

[1]British: table

SECTION 3

Questions 21–23

Answer the questions below.
*Write **NO MORE THAN THREE WORDS AND/OR A NUMBER** for each answer.*

21 When is the research project due? ....

22 Where will the students conduct the interviews? ....

23 How many interviews will they complete all together? ....

Questions 24–30

Complete the outline showing the steps the students will take to complete their projects.
*Write **NO MORE THAN THREE WORDS** for each answer.*

A. Read **24** ....

B. **25** .... their questionnaire

C. Ask the professor to **26** ....

D. Conduct **27** ....

E. Get together to **28** ....

F. Prepare **29** ....

G. Give **30** ....

SECTION 4

Questions 31–40

Complete the timeline below. Write **NO MORE THAN THREE WORDS AND/OR A NUMBER** *for each answer.*

1832	**31** ....
In her teens	Alcott worked to **32** ....
At age 17	Alcott wrote **33** ....
34	Alcott enlisted as an army nurse.
35	Alcott published her letters in a book called *Hospital Sketches*.
36	Alcott returned from her trip to Europe.
37	Alcott published *Little Women*.
1879	**38** .... died.
39	The novel *Jo's Boys* was published.
1888	**40** ....

> Take ten minutes to transfer your answers onto the Answer Sheet on page 95.

ANSWER SHEET
Academic Module
Practice Test 3

IELTS Reading Answer Sheet

	√ 1 X
1	
2	2
3	3
4	4
5	5
6	6
7	7
8	8
9	9
10	10
11	11
12	12
13	13
14	14
15	15
16	16
17	17
18	18
19	19
20	20

	√ 21 X
21	
22	22
23	23
24	24
25	25
26	26
27	27
28	28
29	29
30	30
31	31
32	32
33	33
34	34
35	35
36	36
37	37
38	38
39	39
40	40
Reading Total	

ACADEMIC MODULE TEST 3

Candidate Name _____

International English Language Testing System

ACADEMIC READING

Time: 1 hour

INSTRUCTIONS TO CANDIDATES

Do not open this booklet until you are told to do so.

Write your name in the space at the top of this page.

Start at the beginning of the test and work through it.

You should answer all questions.

If you cannot do a particular question, leave it and go on to the next. You can return to it later.

All answers must be written on the Answer Sheet.

Do not remove this booklet from the examination room.

INFORMATION FOR CANDIDATES

There are **40** questions on this question paper.

The test is divided as follows:

Reading Passage 1	Questions 1–13
Reading Passage 2	Questions 14–27
Reading Passage 3	Questions 28–40

Reading Passage 1

*You should spend about 20 minutes on **Questions 1–13**, which are based on Reading Passage 1 below.*

Questions 1–7

*The following reading passage has seven sections, **A–G**. Choose the correct heading for each section from the list of headings below. Write the correct number, **i–x**, on lines 1–7 on your answer sheet. There are more headings than sections, so you will not use them all.*

1 Section A

2 Section B

3 Section C

4 Section D

5 Section E

6 Section F

7 Section G

LIST OF HEADINGS

i	Scanning the Brain and Chest
ii	The Role of Computers
iii	The CT Scan Is Invented
iv	The High Cost of CT Scans
v	Risks Associated with CT Scans
vi	Emergency Room Care
vii	Faster and More Comfortable
viii	How Doctors Use CT Scans
ix	The Patient Is Photographed
x	Enhancing Scan Images with Dyes

The CT Scanner

A

The computed tomography scanner, better known as the CT scanner, was originally designed to provide cross-sectional images of the brain. The word *tomography* comes from the Greek word *tomos*, meaning "section," and *graphia*, meaning "picture." Godfrey Hounsfield developed the technique in 1972 and was later knighted and awarded the Nobel Peace Prize for his contribution to the medical field. Within four years of this development, CT scans, also called CAT scans (computed axial tomography), were restructured, allowing technicians to scan the entire body for evidence of tumors, injuries, and other abnormalities. Rather than taking a single picture as in an X ray, a CT scanner sends several beams into an area and takes photographs from many different angles.

B

While the original CT scans took Hounsfield several hours to reconstruct into a useful image, today's machines can produce an in-depth image in a fraction of a second. Creating a scanner that could produce images at a faster rate was crucial in the development of tomography, as it reduced the degree of distortion in an image caused when patients breathed and moved. As well as providing images with better resolution, today's scanners also provide more comfort for the patient.

C

During a CT scan, a patient must lie still on a special table while the radiology technician locates the specific area that needs to be photographed. The table slides into a round tunnel (gantry), where it can be rotated or moved forward and backward in order to obtain the necessary view. Inside the donut-shaped[1] machine, a number of X rays are taken, each producing a small slice of the image that doctors require. When passing through dense tissue such as a bone, the X-ray beams are weak and appear white in the CT images. Tissues such as those found in the brain are less dense and appear gray. Images that appear black denote organs such as lungs or others that can fill with air.

D

The CT scanner is made up of several computer systems, including the host computer, which organizes[2] the entire process. One of the computers converts the raw data into an image, while another allows the technician to control the rotation of the gantry. After the information is processed, it is displayed on a monitor for radiologists and physicians to analyze.[3] The information is also saved and printed to keep in a doctor's records and to share and discuss with patients and their family members.

---

[1]British: doughnut-shaped
[2]British: organises
[3]British: analyse

E

Physicians order CT scans for a number of different reasons, including searching for and assessing tumors, cysts, kidney stones, and bone injuries. Without this technology, surgeons would have to perform many needless and costly operations. Brain, chest, and abdominal CT scans are the most common, though physicians also rely on the CT scanner to guide their needles while draining an abscess or performing a biopsy. Most emergency or shock-treatment centers contain a CT scanner in order to assess trauma victims. CT scans can pinpoint internal bleeding both in the brain and throughout the body.

F

In many cases, a patient must be given a contrast material before undergoing a CT scan. During "dynamic CT scanning," iodine dye is either injected into the blood or added to a drink that the patient must ingest approximately forty-five minutes before entering the scanner. The liquid X-ray dye makes it easier to see the organs and blood vessels when the pictures are developed. The intravenous contrast material is typically used for chest or pelvic scans, while oral-contrast material is used for abdominal scans. In some cases, physicians request that pictures be taken both before and after the contrast material enters the patient's body. Patients who receive contrast material in the arm often report feeling a warm sensation, and in rare cases an allergic reaction occurs. Contrast material causes water loss and is avoided when scanning patients who suffer from kidney failure.

G

The danger of radiation exposure caused by X-ray beams is generally considered minimal compared to the benefits that a CT scan can provide. In many cases, especially in the detection of tumors and internal bleeding, CT scans provide information that can save a person's life. Full-body scanning, which is saved for serious conditions such as coronary artery disease, remains a controversial procedure as prolonged exposure to radiation is linked to cancer. Pregnant women are excluded from receiving CT scans, as the X rays can be harmful to the fetus. When pregnant woman require an evaluation, most physicians favor using other procedures such as an ultrasound or an MRI.

Questions 8–10

Which of the following are facts about the original CT scanner mentioned in the passage? Choose **THREE** answers from the list below and write the correct letters, **A–F**, on lines 8–10 on your answer sheet.

A   It made it difficult for patients to breathe.
B   It was created to take pictures of the brain.
C   It was much bigger than current CT scanners.
D   It was developed in 1972.
E   It took several hours to produce a completed image.
F   It produced images in color.

Questions 11–13

Which of the following are facts about contrast materials used for CT scans mentioned in the passage? Choose **THREE** answers from the list below and write the correct letters, **A–F**, on lines 11–13 on your answer sheet.

A   They are bright in color.
B   They can be given by injection.
C   They have a bitter taste.
D   They might cause a feeling of warmth in the arm.
E   They are administered only by a specially trained technician.
F   They may cause allergies in a few patients.

Reading Passage 2

*You should spend about 20 minutes on **Questions 14–27**, which are based on Reading Passage 2 below.*

Nineteenth-Century Paperback Literature

A publishing craze that hit both America and England from the mid- to late nineteenth century attracted the readership of the semiliterate working class. In America, dime novels typically centered on tales of the American Revolution and the Wild West, while British penny bloods (later called penny dreadfuls) told serial tales of horror or fictionalized[1] versions of true crimes. These paperback novels were sold at newsstands and dry goods stores and succeeded in opening up the publishing market for both writers and readers. The industrial revolution facilitated the growth of literacy, making it easier to print and transport publications in large quantities, thus providing inexpensive entertainment for the masses.

Though Johann Gutenberg's printing press was designed in the fifteenth century, it was not until after the first newspapers began circulating in the eighteenth century that it became a profitable invention. Throughout the nineteenth century, commoners in England were becoming educated through normal schools, church schools, and mutual instruction classes, and by the 1830s, approximately 75 percent of the working class had learned to read. In 1870, the Forster Education Act made elementary education mandatory for all children. Though few children's books were available, penny dreadfuls were highly accessible, especially to male youths who created clubs in order to pool their money and start their own libraries. Similar to reading a newspaper, dime novels and penny dreadfuls were meant to be read quickly and discarded, unlike the hardbound high literature that was written in volumes and published for the elite. Struggling authors, many of whom had limited writing and storytelling skills, suddenly found an audience desperate to read their work. When the first typewriter became available in the 1870s, authors were able to maximize[2] their output. Successful authors, some of whom wrote over 50,000 words a month, were able to earn a decent living at a penny per word.

From the 1830s to 1850s, penny bloods featured tales of gore that often depicted the upper class as corrupt. One of the most beloved characters from the penny blood serials was Sweeney Todd. In the original story, *String of Pearls: A Romance*, published in 1846, Sweeney Todd was a demon barber who used his razor to torture his victims before turning them into meat pies. In 1847, hack-playwright George Dibdin Pitt adapted Thomas Prest's story for the stage, renaming it *The String of Pearls: The Fiend of Fleet Street*. With no copyright laws, authors were always at risk of having their ideas pilfered. Pitt's play was released again

---

[1]British: fictionalised
[2]British: maximise

one year later at one of London's "bloodbath" theaters[1] under the name *Founded on Fact*. The Sweeney Todd story also made its way into musicals and comedies. Controversy still exists over whether Thomas Prest's character was based on a real person. No records of a barber shop on Fleet Street, or a barber named Sweeney Todd have been found, though Thomas Prest was known for getting his inspiration from "The Old Bailey" of the *London Times*, a section devoted to real-life horror stories.

Despite the warning from Lord Shaftsbury that the paperback literature was seducing middle-class society into an unproductive life of evil, the penny bloods grew in popularity. They provided a literary voice for commoners at an affordable price. Eventually, penny bloods became known as penny dreadfuls and began to focus more on adventure than horror.

In 1860, Beadle and Adams was the first firm in the United States to publish a title that would be categorized[2] as a dime novel. *Malaeska: The Indian Wife of the White Hunter*, by Anne Stephens, had originally been published twenty years earlier as a series in a magazine. In novel form, approximately 300,000 copies of the story were sold in the first year, paving the way for the new fad in America. Many dime novels were written as serials with recurring characters, such as Deadwood Dick, Commander Cody, and Wild Bill. Originally, the paperbacks were intended for railroad travelers; however, during the Civil War, soldiers quickly became the most avid dime novel readers. Beadle dime novels became so popular that the company had to build a factory of hack writers to mass produce them. As urbanization[3] spread, stories of the Wild West were in less demand, and tales of urban outlaws became popular. At that time, dime novels were chosen for their illustrated covers rather than their sensational stories and characters. Despite their popularity, by the late 1880s dry goods stores were so full of unsold books that prices dropped to less than five cents per copy. Many titles that could still not sell were given away or destroyed. The International Copyright Law, passed by Congress in 1890, required publishers to pay royalties to foreign authors. Selling at less than five cents a copy, the paperback industry was doomed until the arrival of pulp paper.

---

[1]British: theatres
[2]British: categorised
[3]British: urbanisation

Questions 14–19

Which of the characteristics below belongs to which type of literature? On lines 14–19 on your answer sheet write:

> **A**   if it is characteristic of penny bloods
>
> **B**   if it is characteristic of dime novels
>
> **C**   if it is characteristic of both penny bloods and dime novels

14   They were popular in America.

15   They were popular in Britain.

16   They showed members of the upper class as corrupt.

17   They were inexpensive.

18   They featured tales of the Wild West.

19   They were popular among members of the working class.

Questions 20–23

*Match each year with the event that occurred during that year. Choose the correct event, **A–F**, from the box below and write the correct letter on lines 20–23 on your answer sheet. There are more events than years, so you will not use them all.*

> **EVENTS**
>
> **A**   The first dime novel was published in the United States.
>
> **B**   Lord Shaftsbury warned people about the dangers of penny bloods.
>
> **C**   The price of dime novels fell.
>
> **D**   The price of dime novelsl fell.
>
> **E**   A law about copyrights was passed.
>
> **F**   The first Sweeney Todd story was published.

20   1870

21   1846

22   1860

23   1890

Questions 24–27

Do the following statements agree with the information in the reading passage? On lines 24–27 on your answer sheet write:

YES	*if the statement agrees with the views of the writer*
NO	*if the statement disagrees with the views of the writer*
NOT GIVEN	*if there is no information on this in the passage*

24 The literacy rate in England rose in the nineteenth century.

25 Children's books were popular in the nineteenth century.

26 Most people agree that Sweeney Todd was based on a real person.

27 Dime novels were popular among Civil War soldiers.

Reading Passage 3

*You should spend about 20 minutes on **Questions 28–40**, which are based on Reading Passage 3 below.*

Cosmic Black Holes

In 1687, the English scientist Isaac Newton published his monumental work, *Philosophiae Naturalis Principia Mathematica (Mathematical Principles of Natural Philosophy)*, containing his theory of gravitation and the mathematics to support it. In essence, Newton's law of gravitation stated that the gravitational force between two objects, for example, two astronomical bodies, is directly proportional to their masses. Astronomers found that it accurately predicted all the observable data that science at that time was able to collect, with one exception—a very slight variation in the orbit of the planet Mercury around the sun.

It was 228 years before anyone was able to offer a refinement of Newton's law that accounted for the shape of Mercury's orbit. In 1915, Albert Einstein's general theory of relativity was published. Using the equations of general relativity, he calculated the shape of Mercury's orbit. The results predicted astronomical observations exactly and provided the first proof of his theory. Expressing it very simplistically, the general theory of relativity presumes that both matter and energy can distort space–time and cause it to curve. What we commonly call gravity is in fact the effect of that curvature.

Among other phenomena, Einstein's theory predicted the existence of black holes, although initially he had doubts about their existence. Black holes are areas in space where the gravitational field is so strong that nothing can escape them. Because of the immense gravitational pull, they consume all the light that comes near them, and thus they are "black." In fact, neither emitting nor reflecting light, they are invisible. Due to this, they can be studied only by inference based on observations of their effect on the matter—both stars and gases[1]—around them and by computer simulation. In particular, when gases are being pulled into a black hole, they can reach temperatures up to 1,000 times the heat of the sun and become an intensely glowing source of X rays.

Surrounding each black hole is an "event horizon," which defines the area over which the gravitational force of the black hole operates. Anything passing over the lip of the event horizon is pulled into the black hole. Because observations of event horizons are difficult due to their relatively small size, even less is known about them than about black holes themselves.

Black holes exist in three sizes. Compact ones, called star-mass black holes and which have been known to exist for some time, are believed to be the result of the death of a single star. When a star has consumed itself to the point that it no longer has the energy to support its mass, the core collapses and forms a black hole. Shock waves then bounce out, causing the shell of the star to explode. In a way that is not yet understood, the black hole may then reenergize[2] and create multiple explosions within the first few minutes of its existence. So-called super-massive black holes, also well documented, contain the mass of millions or even billions of stars. And just recently one intermediate black hole, with about 500 times the mass of the sun, has been discovered. Scientists have postulated that the intermediate black hole may provide a "missing link" in understanding the evolution of black holes.

Current scientific data suggest that black holes are fairly common and lie at the center of most galaxies. Based on indirect evidence gained using X-ray telescopes, thousands of black holes have been located in our galaxy and beyond. The black hole at the center of the Milky Way, known as Sagittarius A* (pronounced "A-star"), is a supermassive one, containing roughly four million times the mass of our sun. Astronomers suggest that orbiting around Sagittarius A*, 26,000 light years from Earth, may be as many as tens of thousands of smaller black holes. One possible theory to explain this is that a process called "dynamical friction" is causing stellar black holes to sink toward the center of the galaxy.

It is thought that the first black holes came into existence not long after the big bang. Newly created clouds of gases slowly coalesced into the first stars. As these early stars collapsed, they gave rise to the first black holes. A number of theories proposed that the first black holes were essentially "seeds," which then gravitationally attracted and consumed enormous quantities of matter found in adjacent gas clouds and dust. This allowed them to grow into the super-massive black holes that now sit in the centers of galaxies. However, a new computer simulation proposes that such growth was minimal. When the simulated star collapsed and formed a black hole, there was very little matter anywhere near the black hole's event horizon. Being in essence "starved," it grew by less than 1 percent over the course of its first hundred million years. The new simulations do not definitively invalidate the seed theory, but they make it far less likely. On the other hand, it is

---

[1]British: gasses
[2]British: reenergise

known that black holes a billion times more massive than our sun did exist in the early universe. Researchers have yet to discover how these super-massive black holes were formed in such a short time, and the origin of these giants poses one of the most fundamental questions in astrophysics.

It has become practically a hallmark of the research on black holes that with each new study, more is known, more theories are generated, and yet more questions are raised than answered.

Questions 28–34

*Complete each sentence with the correct ending, **A–N**, below.*
*Write the correct letter, **A–N**, on lines 28–34 on your answer sheet.*

A	by observing the matter around them.
B	suggested the presence of black holes in outer space.
C	when a single star collapses.
D	difficult to study.
E	barely visible light.
F	an inescapable gravitational pull.
G	did not apply to most astronomical bodies.
H	by direct observation.
I	could not explain Mercury's path around the sun.
J	caused doubt about the existence of black holes.
K	lose visibility.
L	become very hot.
M	with large event horizons.
N	at the center of each black hole.

28 Newton's law of gravitation

29 Einstein's theory of relativity

30 We define black holes as areas that have

31 Scientists study black holes

32 Gases that are pulled into a black hole

33 Because event horizons are comparatively small, they are

34 Compact black holes occur

Questions 35 and 36

*Choose the correct letter, **A**, **B**, or **C**, and write them on lines 35 and 36 on your answer sheet.*

35 Black holes can be found

  A only in the Milky Way.
  B in most galaxies.
  C close to the sun.

36 Sagittarius A* is

  A a black hole located 26,000 light years from Earth.
  B one of thousands of black holes orbiting Earth.
  C a well-known compact black hole.

Questions 37–40

Do the following statements agree with the information given in the passage? On lines 37–40 on your answer sheet, write:

TRUE	*if the statement agrees with the information*
FALSE	*if the statement contradicts the information*
NOT GIVEN	*if there is no information on this*

37 It is not certain when the big bang occurred.

38 According to the "seed" theory, the first black holes eventually became super-massive black holes.

39 The "seed" theory has been proven true by computer simulation.

40 The black holes that existed in the early universe were all compact black holes.

ANSWER SHEET
Academic Module
Practice Test 3

Writing Answer Sheet

TASK 1

_____

_____

_____

_____

_____

_____

_____

_____

_____

_____

_____

_____

_____

_____

_____

_____

_____

_____

_____

ANSWER SHEET
Academic Module
Practice Test 3

-2-

-3-

TASK 2

ANSWER SHEET
Academic Module
Practice Test 3

-4-

ACADEMIC MODULE TEST 1

Candidate Name _____

International English Language Testing System

ACADEMIC WRITING

Time: 1 hour

INSTRUCTIONS TO CANDIDATES

Do not open this booklet until you are told to do so.

Write your name in the space at the top of this page.

All answers must be written on the separate answer booklet provided.

Do not remove this booklet from the examination room.

INFORMATION FOR CANDIDATES

There are **2** tasks on this question paper.

You must do **both** tasks.

Underlength answers will be penalized.[1]

---

[1]British: penalised

Writing Task 1

You should spend about 20 minutes on this task.

> The charts below show degrees granted in different fields at the National University in the years 1995, 2005, and 2015.
>
> Summarize[1] the information by selecting and reporting the main features, and make comparisons where relevant.

Degrees Granted at the National University

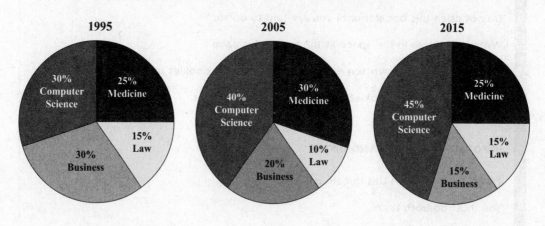

Write at least 150 words.

Writing Task 2

You should spend about 40 minutes on this task.

> Write about the following topic:
>
> All children should study a foreign language in school, starting in the earliest grades.
>
> To what extent do you agree or disagree with this statement? Give reasons for your answer and include any relevant examples from your own knowledge or experience.

Write at least 250 words.

---

[1]British: Summarise

SPEAKING

Examiner questions:

Part 1

Places

Describe a place in your city or town where you like to go in your free time.

Why do you like to go there?

Is there anything you don't like about it?

Is it a popular place for people in your city? Why or why not?

The Internet

How often do you use the Internet?

What are some things you do on the Internet?

Do you prefer shopping online or in real stores? Why?

Part 2

You will have one to two minutes to talk about this topic.

You will have one minute to prepare what you are going to say.

Describe a hobby you enjoy doing.

You should say:

  What the hobby is

  What materials or tools you need for it

  How you learned to do it and explain why you enjoy it

Part 3

Hobbies

What hobbies are common in your culture?

Are there any hobbies that you think are not worthwhile?

Hobbies in Our Lives

Why do people have hobbies?

How important is it to encourage children to take up hobbies?

Hobbies Past and Present

How are hobbies now different from hobbies in the past?

Has modern life limited the time we spend on hobbies?

ANSWER KEY
Practice Test 3

ACADEMIC MODULE TEST 3

Listening

1. February
2. one
3. Wilson
4. 2336189872
5. C
6. F
7. G
8. C
9. A
10. C
11. 18
12. 9
13. Hill Park
14. Bay Bridge
15. Green Street
16. view
17. boats
18. eat
19. baskets/souvenirs
20. theater
21. in three weeks
22. a shopping mall
23. thirty
24. a government study
25. design
26. approve their questionnaire
27. the interviews
28. analyze the results
29. some charts
30. the (class) presentation
31. Alcott was born.
32. support her family.
33. her first novel/The Inheritance
34. 1862
35. after the war
36. 1866
37. 1868
38. May/her younger sister
39. 1886
40. Alcott died.

Reading

1. iii
2. vii
3. ix
4. ii
5. viii
6. x
7. v
8. B
9. D
10. E
11. B
12. D
13. F
14. B
15. A
16. A
17. C
18. B
19. C
20. D
21. F
22. A
23. E
24. Yes
25. No
26. No
27. Yes
28. I
29. B
30. F
31. A
32. L
33. D
34. C
35. B
36. A
37. Not Given
38. True
39. False
40. False

ACADEMIC MODULE—PRACTICE TEST 3

Listening

1. *February.* The man says, "So, that's February 13th and 14th," and the woman confirms this.

2. *one.* The man asks, "And how many guests will there be?" and the woman replies, "Just me," meaning she will be the only guest.

3. *Wilson.* The woman spells her last name.

4. *2336189872.* The woman gives her credit card number, and the man repeats the last four digits.

5. **(C)** The woman says she loves shopping, and the man directs her to a shopping mall.

6. **(F)** The woman asks about a place to eat lunch, and the man tells her about a nearby restaurant.

7. **(G)** The woman says that she will walk in the park after having lunch at the restaurant.

8. **(C)** The woman says that she will be arriving after 10:00 P.M. Choice (A) is confused with when she will have free time, "Friday morning." Choice (B) is not mentioned.

9. **(A)** The man says the subway runs late, and the woman then says, "Then I'll do that," meaning that she will take the subway.

10. **(C)** The man says, "The front desk stays open until two." Choice (A) is the time that the woman will arrive. Choice (B) is how late the subways run.

11. *18.* The speaker says, "The all-day bus pass costs eighteen dollars for adults."

12. *9.* The speaker says, "Children between the ages of five and twelve pay half the adult fare. . . ."

13. *Hill Park.* The speaker says, "the bus goes to the first stop, Hill Park."

14. *Bay Bridge.* The speaker says, "the bus goes on to the third stop, Bay Bridge. . . ."

15. *Green Street.* The speaker says, "then the fifth and last stop is at Green Street."

16. *view.* The speaker says, "At the first stop, you can enjoy a spectacular view of the bay. . . ."

17. *boats.* The speaker says, "At the second stop, you can walk around and look at the boats."

18. *eat.* The speaker says, "You can eat fresh fish here prepared in the traditional local way."

19. *baskets/souvenirs.* The speaker says, "Don't miss the opportunity to purchase some of our city's famous handmade baskets. You'll want to take several home as souvenirs of your visit to our city."

20. *theater.* The speaker says, "Finally, at the last stop on the tour, you can visit one of the oldest buildings in our city, the theater."

21. *in three weeks.* The two students start out by discussing when the project is due, and Student 2 says it's due in "only three more weeks."

22. *a shopping mall.* Student 1 suggests the shopping mall, and Student 2 agrees.

23. *thirty.* They will conduct fifteen interviews each to meet the required total of thirty.

24. *a government study.* The students discuss reading a government study so that they can compare their results to the government study results.

25. *design.* Student 2 says, "Yes, so we'd better read that first and then design our questionnaire."

26. *approve their questionnaire.* Student 1 says, "The professor said she had to approve our questionnaire first, before we actually conducted the interviews."

27. *the interviews.* Student 2 says, "So we'll get her approval and then conduct the interviews."

28. *analyze the results.* Student 2 says, "And let's also plan to get together the next day to analyze the results."

29. *some charts.* Student 1 says, "Well, I think the obvious thing is to prepare some charts showing our results. . . ."

30. *the (class) presentation.* Student 1 says, "All that will be left to do is give the class presentation."

31. *Alcott was born.* The speaker says, "She was born in 1832. . . ."

32. *support her family.* The speaker says, "As a teenager, she worked to support her family. . . ."

33. *her first novel/The Inheritance.* The speaker says, "She wrote her first novel when she was just seventeen years old. . . . It was called *The Inheritance.*"

34. *1862.* The speaker says, "In 1861, the Civil War broke out. . . . The following year, she enlisted as an army nurse."

35. *after the war.* The speaker says, "After the war, she turned the letters into a book, which was published under the title *Hospital Sketches.*"

36. *1866.* The speaker says, "When she returned home from Europe in 1866. . . ."

37. *1868.* The speaker says, "Her big break came in 1868 with the publication of her first novel for girls, *Little Women.*"

38. *May/her younger sister.* The speaker says, "In 1878, her youngest sister, May, got married. A year later, May died. . . ."

39. *1886.* The speaker says, "Alcott was still writing novels for girls including two sequels to *Little Women: Little Men* and *Jo's Boys.* The latter was published in 1886.

40. *Alcott died.* The speaker says, "She died in March of 1888 at the age of 55."

Reading

PASSAGE 1

1. *iii.* Section A explains the origin and development of the CT scanner.

2. *vii.* Section B talks about how CT scanners were developed to work faster so that images were less distorted and patients were more comfortable.

3. *ix.* Section C explains the process of getting X-ray images of the patient.

4. *ii.* Section D explains the computer systems used for CT scans.

5. *viii.* Section E talks about the different circumstances for which CT scans are used.

6. *x.* Section F explains the use of dyes to make CT scan images easier to analyze.

7. *v.* Section G talks about possible dangers to patients receiving CT scans.

8. **(B)** Section A: "The computed tomography scanner, better known as the CT scanner, was originally designed to provide cross-sectional images of the brain."

9. **(D)** Section A: "Godfrey Hounsfield developed the technique in 1972 . . . ."

10. **(E)** Section B: "While the original CT scans took Hounsfield several hours to reconstruct into a useful image . . . ."

11. **(B)** Section F: "During 'dynamic CT scanning,' iodine dye is either injected into the blood . . . ."

12. **(D)** Section F: "Patients who receive contrast material in the arm often report feeling a warm sensation . . . ."

13. **(F)** Section F: "in rare cases an allergic reaction occurs."

PASSAGE 2

14. **(B)** Paragraph 1: "In America, dime novels . . . ."

15. **(A)** Paragraph 1: "while British penny bloods (later called penny dreadfuls) told serial tales of horror or fictionalized versions of true crimes."

16. **(A)** Paragraph 3: "penny bloods featured tales of gore that often depicted the upper class as corrupt."

17. **(C)** Paragraph 1: "thus providing inexpensive entertainment for the masses."

18. **(B)** Paragraph 1: "dime novels typically centered on tales of the American Revolution and the Wild West . . . ."

19. **(C)** Paragraph 1: "A publishing craze that hit both America and England from the mid- to late nineteenth century attracted the readership of the semiliterate working class."

20. **(D)** Paragraph 2: "In 1870, the Forster Education Act made elementary education mandatory for all children."

21. **(F)** Paragraph 3: "In the original story, *String of Pearls: A Romance*, published in 1846, Sweeney Todd . . . ."

22. **(A)** Paragraph 5: "In 1860, Beadle and Adams was the first firm in the United States to publish a title that would be categorized as a dime novel."

23. **(E)** Paragraph 5: "The International Copyright Law, passed by Congress in 1890, required publishers to pay royalties to foreign authors."

24. *Yes.* Paragraph 2: "by the 1830s, approximately 75 percent of the working class had learned to read."

25. *No.* Paragraph 2: "Though few children's books were available . . . ."

26. *No.* Paragraph 3: "Controversy still exists over whether Thomas Prest's character was based on a real person."

27. *Yes.* Paragraph 5: "during the Civil War, soldiers quickly became the most avid dime novel readers."

PASSAGE 3

28. **(I)** Paragraph 1: "Astronomers found that it accurately predicted all the observable data . . . , with one exception—a very slight variation in the orbit of the planet Mercury around the sun."

29. **(B)** Paragraph 3: "Among other phenomena, Einstein's theory predicted the existence of black holes."

30. **(F)** Paragraph 3: "Black holes are areas in space where the gravitational field is so strong that nothing can escape them."

31. **(A)** Paragraph 3: "they can be studied only by inference based on observations of their effect on the matter—both stars and gases—around them and by computer simulation."

32. **(L)** Paragraph 3: "when gases are being pulled into a black hole, they can reach temperatures up to 1,000 times the heat of the sun . . . . "

33. **(D)** Paragraph 4: "Because observations of event horizons are difficult due to their relatively small size, even less is known about them than about black holes themselves."

34. **(C)** Paragraph 5: "Compact ones . . . are believed to be the result of the death of a single star."

35. **(B)** Paragraph 6: "Current scientific data suggest that black holes are fairly common and lie at the center of most galaxies." Choice (A) is contradicted by the information in paragraph 6. Choice (C) is confused with the mention of the sun, but it is used to describe the size, not the location, of a back hole.

36. **(A)** Paragraph 6 explains that Sagittarius A* is a black hole in the center of the Milky Way and 26,000 light years from Earth. Choice (B) uses words from the paragraph, but black holes do not orbit Earth. Choice (C) is incorrect because the paragraph tells us that Sagittarius A* is a super-massive, not a compact, black hole.

37. *Not Given.* The big bang is mentioned, but the time of its occurrence is not.

38. *True.* Paragraph 7: "A number of theories proposed that the first black holes were essentially "seeds," which then gravitationally attracted . . . matter . . . . This allowed them to grow into the super-massive black holes."

39. *False.* Paragraph 7: "The new simulations do not definitively invalidate the seed theory, but they make it far less likely."

40. *False.* Paragraph 7: "it is known that black holes a billion times more massive than our sun did exist in the early universe."

Writing

These are models. Your answers will vary. See page 2 in the Introduction to see the criteria for scoring.

WRITING TASK 1

The three pie charts show the different kinds of degrees granted by the National University in three different years. The fields of study shown are Medicine, Law, Business, and Computer Science. The percentage of the total degrees granted for each field changes over the three years shown.

In 1995, Business and Computer Science were the most popular fields of study. Thirty percent of the degrees granted were in Business, and another 30 percent were in Computer Science. Medicine accounted for 25 percent of the degrees, and Law accounted for only 15 percent.

The figures changed somewhat in 2005. Computer Science had gained popularity, with 40 percent of the degrees granted in this field. Business had dropped to 20 percent, and Law had dropped to 10 percent. Medicine accounted for 30 percent of the degrees.

By 2015, the popularity of Computer Science had risen even more, with 45 percent of total degrees in this field. Meanwhile, Business and Medicine had dropped to 15 percent and 25 percent, respectively. Law, however, had risen to 15 percent. The only field that consistently grew in popularity in the time period shown was Computer Science.

WRITING TASK 2

I strongly agree that all children should study a foreign language in school, starting from their first day of school. Learning how to communicate with people in other countries is very important in the modern world, and we need to speak different languages in order to do this. Childhood is the best time to learn foreign languages.

Modern technology has made the world smaller. By airplane, we can travel to faraway countries in just a few hours. With the Internet, we can communicate instantly with people on the other side of the world. People do business with people in other countries, buy products from other countries, and, unfortunately, have wars with foreign countries. None of these activities are new, but they have become easier to do and more common because of modern technology. Therefore, it is now more important than ever to know how to speak one, two, or more foreign languages.

To learn a foreign language well, it is best to start in childhood. Children's brains are made for learning. Children are eager to absorb new information. Children can learn to speak foreign languages as well as their native language. It is difficult to learn a foreign language quite as well if you start studying it at a later age. Therefore, the best way to learn a foreign language is to start studying it during the first years of school.

The healthy future of our planet depends on people everywhere being able to communicate well. Teaching children to speak foreign languages from the first years of school will go a long way toward achieving this goal.

Speaking

These are models. Your answers will vary. See page 2 in the Introduction to see the criteria for scoring.

PART 1

Describe a place in your city or town where you like to go in your free time.

There's a huge shopping mall just outside my city. It's one of the biggest in the country, and people come from all over, even from faraway places, to shop there. It has hundreds of stores of all different kinds. It also has restaurants, clubs, and movie theaters. It also has a couple of areas kind of like indoor parks where you can sit on benches and watch a water fountain. There's a lot you can do there.

Why do you like to go there?

I like to go there because there are so many different things to do. Whatever I may need to buy, I can buy it there. If I want to get together with my friends, it's a good place for us to meet. We have our choice of restaurants, movies, and clubs. It's kind of like a little city all under one roof. I especially like to go there in the winter when it's too cold to be outside.

Is there anything you don't like about it?

I can only think of one thing I don't like about it, and that's the parking situation. The parking garage is very crowded and sometimes I spend a long time driving around looking for an empty spot. That really annoys me. They should have a system to let people know where the empty spaces are so we can go right to them without driving around and around.

Is it a popular place for people in your city? Why or why not?

It's a very popular place for people in my city. The main reason is because there are so many different things to do and buy there. There's something for everyone. Another reason people like it is because it's all indoors. We live in a cold climate, and the winters can be very, very cold. No one likes to walk around outside then. If you go to the shopping mall, you don't have to go outside to get from place to place.

How often do you use the Internet?

I use the Internet quite frequently. I use it in the course of my work every day. For example, I frequently use e-mail to discuss things with my colleagues. I often have to look for information online, for both work and personal reasons. So, I'd have to say I use the Internet several times a day.

What are some things you do on the Internet?

Besides e-mailing my colleagues and my friends and relatives, I use the Internet for a number of other things. I often use it to find information I need for my work. I also use it to research products before I make a big purchase; I mean something expensive. Last year I had to buy a new refrigerator, so I did some research online to figure out what kind I wanted and what it should cost. I often read the news online, and I find out about movies I want to see and books I want to buy. I do a lot on the Internet.

Do you prefer shopping online or in real stores? Why?

As I mentioned, I like to research products online before I make a major purchase, but usually I prefer to buy things in a regular store. Especially if I'm buying something expensive, I like to see it before I buy it. Also, shipping costs can be very high, and you don't have to pay them if you buy from a store. Sometimes it's hard to find things locally, and sometimes you can find a really, really good price online, so sometimes I buy things that way. But usually I go to stores.

PART 2

A hobby I enjoy is painting. I can't say I'm very artistic, but I like painting. I do watercolor paintings, so the materials I need are paint and brushes, water, and special watercolor paper. I learned to paint by taking classes. Frankly, I can't remember how I got the idea to learn to paint, but once I decided I wanted to do it, I looked for classes at the local community center. I've taken several painting classes there, and I've learned a lot. I enjoy painting because it's very relaxing. When I paint, I can take my mind off my work and off personal problems. I just think about my painting. I also like the challenge. It's a challenge to try to make a painting look the way I want it to look. I work all the time to improve my technique. I've had a lot of frustrations, but when I feel like I've finally made a painting look the way I want it to look, I feel really happy. It's a satisfying feeling. Another thing I like about painting is that it gives me something to hang on the walls of my apartment! Of course, I only hang up the successful paintings.

PART 3

What hobbies are common in your culture?
People in my country enjoy all kinds of hobbies. One hobby that is very popular now is collecting comic books. Comics are very popular and some people try to collect different comics, including comics from other countries. People enjoy collecting other things, too, like coins and stamps and other types of things. Some people are very artistic and they like painting and drawing.

Are there any hobbies that you think are not worthwhile?
For me, some hobbies would be a real waste of time. I would not enjoy collecting baseball cards, for example, because I am completely uninterested in baseball. But I can't say that it wouldn't be worthwhile for somebody who likes baseball. I think any hobby is fine as long as it isn't harmful to other people. I don't think you have to learn anything special from a hobby. You just have to have fun. As long as your hobby is fun for you, then I think it's worthwhile for you to do it.

Why do people have hobbies?
I think the main reason people have hobbies is to relax. After working or studying all week, people want to do something relaxing in their free time, to enjoy themselves. Sometimes people have hobbies because they want to develop special skills, like drawing or sewing or carpentry, so that's another reason to have a hobby. Also, having a hobby can be a way to make new friends. You can join clubs or groups of people who have the same hobby as you do, then you can meet new people.

How important is it to encourage children to take up hobbies?
I think it's a good idea to encourage children to take up hobbies. Then they will have a good way to spend their free time. Instead of watching TV or sitting around feeling bored, children with hobbies can have fun and interesting experiences during their free time. They can also learn skills through hobbies. Even if their hobby is collecting baseball cards, which may seem

like an unimportant thing to do, they can learn skills like organizing, or setting goals and reaching them, all kinds of skills that will help them in life.

How are hobbies now different from hobbies in the past?

In the past people probably did a lot more handcrafts, like knitting and sewing or making things for the house. A lot of women my grandmother's age know how to knit and sew, but not many young women know how to do these things now. I think now people are more interested in things that are related to the modern world, like collecting music that is currently popular, or playing the sports that famous athletes play. We see a lot of things on TV, and that influences our interests. I think in the past people were more interested in the home and their hobbies reflected this. Now we are interested in what's going on in the world so our hobbies are about the outside world.

Has modern life limited the time we spend on hobbies?

I think we have less time for hobbies than we did in the past. People work a lot now and also we have the Internet and TV. We spend a lot of time watching TV or doing things online and less time making things or learning new skills. If we learn new skills, they are skills we need for our jobs.

Academic Module

PRACTICE TEST 4

ANSWER SHEET
Academic Module
Practice Test 4

IELTS Listening Answer Sheet

		√	X
1		1	
2		2	
3		3	
4		4	
5		5	
6		6	
7		7	
8		8	
9		9	
10		10	
11		11	
12		12	
13		13	
14		14	
15		15	
16		16	
17		17	
18		18	
19		19	
20		20	

		√	X
21		21	
22		22	
23		23	
24		24	
25		25	
26		26	
27		27	
28		28	
29		29	
30		30	
31		31	
32		32	
33		33	
34		34	
35		35	
36		36	
37		37	
38		38	
39		39	
40		40	

Listening Total

ACADEMIC MODULE TEST 4

Candidate Name _____

International English Language Testing System

LISTENING

Time: Approx. 30 minutes

INSTRUCTIONS TO CANDIDATES

Do not open this booklet until you are told to do so.

Write your name in the space at the top of this page.

You should answer all questions.

All the recordings will be played ONCE only.

Write all your answers on the Question Paper.

At the end of the test, you will be given ten minutes to transfer your answers to an Answer Sheet.

Do not remove this booklet from the examination room.

INFORMATION FOR CANDIDATES

There are **40** questions on this question paper.

The test is divided as follows:

Section 1	Questions 1–10
Section 2	Questions 11–20
Section 3	Questions 21–30
Section 4	Questions 31–40

SECTION 1

Questions 1–10

TIP

If you do not have access to the MP3 files on the enclosed disk, please refer to the audioscripts starting on page 421 when prompted to listen to an audio passage.

Complete the form below.

*Write **NO MORE THAN TWO WORDS AND/OR A NUMBER** for each answer.*

Example	ClearPoint ..Telephone Company....

Customer Order Form

Order taken by:	Ms. Jones ....
Name:	Harold **1**.............................
Address:	**2**.............................. Fulton Avenue, apartment 12
Type of service:	**3**.............................
Employer:	Wrightsville Medical Group
Occupation:	**4**.............................
Work phone:	**5**.............................
Time at current job:	**6**.............................
Special services:	**7**............................. **8**.............................
Installation scheduled for:	Day **9**.............................
	Time of day **10**.............................

SECTION 2

Questions 11–14

*Choose the correct letter, **A**, **B**, or **C**.*

11 The fair will take place at the

    A fairgrounds.

    B park.

    C school.

12 The fair will begin on Friday

    A morning.

    B afternoon.

    C evening.

13 The fair will begin with a

    A parade.

    B dance performance.

    C speech by the mayor.

14 There will be free admission on

    A Friday.

    B Saturday.

    C Sunday.

Questions 15–20

Complete the chart[1] below.

*Write **NO MORE THAN ONE WORD** for each answer.*

Day/Time	Event
Saturday afternoon	15 .... show
Saturday evening	16 .... by the lake
Sunday afternoon	17 .... contest
Sunday evening	18 .... food
	19 .... for children
	20 .... for sale

---

[1]British: table

SECTION 3

Track 16

Questions 21–23

Complete the information below.
*Write **NO MORE THAN TWO WORDS** for each answer.*

How to get academic credit for work experience

First, read the **21** .... Find courses that match your work

experience. Then write **22** .... of your work experience. Submit

that together with a letter from your **23** .... to the university

admissions office.

Questions 24–28

Where can the student go to get the information and items listed below?

A	Student Services Center
B	university website
C	library

---

*Write the correct letter, **A, B,** or **C,** next to **Questions 24–28.***

24 course catalog[1] ....

25 admissions form ....

26 admissions requirements ....

27 information about professors ....

28 parking pass ....

---
[1]British: catalogue

Questions 29 and 30

*Choose the correct letter, **A**, **B**, or **C**.*

29 What are full-time students eligible for?

   A Discounted books
   B The work-study program[1]
   C A free bus pass

30 How can a student get financial assistance?

   A Speak with a counselor[2]
   B Apply to the admissions office
   C Make arrangements with a bank

SECTION 4

Questions 31–35

Complete the chart with information about the black bear.
*Write **NO MORE THAN TWO WORDS** for each answer.*

Range	Lives in 31 .... of North America
Diet	Ninety percent of diet consists of 32 ....
	Also eats 33 .... and ....
Cubs	Baby bear cubs are born during the 34 ....
Life span	Black bears live for about 35 .... in the wild.

---

[1]British: programme
[2]British: counsellor

Questions 36–40

Which characteristics fit black bears and which fit grizzly bears?
*Write **A** if it is a characteristic of black bears. Write **B** if it is a characteristic of grizzly bears.*

36 Has a patch of light fur on its chest   ....

37 Weighs 225 kilos   ....

38 Has a shoulder hump   ....

39 Has pointed ears   ....

40 Has shorter claws   ....

> **Take ten minutes to transfer your answers onto the Answer Sheet on page 135.**

ANSWER SHEET
Academic Module
Practice Test 4

IELTS Reading Answer Sheet

#		✓ ✗	#		✓ ✗
1		✓ 1 ✗	21		✓ 21 ✗
2		2	22		22
3		3	23		23
4		4	24		24
5		5	25		25
6		6	26		26
7		7	27		27
8		8	28		28
9		9	29		29
10		10	30		30
11		11	31		31
12		12	32		32
13		13	33		33
14		14	34		34
15		15	35		35
16		16	36		36
17		17	37		37
18		18	38		38
19		19	39		39
20		20	40		40
			Reading Total		

ACADEMIC MODULE TEST 4

Candidate Name _____

International English Language Testing System

ACADEMIC READING

Time: 1 hour

INSTRUCTIONS TO CANDIDATES

Do not open this booklet until you are told to do so.

Write your name in the space at the top of this page.

Start at the beginning of the test and work through it.

You should answer all questions.

If you cannot do a particular question, leave it and go on to the next. You can return to it later.

All answers must be written on the Answer Sheet.

Do not remove this booklet from the examination room.

INFORMATION FOR CANDIDATES

There are **40** questions on this question paper.

The test is divided as follows:

Reading Passage 1	Questions 1–13
Reading Passage 2	Questions 14–27
Reading Passage 3	Questions 28–40

Reading Passage 1

*You should spend about 20 minutes on **Questions 1–13**, which are based on Reading Passage 1 below.*

The Gulf Stream and Global Warming

Labrador and London lie at about the same latitude, but Labrador is frigid and has only 30 miles of paved roads while London is one of the major centers[1] of civilization.[2] Why do two places, equidistant from the Arctic Circle, have such disparate climates? The Gulf Stream that flows by the British Isles makes all the difference: Its warm waters make northwestern Europe so abundant with life that palm trees can actually grow on the southern shores of England.

This life-giving Gulf Stream is warm, salty water, which travels along the surface of the Atlantic Ocean from the Caribbean, along the east coast of the United States, and then veers toward Europe. In the tropics, this water is warmed by the sun and becomes saltier because of the higher rate of evaporation in the heat. The Gulf Stream divides as it travels, but the majority of the stream moves north and east. As it travels past Europe, the Gulf Stream warms the atmosphere, and the prevailing westerly winds bring the warmed air to all of northwestern Europe, making the area suitable for intense agriculture. The Gulf Stream makes it possible for Europe to feed an increasingly large population.

After the Gulf Stream reaches southeast Greenland and western Iceland, much of the heat of the stream is gone, and the colder, denser water then sinks. The bulk of the Gulf Stream is carried down toward the ocean floor into as many as seven large vortices, called chimneys. They suck the Gulf Stream waters down over a mile deep, where the water is then drawn into another dynamic ocean current. Almost 2 miles below the surface, this cold water current flows in reverse, from the north southward. When this cold water nears the equator, it is again pulled up from the bottom of the ocean as the surface water is heated and starts its journey north. This upwelling brings with it minerals and food from the detritus at the bottom of the ocean to refresh food supplies for fish and other marine creatures.

This stream of water—the warm water traveling[3] north along the surface and the cold water traveling south along the floor—has become known as the Great Ocean Conveyor Belt. This flow of ocean currents has been extremely important in regulating the temperature of the globe and in making life possible. These currents in the North Atlantic are part of the Great Conveyor Belt that flows through all the oceans of the world. The least stable section of this global current is in the North Atlantic. The Gulf Stream is the most unstable of all.

Predictions of the effects of global warming on the Gulf Stream are based on computer models, which differ to some extent. But several important facts are

---

[1]British: centres
[2]British: civilisation
[3]British: travelling

known. South of Greenland, there used to be as many as seven chimneys that pulled water from the Gulf Stream down toward the ocean floor. In the last several years, only one remained, and then, in 2007, that one disappeared. The causes for the demise of the chimneys may include the increase in fresh water from glacial melt. In recent winters, glacial melt has released record amounts of fresh water into the oceans. As the North Atlantic waters, including fresh water from rivers as well as the increased amount of glacial melt, mix with the Gulf Stream, the salt water is diluted. Because fresh water is not as dense as salt water, it does not sink, which impairs the natural mechanism for forming the chimneys. As the chimneys have disappeared, the Gulf Stream has slowed. About 30 percent of the water from the Gulf Stream that used to reach Europe travels elsewhere or is lost in the disintegration of the current, a loss of over six million tons of water flow every second. Without a strong Gulf Stream, the slow, cold water of the lower part of the conveyor belt fails to rise, which reduces the circulation of nutrients for marine life. The problem of warming then worsens: As less surface water, which is full of carbon dioxide from the atmosphere, siphons into the depths of the ocean, less carbon dioxide is removed from the atmosphere, thus increasing global warming.

Ocean sediments and glacial cores show that there have been global swings in temperature in the past. The last Ice Age, when much of North America and northern Europe were covered in glaciers 2 miles thick, occurred when the average temperature dropped about 5 degrees Celsius. That ice age ended about 20,000 years ago. The last "Little Ice Age," when the average temperature dropped only 1 to 2 degrees Celsius, occurred in the sixteenth and seventeenth centuries, hitting Europe hardest. At that time, the Gulf Stream had slowed to about half its usual rate.

Core samples also show that the changes in temperature have been abrupt, not gradual. There would be little time to prepare for the devastating changes resulting from the weakening of the Gulf Stream. The good news is that in the winters of 2008 and 2009, one of the chimneys off southeastern Greenland suddenly burst into action again, bringing the Gulf Stream waters down deep enough to be caught in the conveyor and to keep the ocean currents in the North Atlantic flowing.

Questions 1–7

*Write the correct letter, **A**, **B**, or **C**, on lines 1–7 on your answer sheet.*

1 Labrador and London are similar in

   A climate.
   B distance from the North Pole.
   C abundance of wildlife.

2 Europe can support a large population because

   A it has a lot of fresh water.
   B it is at the proper latitude.
   C it has a good climate for farming.

3 When the Gulf Stream reaches the North Atlantic, it sinks because

   A it has become colder.
   B it has become less salty.
   C it is blown by the winds.

4 Ocean currents help make life on Earth possible because they

   A enable marine life to travel.
   B maintain suitable temperatures.
   C regulate glacial melt.

5 In 2007, the number of vortices, or chimneys, that pulled the waters of the Gulf Stream down toward the ocean floor was

   A zero.
   B one.
   C seven.

6 During the most recent Little Ice Age,

   A the Gulf Stream slowed down significantly.
   B Europe was affected only slightly.
   C glaciers covered much of North America.

7 In the past, climate change has happened

   A at regular intervals.
   B gradually over time.
   C very quickly.

Questions 8–13

*The flow chart below shows a possible effect of global warming on the Gulf Stream. Complete the flow chart using the list of words, **A–L**, below.*

*Write the correct letter, **A–L**, on lines 8–13 on your answer sheet.*

A less salty	**E** rise	**I** food
B colder	**F** weakened	**J** melt
C warmer	**G** strengthened	**K** air
D sink	**H** heated	**L** form

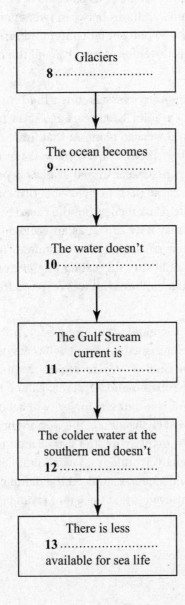

Glaciers
8 ....

↓

The ocean becomes
9 ....

↓

The water doesn't
10 ....

↓

The Gulf Stream current is
11 ....

↓

The colder water at the southern end doesn't
12 ....

↓

There is less
13 ....
available for sea life

READING PASSAGE 2

*You should spend about 20 minutes on **Questions 14–27**, which are based on Reading Passage 2 below.*

Chocolate—Food of the Gods

The cacao plant is believed to have evolved at least 4,000 years ago. It is a small evergreen tree, 15–25 feet high, which grows in the tropical forest understory, where it is protected by the shade of larger trees. The scientific name for the cacao plant is *Theobroma*, which means "food of the gods." Native to the Amazon and Orinoco River basins, it requires a humid climate and regular rainfall. Small pink flowers grow directly on the trunk and older branches. The fruit, a cacao pod, is melon shaped and weighs roughly 1 pound when fully ripened. A mature tree may have as many as 6,000 flowers but will only produce about twenty pods. Each pod contains between twenty and sixty seeds, called beans. The beans have a 40–50 percent fat content, referred to as *cocoa butter*. (*Cacao* is the plant; *cocoa* is the edible derivative and the primary ingredient in chocolate.)

Chemical analysis of pottery vessels unearthed in Puerto Escondido, Honduras, and dating from around 3,100 years ago show traces of a compound that is found exclusively in the cacao plant. At that time, the plant was already being used as a beverage ingredient. However, it was not the cacao beans that were first used. Instead, the first cacao-based drink was probably produced by fermenting the pulp in the cacao pods to yield a beerlike beverage. Researchers speculate that the chocolate drink made from the cacao beans and known later throughout Mesoamerica may have arisen as an accidental by-product of the brewing process. In all, ten small, beautifully crafted drinking vessels were found at the Puerto Escondido site, suggesting that even then the cacao brew was not consumed on a frequent basis but was reserved for important feasts or ceremonial events.

The villagers of Puerto Escondido had likely been influenced by the great Olmec civilization,[1] which flourished for about 800 years beginning 3,200–2,400 years ago in the southern Gulf of Mexico region. Although centered in the modern Mexican states of Tabasco and Veracruz, Olmec influence reached as far south as El Salvador and Honduras. A majority of scholars concur that the Olmec people created the first civilization in the western hemisphere. They built large cities with significant architecture and established commerce extending over hundreds of miles. Relatively little is known about Olmec society because very little archeological[2] evidence has survived the damp climate of the Gulf of Mexico. What is known, however, is that the later Mayan peoples, who did leave

---

[1]British: civilisation
[2]British: archaeological

behind a great deal of cultural evidence, based much of their high culture on earlier Olmec traditions.

Mayan civilization flourished in southern Mexico and Central America from around 500 B.C.E.[1] to around 1500, and the word *cacao* comes from the Mayan word *Ka'kau'*. However, this is not a native Mayan word but is derived from the Olmec language. To the Mayans, the cacao pod symbolized[2] life and fertility. Many of the bas-reliefs carved on their palaces and temples show cacao pods. It is believed that the Mayans took the cacao tree from its native rain forest and began to cultivate it in plantations. After harvesting the seed pods, they scooped out the contents—the cacao beans embedded in a sticky, white flesh—and allowed it all to ferment until the seeds turned dark brown. The seeds were then roasted and ground into a thick chocolate paste.

From the paste, the Mayans made a hot chocolate drink. However, it was very different from contemporary hot chocolate. The basic drink was made by mixing the paste with water, chili powder, cornmeal, and other ingredients and heating it. Then the liquid was poured back and forth from one vessel held at arm's height to another resting on the ground. This created a chocolate drink with a thick head of dark foam—considered the best part of the drink. Among the Mayans, as the chocolate drink grew more popular and the ingredients more readily available, people from all levels of society enjoyed it at least on occasion.

The Maya preserved their knowledge of cacao use through stone carvings, some in jade and obsidian, pottery decorations, and written documents that detailed the use of cacao, described in Mayan as "food of the gods." Cacao was used in ceremonies, medical treatments, and daily life centuries before the discovery of the New World by Europeans. Certain recipes for cacao drinks included vanilla, nuts, honey from native bees, and various flowers.

Ek Chuah (meaning "black star" in Yucatec Maya) was the patron god of merchants and commerce. Because cacao seeds were light in weight, easily transported, and of great value, they were used as currency throughout Mesoamerica. Thus *Ek Chuah* also became the patron god of cacao. Each April, the Maya held a festival to honor[3] this deity. The celebration included offerings of cacao, feathers, and incense, the sacrifice of a dog with cacao-colored[4] markings, other animal sacrifices, and an exchange of gifts. Given that the chocolate drink could be made only through the direct destruction of currency, one can understand why it was called the "food of gods." The immortals could easily afford it, while for humans it was a precious commodity indeed.

---

[1]B.C.E. is the abbreviation for "Before the Common Era," that is, before the year 0.
[2]British: symbolised
[3]British: honour
[4]British: coloured

Questions 14–18

Do the following statements agree with the information in the passage? On lines 14–18 on your answer sheet, write:

TRUE	*if the statement agrees with the information*
FALSE	*if the statement contradicts the information*
NOT GIVEN	*if there is no information on this*

14 The mature cacao plant produces about 6,000 pods.

15 The cacao plant prefers wet weather.

16 Each flower on the cacao plant produces twenty pods.

17 Cacao drinks were originally made using the pulp from the pod.

18 In ancient Puerto Escondido, cacao drinks were served hot.

Questions 19–25

According to the information in Reading Passage 2, which ancient civilizations do the following phrases describe? On lines 19–25 on your answer sheet, write:

A if the phrase describes the ancient Olmec civilization only

B if the phrase describes the ancient Mayan civilization only

C if the phrase describes both the Olmec and the Mayan civilizations

19 collapsed around 2,400 years ago

20 was located in Mexico

21 grew cacao on large farms

22 left behind little concrete evidence of their culture

23 influenced the ancient inhabitants of Puerto Escondido

24 carved images of cacao pods

25 made a drink by mixing cacao with chili powder and cornmeal

Questions 26 and 27

Write the correct letter, A, B, or C, on lines 26 and 27 on your answer sheet.

26 The ancient Maya used cacao seeds as

    A decorations.

    B a dye.

    C money.

27 In April, the ancient Maya celebrated

    A dogs.

    B a god.

    C stars.

Reading Passage 3

*You should spend about 20 minutes on **Questions 28–40**, which are based on Reading Passage 3 below.*

The Intelligence of Corvids

For hundreds of years humans thought that tool making was a uniquely human trait. In 1960, Jane Goodall observed chimpanzees using tools in the wild, a discovery to which Goodall's mentor Louis Leakey famously responded, "We must redefine tool, redefine man, or accept chimpanzees as human." It is now commonly accepted that various primates engage in tool making, and there is a growing body of evidence that many corvids, a group of bird species that includes crows, jays, rooks, ravens, and magpies, are also tool makers, and that they show many other signs of possessing high intelligence.

Scientists have observed wild New Caledonian crows making hooks out of twigs to pull grubs from tree holes that are too deep for their beaks. New Caledonian crows also sometimes use their beaks to create small spears from leaves for collecting insects. Because New Caledonian crows are highly social and because tool design varies from area to area, most researchers assume the birds' tool use is cultural; that is, the tool use is learned from other crows.

In 2002, however, three researchers at Oxford University reported in *Science* a startling new twist to tool making in corvids: A New Caledonian crow that had been captured in 2000 as a juvenile had invented a new tool from materials not found in her natural habitat without observing the behavior[1] in other crows. The crow, named Betty, shared space with a male crow named Abel. The researchers had set up an experiment in which both crows were presented with a straight wire

---

[1]British: behaviour

and a hooked wire and food that could most easily be retrieved with a hooked wire. When Abel flew away with the hooked wire, Betty bent the straight wire and successfully lifted the bucket of food with her hook. The researchers then set out to see whether they could get Betty to replicate the behavior. Ten times, they set out a single straight wire and food to be retrieved. Betty retrieved the food nine times by bending the wire; once she managed to retrieve the food with the straight wire. Alex Kacelnik, one of the researchers who worked with the crows, noted that she had solved a new problem by doing something she had never done before.

Professor John Marzloff, at the University of Washington in Seattle, demonstrated another interesting ability in American crows: recognizing[2] faces of individual humans. In 2005, he and other researchers each wore a caveman mask when they captured, tagged, and then released crows on campus. Then Marzloff and other researchers took turns wearing the mask and walking around campus. Over time, increasing numbers of crows flocked together and cawed at anyone wearing the caveman mask, regardless of the size, gender, and skin color of the mask wearer or whether the wearer was one of the researchers who had originally captured crows. When the same people did not wear the mask, they got no reaction from the crows. This showed that it was clearly the face that was identified as a threat to the flock. Crows that had not originally been captured were joining the harassment of the perceived threat. When Marzloff suggested that researchers try wearing the caveman mask upside down, some crows actually turned their heads upside down to better identify the face of the "enemy."

In their studies of western scrub jays published in *Science* in May 2006, Johann Dally, Nathan Emery, and Nicola Clayton showed that jays have the ability to remember whether a specific other jay saw them hide food for later use. When it became clear that a jay that observed the hiding might have access to the cache, the hiders retrieved their food and re-hid it when given the opportunity to do so without observation. They did not re-hide food when other jays were introduced to the situation. Similarly, ravens in the wild have been observed misleading other ravens by pretending to hide food in one location then flying off to hide it elsewhere when the other raven goes to investigate the false cache.

Corvids are also capable of fooling humans. Marzloff tells the story of a pair of crows that built a fake nest that they always flew to when researchers were in their area. The crows' actual nest with their young was nearby, but the humans never saw the crows actually fly to it.

In an experiment to test social cooperation in rooks, University of Cambridge researchers found that pairs of rooks quickly figured out how to pull on ropes at the same time to bring food that could not be gained through the individual effort of one rook.

Otto Koehler tested the ability of captive jackdaws to count, a skill apparently related to their communication often being based on the number of calls. First, Koehler trained jackdaws to expect five food rewards. Then the jackdaws were given a number of boxes, some of which contained food. They proceeded to open

---

[2]British: recognising

the boxes until they had found five pieces of food, at which point they stopped opening boxes because they knew they had reached five. In another experiment Koehler also trained jackdaws to choose a box with the same number of dots on the lid as the number of dots on a cue card.

Tool makers, tricksters, cooperators, mathematicians—the corvids are far from "bird brains." In fact, their intelligence, in many cases, appears to equal or even surpass that of many of our primate "cousins."

Questions 28–33

Complete the summary using the list of words and phrases, A–N, below. Not all letters are used.

Write the correct letter, A–N, on lines 28–33 on your answer sheet.

A	learn from other birds	H	hooks
B	twigs	I	try to take away
C	humans	J	modify
D	repeat	K	chimpanzees
E	spears	L	grubs
F	are born knowing	M	teach her how to make
G	leaves	N	corvids

Jane Goodall's work in 1960 showed that **28** .... were not the only ones to make tools. Since then, scientists have observed different kinds of animals making tools. New Caledonian crows, for example, make tools in order to retrieve the **29** .... that they eat in the wild. Scientists believe that generally these birds **30** .... how to make tools. In 2002, a captive New Caledonian crow named Betty invented a new tool. Scientists observed Betty use pieces of wire to make **31** ...., which she used to retrieve food. The interesting thing is that other crows did not **32** .... the tools. Once the scientists saw Betty make a tool, they tried to get her to **33** .... the behavior, which she did successfully.

Questions 34–36

*Write the correct letter, **A**, **B**, or **C**, on lines 34–36 on your answer sheet.*

34 Researchers wore a mask when working with crows in order to

   A conceal their true identity from the crows.

   B find out whether crows would recognize the mask in another situation.

   C protect their faces from aggressive crows.

35 Crows harassed researchers wearing the mask because the researchers

   A had worn the mask when handling crows.

   B were of a size and skin color that crows feared.

   C took turns wearing the mask while walking around campus.

36 When researchers removed the mask,

   A the crows did not harass them.

   B they were attacked by the entire flock of crows.

   C they could more easily tag the crows.

Questions 37–40

Match each corvid action described by researchers below with the information it shows us about corvid intelligence.

*Write the correct letter, **A–F**, on lines 37–40 on your answer sheet. There are more types of information listed than actions, so you will not use them all.*

INFORMATION ABOUT CORVID INTELLIGENCE

A Corvids can count.

B Corvids recognize individual birds.

C Corvids are good at discovering food sources.

D Corvids can work together to achieve a goal.

E Corvids protect themselves by tricking their enemies.

F Corvids are skilled at remembering where they hid things.

---

37 Birds opened boxes to obtain food.

38 Birds pulled ropes to get food.

39 Birds hid food from other birds.

40 Birds built a nest that was not real.

Writing Answer Sheet

TASK 1

_____

_____

_____

_____

_____

_____

_____

_____

_____

_____

_____

_____

_____

_____

_____

_____

_____

_____

_____

ACADEMIC MODULE TEST 4

-2-

ACADEMIC MODULE TEST 4

-3-

TASK 2

_____

_____

_____

_____

_____

_____

_____

_____

_____

_____

_____

_____

_____

_____

_____

_____

_____

_____

_____

_____

-4-

ACADEMIC MODULE TEST 4

Candidate Name _____

International English Language Testing System

ACADEMIC WRITING

Time: 1 hour

INSTRUCTIONS TO CANDIDATES

Do not open this booklet until you are told to do so.

Write your name in the space at the top of this page.

All answers must be written on the separate answer booklet provided.

Do not remove this booklet from the examination room.

INFORMATION FOR CANDIDATES

There are **2** tasks on this question paper.

You must do **both** tasks.

Underlength answers will be penalized.[1]

---

[1]British: penalised

Writing Task 1

You should spend about 20 minutes on this task.

> The graph below shows the average number of movies seen in a theater per year, by age group.
>
> Summarize[1] the information by selecting and reporting the main features, and make comparisons where relevant.

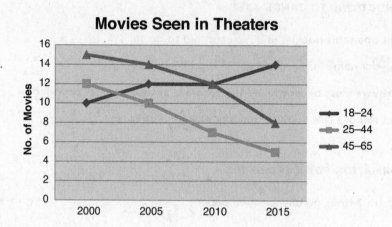

Movies Seen in Theaters

Write at least 150 words.

---
[1]British: Summarise

Writing Task 2

You should spend about 40 minutes on this task.

> *Write about the following topic:*
>
> *The large number of private cars on the roads in many parts of the world has led to serious problems of pollution and may contribute to global warming. Some people think that governments should spend money for the development of public transportation systems in order to help solve this problem. Others think it is better to spend money for the development of electric and other types of cars that may cause less pollution.*
>
> *Discuss both these views and give your own opinion. Give reasons for your answer and include any relevant examples from your own knowledge and experience.*

Write at least 250 words.

SPEAKING

Examiner questions:

Part 1

Being Near the Ocean

How much time have you spent by the ocean?

Why do people like being near the ocean?

What do you like about the ocean?

Would you like to live near the ocean?

Do you prefer to spend your leisure time indoors or outdoors?

Is there anything you don't like about being indoors (outdoors)?

What are some activities you do indoors (outdoors)?

What do you enjoy about these activities?

Part 2

You will have one to two minutes to talk about this topic.

You will have one minute to prepare what you are going to say.

Leisure Time

> Describe a book you read recently.
>
> You should say:
>
> > The title and author of the book
> > What the book was about
> > Why you decided to read it and explain why you enjoyed/didn't enjoy reading it

Part 3

Reading Habits

What are some of the reasons that people read?

What types of books are most popular in your culture?

What other things, besides books, do people read these days?

Reading Past, Present, and Future

Do you think people read more in the past than they do now? Why?

How has technology influenced people's reading habits?

ANSWER KEY
Practice Test 4

Listening

1. Kramer
2. 58
3. residential
4. office manager
5. 637-555-9014
6. nine years
7. long distance
8. Internet
9. Friday
10. morning
11. B
12. C
13. B
14. A
15. clown
16. concert
17. singing
18. international
19. games
20. crafts
21. university catalog
22. a summary
23. work supervisor
24. B
25. B
26. C
27. C
28. A
29. B
30. A
31. forested area
32. plant foods
33. insects/fish
34. winter
35. twenty-five years
36. A
37. B
38. B
39. A
40. A

Reading

1. B
2. C
3. A
4. B
5. A
6. A
7. C
8. J
9. A
10. D
11. F
12. E
13. I
14. False
15. True
16. False
17. True
18. Not Given
19. A
20. C
21. B
22. A
23. A
24. B
25. B
26. C
27. B
28. C
29. L
30. A
31. H
32. M
33. D
34. B
35. A
36. A
37. A
38. D
39. B
40. E

ACADEMIC MODULE—PRACTICE TEST 4

Listening

1. *Kramer.* The man spells his name.

2. *58.* The man gives his address, "That would be number 58 Fulton Avenue, apartment 12."

3. *residential.* The woman asks, "Then the type of phone service you want is residential, not business?" Then the man confirms that it is for his home.

4. *office manager.* The woman asks about the man's occupation, and the man says, "I'm the office manager."

5. *637-555-9014.* The man gives his work phone number, and the woman repeats the last part of it.

6. *nine years.* The man thinks about it then says that he has been at his current job for nine years.

7. *long distance.* The speakers discuss the special services offered. The woman says, "Then I'll put you down for long-distance service."

8. *Internet.* The speakers discuss voicemail and Internet, and the man says, "Please put me down for Internet as well as phone service."

9. *Friday.* The woman suggests Friday, and the man says, "That would be fine."

10. *morning.* The man says, "Morning would be best."

11. **(B)** The woman says, "So we've moved the fair to City Park." Choice (A) is where the fair has been held in the past. Choice (C) is near the fairgrounds.

12. **(C)** The man mentions Friday morning, but the woman says, "it won't begin until that evening. . . ." Choice (A) is when the man thinks the fair will begin. Choice (B) is not mentioned.

13. **(B)** The woman says, "this year our opening event will be a special dance performance. . . ." Choice (A) is what the traditional opening event has been. Choice (C) mentions the mayor, who will participate in the dance performance, but a speech is not mentioned.

14. **(A)** The woman says, "The opening event on Friday. . .doesn't cost anything to attend. . . ." Choices (B) and (C) are incorrect because the woman mentions admission fees for those days.

15. *clown.* The woman says, "There are a number of events especially for children, including a clown show on Saturday afternoon."

16. *concert.* The woman says, "On Saturday evening we've got an event that can be enjoyed by the whole family—a concert by the lake."

17. *singing.* The woman says, "There will be a singing contest in the afternoon."

18. *international.* The woman says, "international food will be served."

19. *games.* The woman says, "There will also be special games for children at different locations around the fair."

20. *crafts.* The woman says, "We have a large area set aside where there will be crafts for sale."

21. *university catalog.* The advisor explains, "First, you'll need to read the university catalog to see if any of the course descriptions match your specific job experience."

22. *a summary.* The advisor explains, "You would write a summary of your work experience, relating it to specific courses we offer."

23. *work supervisor.* The advisor explains, "Submit that to the admissions office with a letter from your work supervisor confirming your experience."

24. **(B)** While discussing the course catalog, the advisor says, "Just go to the university website and you'll find it there."

25. **(B)** The advisor says, "Well, first you'll need to fill out an admissions form and submit it. That's on the website, as well."

26. **(C)** The advisor says that the requirements will be explained at a special session next Wednesday and later tells the student that this will be held in the meeting room in the basement of the library.

27. **(C)** The advisor explains that at the session that will be held in the library the student will have the chance to meet professors and learn more about them.

28. **(A)** When the student asks where to get a parking pass, the advisor says, "You have to get it in person from the Student Services Center."

29. **(B)** After the student says that he wants to be a full-time student, the advisor says, "Then you'll qualify for the work-study program." Choice (A) is confused with the advisor saying that the student can apply for assistance to help pay for books, but a discount is not mentioned. Choice (C) is what the advisor says is not available.

30. **(A)** While discussing financial assistance, the advisor says, "You'll need to make an appointment with a counselor." Choice (B) is what the student thinks. Choice (C) is plausible but is not mentioned.

31. *forested areas.* The speaker says, "The black bear, or *Ursus americanus*, has a wide range, inhabiting forested areas of North America."

32. *plant foods.* The speaker says, "plant foods make up 90 percent of the bear's diet."

33. *insects/fish.* The speaker says, "The rest of its meals consist of animal foods such as insects and fish."

34. *winter.* The speaker says, "but bear cubs aren't born until the following winter."

35. *twenty-five years.* The speaker says, "Wild black bears can live as long as twenty-five years."

36. **(A)** The speaker says, "Many black bears, however, have a patch of fur on their chests that's lighter in color than the rest of their fur."

37. **(B)** The speaker says, "grizzly bears are usually heavier, with an average weight of 225 kilos."

38. **(B)** The speaker explains that grizzly bears spend time digging so "The large muscles they need for this give them a distinct shoulder hump."

39. **(A)** The speaker says, "Black bears, on the other hand, have a straighter profile and longer, more pointed ears."

40. **(A)** In paragraph 3, the speaker says, "Black bears have shorter claws, which are better suited for climbing trees."

Reading

PASSAGE 1

1. **(B)** Paragraph 1: "Labrador and London lie at about the same latitude . . . two places, equidistant from the Arctic Circle . . . ." Choice (A) contradicts the information given in the paragraph. Choice (C) is confused with the mention of the abundance of palm trees on England's southern shores, but wildlife and Labrador are not mentioned.

2. **(C)** Paragraph 2: "the Gulf Stream warms the atmosphere, and the prevailing westerly winds bring the warmed air to all of northwestern Europe, making the area suitable for intense agriculture." Choices (A) and (B) are related to the discussion but are not given as reasons.

3. **(A)** Paragraph 3: "After the Gulf Stream reaches southeast Greenland and western Iceland, . . . the colder, denser water then sinks." Choices (B) and (C) are related to the discussion but are not given as reasons.

4. **(B)** Paragraph 4: "This flow of ocean currents has been extremely important in regulating the temperature of the globe and in making life possible." Choices (A) and (C) are plausible but are not given as conditions that make life possible.

5. **(A)** Paragraph 5: "there used to be as many as seven chimneys . . . in the last several years, only one remained, and then, in 2007, that one disappeared." Choices (B) and (C) were true prior to 2007.

6. **(A)** Paragraph 6: "At that time, the Gulf Stream had slowed to about half its usual rate." Choice (B) contradicts facts in the paragraph. Choice (C) was true during a previous ice age.

7. **(C)** Paragraph 7: "Core samples also show that the changes in temperature have been abrupt, not gradual." Choices (A) and (B) are plausible but not mentioned.

8. **(J)** Paragraph 5: "In recent winters, glacial melt has released record amounts of fresh water into the oceans."

9. **(A)** Paragraph 5: "As the North Atlantic waters, including fresh water from rivers as well as the increased amount of glacial melt, mix with the Gulf Stream, the salt water is diluted."

10. **(D)** Paragraph 5: "Since fresh water is not as dense as salt water, it does not sink, and the mechanism for forming the chimneys is impaired."

11. **(F)** Paragraph 5: "As the chimneys have disappeared, the Gulf Stream has slowed."

12. **(E)** Paragraph 5: "Without a strong Gulf Stream, the slow, cold water of the lower part of the conveyor belt fails to rise . . . ."

13. **(I)** Paragraph 5: "which reduces the circulation of nutrients for marine life."

PASSAGE 2

14. *False.* According to paragraph 1, the cacao tree produces 6,000 flowers but only about twenty pods.

15. *True.* Paragraph 1: "it requires a humid climate and regular rainfall."

16. *False.* According to paragraph 1, the entire plant, with 6,000 flowers, produces only twenty pods.

17. *True.* Paragraph 2: "Instead, the first cacao-based drink was probably produced by fermenting the pulp . . . ."

18. *Not Given.* There is no mention of whether the drinks were served hot or cold.

19. **(A)** According to paragraph 3, the Olmec civilization lasted until around 2,400 years ago.

20. **(C)** According to paragraph 3, Olmec civilization was "centered in the modern Mexican states of Tabasco and Veracruz" and "Mayan civilization flourished in southern Mexico and Central America . . . ."

21. **(B)** Paragraph 4: "It is believed that the Mayans took the cacao tree from its native rain forest and began to cultivate it in plantations."

22. **(A)** Paragraph 3: "Relatively little is known about Olmec society because very little archeological evidence has survived . . . ."

23. **(A)** Paragraph 3: "The villagers of Puerto Escondido had likely been influenced by the great Olmec civilization . . . ."

24. **(B)** Paragraph 4: "Many of the bas-reliefs carved on their palaces and temples show cacao pods."

25. **(B)** Paragraph 5: "The basic drink was made by mixing the paste with water, chili powder, cornmeal, and other ingredients and heating it."

26. **(C)** According to paragraph 7, the ancient Mayans used cacao seeds as currency, or money. Choices (A) and (B) are plausible but are not mentioned.

27. **(B)** According to paragraph 7, the ancient Mayans held a festival in honor of the deity Ek Chuah every April. Choice (A) is the animal sacrificed during the festival. Choice (C) is part of the meaning of the deity's name.

PASSAGE 3

28. **(C)** Paragraph 1: "In 1960, Jane Goodall observed chimpanzees using tools in the wild. . . ."

29. **(L)** Paragraph 2: "Scientists have observed wild New Caledonian crows making hooks out of twigs to pull grubs from tree holes that are too deep for their beaks."

30. **(A)** Paragraph 2: "most researchers assume the birds' tool use is cultural; that is, the tool use is learned from other crows."

31. **(H)** Paragraph 3: "Betty bent the straight wire and successfully lifted the bucket of food with her hook."

32. **(M)** Paragraph 3: "invented a new tool from materials not found in her natural habitat without observing the behavior in other crows."

33. **(D)** Paragraph 3: "The researchers then set out to see if they could get Betty to replicate the behavior."

34. **(B)** Paragraph 4 explains the experiment. Researchers wore a mask when handling crows, an upsetting experience for the crows. When crows saw the mask later in other

places, they attacked it, showing that they remembered and associated it with their bad experience. Choices (A) and (C) are plausible reasons but are not the correct answer.

35. **(A)** The crows associated the mask with the bad experience of being handled, so they attacked whoever was wearing it. Choice (B) is about features of the masks that had no effect on the crows. Choice (C) is true but is not the reason for the crows' behavior.

36. **(A)** Paragraph 4: "When the same people did not wear the mask, they got no reaction from the crows." Choice (B) is the opposite of what actually happened. Choice (C) is something the researchers did but was not related to the crow's reaction to the masks.

37. **(A)** Paragraph 8 describes the experiment where jackdaws, trained to expect five rewards, stopped opening boxes after they had found five that contained food.

38. **(D)** Paragraph 7 describes an experiment with pairs of rooks, which figured out that they had to pull ropes together, not alone, to get food.

39. **(B)** Paragraph 5 describes observations by researchers who saw scrub jays re-hide food when they noticed that another bird had seen the original hiding place.

40. **(E)** Paragraph 6 describes the observation of researchers who saw that a pair of crows always flew to a fake nest when the researchers were present, thus hiding the location of their true nest.

Writing

These are models. Your answers will vary. See page 2 in the Introduction to see the criteria for scoring.

WRITING TASK 1

The graph shows the average number of movies people of different ages saw in theaters in four different years. In the time period shown, the number changed in different ways for each age group.

For the two older age groups, the number of movies seen in theaters fell over the time period from 2000 to 2015. People in the 25–44 age group saw an average of 12 movies a year in theaters in 2000. That number fell steadily until it reached 5 in 2015. People in the 45–65 age group saw an average of 15 movies a year in theaters in 2000, and that number fell steadily to 8 in 2015. The numbers fell at a similar rate for both groups, although it remained consistently higher for the older age group.

In the youngest age group, 18–24, the average number of movies seen in theaters rose. People in this group saw an average of 10 movies in theaters in 2000, lower than the number for the other two age groups in that year. The number rose to 12 in 2005 and remained steady through 2010, then rose to 14 in 2015. In that year, the average number of movies seen in theaters by the youngest group was higher than it was for both the other age groups. Overall, seeing movies in theaters became a less popular activity for older people and a more popular one for younger people.

WRITING TASK 2

Pollution caused by cars is a serious problem in the modern world. Developing better public transport systems is one answer to this problem. However, I think it is even more important for governments to spend money on developing cars that pollute less. In the first place, I believe that most people enjoy having their own cars. In addition, any technology that is developed to improve cars can also improve public transportation.

Many people in the world these days have their own car, and many others aspire to have one. Owning a car is convenient. You can go anywhere you want whenever you want. You are not limited to the places the bus and subway routes take you. You do not have to rely on bus or subway schedules. Everyone enjoys the freedom a car gives. Better public transportation systems may be put in place, but I think people will still prefer driving their own cars.

The same technology that is developed to improve cars can also be used to improve public transportation. Buses can run on electricity or hydrogen as well as cars can. Any money spent to make cars less polluting can also be used to make public transportation less polluting, so the benefit is doubled. Then, people can choose to drive cars or ride buses and either way, pollution will be reduced.

It is a nice idea to improve public transportation systems, but I feel that it is unrealistic. People will always choose to drive their own cars whenever they can. Therefore, I think it is much wiser to spend money on improving cars. The benefit will be much greater.

Speaking

These are models. Your answers will vary. See page 2 in the Introduction to see the criteria for scoring.

PART 1

How much time have you spent by the ocean?
When I was a child, I spent a great deal of time by the ocean. My family usually went to the ocean every summer. We spent two weeks there. Usually, my parents rented a small house for us right near the beach. We spent most of our time on the beach, swimming in the ocean and playing in the sand. Some of my best childhood memories are of those days we spent our vacations by the ocean. These days, unfortunately, I don't have much time to go to the ocean. I go when I can, but it's not very often.

Why do people like being near the ocean?
One reason people like the ocean is that it's very beautiful, no matter what the weather. When the day is calm, the ocean looks beautiful sparkling in the sun. When there's a storm, the waves and color of the ocean are dramatic. I think people also like being near the ocean because there are so many fun things to do. You can swim, fish, ride in a boat, or just relax in the sun.

What do you like about the ocean?

The thing I like most about the ocean is swimming. I love the feel of salt water, and I like the fun and the challenge of swimming in the ocean waves. It's so much better than swimming in a pool. The water in a pool is unnatural because it has chlorine, and the water is completely calm. It's very boring. The ocean, on the other hand, is natural and exciting. It's the best place to swim.

Would you like to live near the ocean?

Even though I love the ocean, I don't think I would like to live near it. For one thing, towns near the ocean are usually crowded with tourists on vacation. Tourists at the beach are always in a relaxed, party mood. I think that's fun sometimes, but I wouldn't like to live around it all the time. Also, in towns near the ocean there often isn't much to do besides go to the beach. I love the beach, but I prefer living in a city where there's a wide variety of things to do and many more opportunities for jobs and studies and things like that.

Do you prefer to spend your leisure time indoors or outdoors?

I definitely prefer to spend my leisure time outdoors. I work all week in an office, so when the weekend comes, I want to spend as much time as possible outdoors in the sun and fresh air. It feels good to be outdoors, and there are a lot of outdoor activities that I enjoy doing.

Is there anything you don't like about being outdoors?

I suppose sometimes it can be uncomfortable to be outdoors. I don't like it when the weather is bad. I don't like getting wet from the rain or too hot when the temperature is high. I don't like to be outdoors when it's mosquito season. That's a very uncomfortable time! But usually these things aren't much of a problem. Usually I feel very happy outdoors.

What are some activities you do outdoors?

I enjoy a lot of outdoor activities. I like walking, which is good because I live in a city and that's a great way to be outdoors in a city. There are so many places to walk. I also like to go to the park with my friends. Sometimes, we bring food and have a picnic, and sometimes we just hang out and relax. Another thing I like doing outdoors is playing tennis. I play several times a week when the weather is nice.

What do you enjoy about these activities?

The first thing I like about these activities is that they're outdoors. That's why I do them. Another thing I like is that they're relaxing. I can leave my worries behind at the office or at home and take a relaxing walk, or enjoy the nice weather in the park or a good tennis game. Also, they're a good way to spend time with my friends. We enjoy walking together or being in the park together. I think we enjoy each other's company more when we're in a pleasant out-door place rather than being in some crowded, noisy indoor place like a shopping mall.

PART 2

A book I read recently was *Gone with the Wind* by Margaret Mitchell. This is a well-known novel written in the 1930s, and the main character, Scarlett O'Hara, is also well known. The novel takes place in the United States around the time of the Civil War. Partly it's a romance novel, and it's also about history and the effects of war. I decided to read it because I saw the movie, which is from the 1930s, too. I was going on vacation, and I always like to take along a nice, long novel to read when I travel. I really enjoyed the book at first. There are very interesting descriptions of life at that time, and it was also interesting to get an idea of what the Civil War was like, especially how it affected daily life. But I have to admit that after a while I got bored. I didn't really like the main character. She kept doing the wrong thing and ruining her happiness. Since I'd seen the movie, I knew what was going to happen, so I didn't finish the book.

PART 3

What are some of the reasons that people read?
I think people read mostly for information. They want to find out the news, what's happening in the world. Or if they're students, they read to learn about the subjects they're studying. If they're looking for a job, they read to find out what positions are available or they might read advice about how to find a job. People also read for leisure. A lot of people like to relax by reading stories or novels.

What types of books are most popular in your culture?
Comic books are very popular in my country. Everybody is reading them these days, even adults. There are some very good ones now. They're not all about Superman or things like that. Romance novels are also very popular. You see people everywhere reading them. I think those two types of books are the most popular, although, of course, people like to read all kinds of things—classic literature, politics, history, even poetry.

What other things, besides books, do people read these days?
I think people mostly read things on the Internet. You can find anything there—news stories, magazine articles, book reviews—all kinds of things. So I would say that people are most interested in reading about what is happening now and the Internet is where you can find that kind of reading.

Do you think people read more in the past than they do now? Why?
I think people read for relaxation more in the past. I think people do other things for relaxation now, but I think people still read a lot. However, now we read for information rather than for fun. So, I think we read more now than we did in the past, but it's a different kind of reading.

How has technology influenced people's reading habits?
On the one hand, technology has provided us with a lot of things to do in our free time besides reading. People relax with TV, movies, or computers more often than they do with a book. On the other hand, because of the Internet, it's easy to find almost anything you want to read. You can find news and information about any topic you are interested in and you can find any book you want. So technology has made it a lot easier to read. If you want to learn about any topic, just go online and start reading.

Academic Module

PRACTICE TEST 5

ANSWER SHEET
Academic Module
Practice Test 5

IELTS Listening Answer Sheet

		√ 1 ✗
1		
2		▭ 2 ▭
3		▭ 3 ▭
4		▭ 4 ▭
5		▭ 5 ▭
6		▭ 6 ▭
7		▭ 7 ▭
8		▭ 8 ▭
9		▭ 9 ▭
10		▭ 10 ▭
11		▭ 11 ▭
12		▭ 12 ▭
13		▭ 13 ▭
14		▭ 14 ▭
15		▭ 15 ▭
16		▭ 16 ▭
17		▭ 17 ▭
18		▭ 18 ▭
19		▭ 19 ▭
20		▭ 20 ▭

		√ 21 ✗
21		
22		▭ 22 ▭
23		▭ 23 ▭
24		▭ 24 ▭
25		▭ 25 ▭
26		▭ 26 ▭
27		▭ 27 ▭
28		▭ 28 ▭
29		▭ 29 ▭
30		▭ 30 ▭
31		▭ 31 ▭
32		▭ 32 ▭
33		▭ 33 ▭
34		▭ 34 ▭
35		▭ 35 ▭
36		▭ 36 ▭
37		▭ 37 ▭
38		▭ 38 ▭
39		▭ 39 ▭
40		▭ 40 ▭
Listening Total		

ACADEMIC MODULE TEST 5

Candidate Name _____

International English Language Testing System

LISTENING

Time: Approx. 30 minutes

INSTRUCTIONS TO CANDIDATES

Do not open this booklet until you are told to do so.

Write your name in the space at the top of this page.

You should answer all questions.

All the recordings will be played ONCE only.

Write all your answers on the Question Paper.

At the end of the test, you will be given ten minutes to transfer your answers to an Answer Sheet.

Do not remove this booklet from the examination room.

INFORMATION FOR CANDIDATES

There are **40** questions on this question paper.

The test is divided as follows:

Section 1	Questions 1–10
Section 2	Questions 11–20
Section 3	Questions 21–30
Section 4	Questions 31–40

SECTION 1

Questions 1–4

Complete the form below.

*Write **NO MORE THAN ONE WORD AND/OR A NUMBER** for each answer.*

Example	...Global... Bicycle Tours

Tour name: River Valley tour .. Tour month: **1** ....

Customer Name: **2** .... Schmidt

Address: P.O. Box **3** ....

....

Bicycle rental required? ....Yes ..X..No

Dietary restrictions: **4** ....

Questions 5–7

*Choose the correct letter, **A**, **B**, or **C**.*

5 What size deposit does the caller have to pay?

   A 5 percent
   B 30 percent
   C 50 percent

6 When does the deposit have to be paid?

   A Two weeks from now
   B Four weeks from now
   C Six weeks from now

7 How will the luggage be carried?

   A By bus
   B By bicycle
   C By van

Questions 8–10

Choose **THREE** *letters, A–F.*
Which **THREE** *things should the caller take on the tour?*

A   raincoat
B   spare tire
C   maps
D   water bottle
E   camera
F   guide book

SECTION 2

Questions 11–15

What change has been made to each part of the health club?
Write the correct letter, A–F, next to **Questions 11–15**.

HARTFORD HEALTH CLUB

A   installed a new floor
B   repainted
C   moved to a new location
D   rebuilt
E   enlarged
F   replaced the equipment

Part of the health club

11   swimming pools ....

12   locker rooms ....

13   exercise room ....

14   tennis court ....

15   club store ....

Questions 16–18

Complete the sentences below.
*Write **NO MORE THAN TWO WORDS** for each answer.*

16 Tomorrow, ..Manchester......... for adults and children will start.

17 On Wednesday, there will be a ....

18 A............................... is planned for next weekend.

Questions 19 and 20

Answer the questions below.
*Choose the correct letter, **A**, **B**, or **C**.*

19 How many months did it take to complete the renovation work?

   A Three
   B Nine
   C Twelve

20 What project is planned for next year?

   A An indoor pool
   B An outdoor tennis court
   C An outdoor pool

SECTION 3

Questions 21–25

*Choose **FIVE** letters, **A–I**.*
*What **FIVE** things will the students do during their museum internship?*

   A art conservation
   B administrative duties
   C guide tours
   D attend board meetings
   E give classes
   F research
   G write brochures
   H plan a reception
   I meet artists

Questions 26–30

Complete the notes below.

*Write **NO MORE THAN TWO WORDS AND/OR A NUMBER** for each answer.*

City Art Museum

Construction of the main museum happened in **26** ....

Construction of the **27** .... happened sixty years later.

Collections: modern art, works by **28** ...., sculpture, European art.

Classes: **29** .... classes for adults
Arts and crafts workshops for children

Weekly **30** .... in the fall and winter

---

SECTION 4

Questions 31–35

*Choose the correct letter, **A**, **B**, or **C**.*

31 The tomato originally came from

  A Mexico.
  B Spain.
  C Peru.

32 The original color[1] of the tomato was

  A red.
  B green.
  C yellow.

33 The Aztec word for *tomato* means

  A golden apple.
  B plump thing.
  C small fruit.

---

[1]British: colour

34 In the 1500s, people in Spain and Italy

    A enjoyed eating tomatoes.

    B used tomatoes as ornamental plants.

    C made medicine from tomatoes.

35 In the 1600s, the British

    A saw tomatoes as poisonous.

    B published tomato recipes.

    C ate tomato sauce daily.

Questions 36–40

Complete the timeline with information about the history of the tomato in the United States.
*Write **NO MORE THAN TWO WORDS** for each answer.*

1806   Tomatoes were mentioned as food in **36** ....

1809   Thomas Jefferson **37** .... at his home in Virginia.

1820   A man proved that tomatoes were not poisonous by eating them
            38 ....

1830s   **39** .... appeared in newspapers and magazines.

1930s   People began to eat **40** ....

> **Take ten minutes to transfer your answers onto the Answer Sheet on page 177.**

ANSWER SHEET
Academic Module
Practice Test 5

IELTS Reading Answer Sheet

	√ 1 X
1	
2	▭ 2 ▭
3	▭ 3 ▭
4	▭ 4 ▭
5	▭ 5 ▭
6	▭ 6 ▭
7	▭ 7 ▭
8	▭ 8 ▭
9	▭ 9 ▭
10	▭ 10 ▭
11	▭ 11 ▭
12	▭ 12 ▭
13	▭ 13 ▭
14	▭ 14 ▭
15	▭ 15 ▭
16	▭ 16 ▭
17	▭ 17 ▭
18	▭ 18 ▭
19	▭ 19 ▭
20	▭ 20 ▭

	√ 21 X
21	
22	▭ 22 ▭
23	▭ 23 ▭
24	▭ 24 ▭
25	▭ 25 ▭
26	▭ 26 ▭
27	▭ 27 ▭
28	▭ 28 ▭
29	▭ 29 ▭
30	▭ 30 ▭
31	▭ 31 ▭
32	▭ 32 ▭
33	▭ 33 ▭
34	▭ 34 ▭
35	▭ 35 ▭
36	▭ 36 ▭
37	▭ 37 ▭
38	▭ 38 ▭
39	▭ 39 ▭
40	▭ 40 ▭
Reading Total	

ACADEMIC MODULE TEST 5

Candidate Name _____

International English Language Testing System

ACADEMIC READING

Time: 1 hour

INSTRUCTIONS TO CANDIDATES

Do not open this booklet until you are told to do so.

Write your name in the space at the top of this page.

Start at the beginning of the test and work through it.

You should answer all questions.

If you cannot do a particular question, leave it and go on to the next. You can return to it later.

All answers must be written on the Answer Sheet.

Do not remove this booklet from the examination room.

INFORMATION FOR CANDIDATES

There are **40** questions on this question paper.

The test is divided as follows:

Reading Passage 1	Questions 1–14
Reading Passage 2	Questions 15–27
Reading Passage 3	Questions 28–40

Reading Passage 1

*You should spend about 20 minutes on **Questions 1–14**, which are based on Reading Passage 1 below.*

Candle Making in Colonial America

The primary material used in making candles today is paraffin[1] wax, which is derived from petroleum. In the process of refining crude oil, refiners "crack" the oil, thereby separating it into different products such as gasoline, heating oil, and kerosene. Paraffin wax, originally produced by plants that lived 100 to 700 million years ago to protect their leaves, is inert and remains suspended in the decayed vegetable matter that eventually becomes crude oil. In the refining process, paraffin wax is separated out and sold as a by-product.

Paraffin was not discovered until the early 1800s. At that time, paraffin was derived by a process of distilling bituminous schist, now known as shale oil. In 1850, Dr. James Young, a Scottish industrial chemist, applied for a patent for obtaining paraffin oil and paraffin from bituminous coals. Shortly after that, under a license from Young, paraffin was being produced from coal on a large scale in the United States. Because petroleum is now readily available, Young's original process for obtaining paraffin is no longer profitable, and paraffin is currently produced from crude oil.

Before the discovery of paraffin, candle making had for centuries relied on different materials. Chemically, those materials were also hydrocarbons; however, they were derived directly from insects, animals, or plants.

In colonial times in America, beeswax was highly valued for making candles. Even today beeswax, though more expensive, is highly regarded because pure beeswax candles emit no smoke when burning, whereas paraffin candles produce a black, slightly oily soot. Beeswax is secreted only by female worker bees. As a worker bee eats honey, her wax glands exude the wax as oval flakes that form on the underside of her last four abdominal segments. The bee then removes the wax flakes and chews them, mixing the wax flakes with her saliva to soften them. When the wax is sufficiently pliable, she attaches it to the honeycomb. As the wax comb is built up, each pocket is filled with honey and then sealed with more wax.

Given the numerous uses and considerable value not only of honey but also of the bees themselves and their beeswax, beekeeping was an important part of American life in the seventeenth and eighteenth centuries. Many of the early settlers brought honeybee hives with them from Europe. Not indigenous to North America, the honeybees nonetheless thrived and often escaped into the wild. In 1785, writing in *Notes on the State of Virginia*, Thomas Jefferson observed, "The bees have generally extended themselves into the country, a little in advance of the white settlers. The Indians therefore call them the white man's fly, and consider their approach as indicating the approach of the settlements of the whites."

---

[1]This paraffin is different from the British word *paraffin*, which is called kerosene in the United States.

Eventually, the Native Americans as well as the colonists used beeswax and honey in the frontier bartering system that grew up in the absence of readily available coinage.

Another source of colonial candle material was animal fat or tallow. Cattle and sheep were the most common sources of tallow. Pork fat was not used because candles made from it dripped too much and were dangerous. Additionally, the odor[1] of burning pork tallow was particularly offensive. Chicken and duck fat were too soft to make candles. The tallow was rendered—heated in a cauldron until the fat melted—and then strained numerous times to remove any gristle, meat fibers,[2] and as many impurities as possible. Straining reduced, but did not entirely eliminate, the extent to which the candles smoked and emitted a noxious odor. Tallow candles needed to be stored in tightly closed containers, usually made of tin or wood, to keep out rodents and other animals that might eat them.

In the New World, the colonists discovered a native plant high in a natural waxy substance that could be extracted and used for candle making. The plant is the bayberry shrub, also known as candleberry. Bayberry shrubs are dense and semievergreen. The plants are extremely hardy, grow to as much as nine feet high, and do well even in salt-laden, coastal soil unsuitable for other horticulture. In winter, the female plants bear clusters of blue-gray berries, which lend their color to the wax. The colonists boiled the berries to separate the waxy matter from the pulp and then skimmed the wax off the top. Although making bayberry candles was more labor[3] intensive than making tallow candles, bayberry candles were considerably superior, burning longer and producing less smoke. Further recommending them, they had a pleasing scent. Compared to beeswax, bayberries were available in greater quantities, and the colonists found that bayberry wax was harder than beeswax and thus also burned longer.

Because the bayberry clusters were harvested in winter and because making the candles was very time-consuming, the candles were often saved for special occasions, particularly Christmas and New Year's Eve. Eventually, they became a holiday tradition and gave rise to the saying, "Bayberry candles burned to the socket, puts luck in the home, food in the larder, and gold in the pocket." Fortunate indeed was the colonial household with brightly burning candles and a holiday feast.

[1]British: odour
[2]British: fibres
[3]British: labour

Questions 1–3

*Write the correct letter, **A**, **B**, or **C**, on lines 1–3 on your answer sheet.*

1 Paraffin is

    A a petroleum by-product.
    B found in rocks.
    C from a type of vegetable.

2 Paraffin was first obtained from

    A crude oil.
    B rotten vegetables.
    C bituminous coal.

3 James Young was

    A a candle maker.
    B an oil producer.
    C a scientist.

Questions 4–14

Classify the following as descriptive of

A	paraffin
B	beeswax
C	tallow
D	bayberry wax

*Write the correct letter, **A**, **B**, **C**, or **D**, in boxes 4–14 on your answer sheet.*

4 was often made from the fat of cows

5 is made from a bush that grows near the sea

6 needs to be filtered before being made into candles

7 was not used before the nineteenth century

8 produces smokeless candles

9 produced candles that were attractive to hungry mice and rats

10 is bluish in color

11 was brought to colonial America by European settlers

12 was often reserved for holiday use

13 has a pleasing aroma

14 was often used for trading in place of money

Reading Passage 2

*You should spend about 20 minutes on **Questions 15–27**, which are based on Reading Passage 2 below.*

Caffeine

Almost 200 years ago, a young German chemist named Friedrich Ferdinand Runge isolated a molecule from coffee beans; he named the substance *kaffein*. Today, scientists are still studying the properties of this bitter, white powder. More than sixty plants are known to produce caffeine, whose pungent taste helps protect them from insect predators.

Caffeine is probably the most widely used drug in the world. Humans have been consuming caffeine for hundreds of years, primarily in the form of coffee, tea, and cocoa. Today, it is also added to soft drinks and energy drinks and is a component of some over-the-counter medications. Many of the world's people, including children, ingest it in some form daily.

The body absorbs caffeine in less than an hour, and it remains in the system for only a few hours, passing from the gastrointestinal tract into the bloodstream within about ten minutes and circulating to other organs, including the brain. Caffeine molecules are small and soluble in fat, properties that allow them to pass through a protective shield known as the blood–brain barrier and directly target the central nervous system.

Caffeine acts on the body in many ways, some of them probably still unknown. However, caffeine accomplishes its principal action as a stimulant by inhibiting adenosine, a chemical that binds to receptors on nerve cells and slows down their activity. Caffeine binds to the same receptors, robbing adenosine of the ability to do its job and leaving caffeine free to stimulate nerve cells, which in turn release epinephrine (also known as adrenaline), a hormone that increases heart rate and blood pressure, supplies an energy boost, and in general makes people feel good.

For all its popularity, caffeine retains a somewhat negative image. It is, after all, a mildly habit-forming stimulant that has been linked to nervousness and anxiety and that causes insomnia. It affects most of the body's major organs. Recent research casts doubt on the magnitude of many of these seemingly undesirable effects and even suggests that a daily dose of caffeine may reduce the risk of some chronic diseases, while providing short-term benefits as well.

Daily caffeine consumption has been associated with lowered incidence of Type 2 diabetes, Parkinson's disease, and Alzheimer's disease. How caffeine works to thwart diabetes, a condition characterized[1] by high levels of glucose in the blood, remains unknown, but glucose tolerance or more efficient glucose metabolism may be involved. Parkinson's disease, a central nervous system disorder that causes tremor and joint stiffness, is linked to insufficient amounts of

---

[1]British: characterised

a substance called dopamine in the brain. Caffeine may interact with brain cells that produce dopamine and help maintain a steady supply. The role of caffeine in Alzheimer's disease, which damages the brain and causes memory loss and confusion, may be related to a problem in the blood–brain barrier, possibly a contributor in Alzheimer's, if not the major cause. Caffeine has been found to protect the barrier against disruption resulting from high levels of cholesterol.

Habitual coffee and tea drinkers had long been observed to have a lower incidence of non-melanoma skin cancers, although no one knew why. A recent study found that caffeine affects skin cells damaged by ultraviolet radiation, a main cause of skin cancer. Caffeine interferes with a protein that cancerous cells need to survive, leaving the damaged cells to die before they become cancerous. Drinking caffeinated coffee has also been associated with a decreased incidence of endometrial cancer—that is, cancer of the cells lining the uterus. The strongest effect appears to be in overweight women, who are at greatest risk for the disease. Researchers believe blood sugar, fat cells, and estrogen may play a role. Although the mechanism remains unknown, people who drink more than two cups of coffee or tea a day reportedly have about half the risk of developing chronic liver disease as those who drink less than one cup of coffee daily; caffeinated coffee has also been associated with lowered risk of cirrhosis and liver cancer.

While many of caffeine's undesirable effects, such as elevated heart rate and blood pressure, are brief, some short-term benefits, including pain relief, increased alertness, and increased physical endurance, have also been attributed to caffeine. As a component of numerous over-the-counter diet pills and pain relievers, caffeine increases their effectiveness and helps the body absorb them more quickly. By constricting blood vessels in the brain, it can alleviate headaches—even migraines—and can help counter the drowsiness caused by antihistamines.

Caffeine does not alter the need for sleep, but it does offer a temporary solution to fatigue for people who need to stay alert. Research has shown that sleep-deprived individuals who consumed caffeine had improved memory and reasoning abilities, at least in the short term. Studies of runners and cyclists have shown that caffeine can improve their stamina—hence its addition to energy-boosting sports drinks.

People who consume a lot of caffeine regularly may develop temporary withdrawal symptoms, headache being the most common, if they quit or cut back on it abruptly. Fortunately, these symptoms last only a day or two in most cases. Individuals who are more sensitive to the stimulatory side effects of caffeine may want to avoid it, but most doctors agree that the equivalent of three cups of coffee a day does not harm healthy people. There is no medical basis to give up daily caffeine and many reasons to include a moderate amount in one's diet.

Questions 15–23

Do the following statements agree with the information given in the passage? On lines 15–23 on your answer sheet, write

TRUE	*if the statement agrees with the information*
FALSE	*if the statement contradicts the information*
NOT GIVEN	*if there is no information on this*

15 Before 200 years ago, people did not drink coffee regularly.

16 Children generally do not consume caffeine.

17 The nervous system is affected by caffeine.

18 Caffeine causes the heart to beat faster.

19 Caffeine can be addictive.

20 Alzheimer's disease may be caused in part by caffeine consumption.

21 Drinking coffee can help protect against some skin cancers.

22 Caffeine may increase the incidence of endometrial cancer.

23 Caffeine can help some medications work faster.

Questions 24–27

*Write the correct letter, **A**, **B**, or **C**, on lines 24–27 on your answer sheet.*

24 Caffeine is used to treat

A high blood pressure.
B liver cancer.
C headaches.

25 Some athletes use caffeine to

A increase their endurance.
B improve their speed.
C maintain their alertness.

26 Symptoms of caffeine withdrawal

A can become an ongoing problem.
B may last as long as a week.
C are usually short-lived.

27 Drinking three cups of coffee a day

A may be recommended by a doctor.
B will probably not cause problems.
C is harmful to the health.

Reading Passage 3

*You should spend about 20 minutes on **Questions 28–40**, which are based on Reading Passage 3 below.*

Animal Camouflage

The theory of natural selection, proposed by Charles Darwin almost 150 years ago, hypothesizes[1] that organisms with traits that give them a survival advantage tend to live longer and produce more offspring. Over many thousands of years of evolution, those beneficial characteristics dominate the gene pool. Animals that use camouflage to conceal themselves from their enemies, predator and prey alike, provide a classic example of natural selection at work. Creatures with some type of protective coloring pass along the genes responsible, with each generation fine-tuning them along the way, eventually providing the most effective coloring for their environment and lifestyle. Scientists have described four types of camouflage that animals use: background matching, disruptive coloration, countershading, and mimicry.

From dirt-colored chipmunks and gophers to leaf-green praying mantises and tree frogs to ocean-gray mackerel and sharks, all sorts of wildlife use background matching, also known as *crypsis*, to blend in with their surroundings. Some animals have the ability to alter their coloring as their environment changes seasonally or as they change locations. The arctic fox and the snowshoe hare both have white winter fur that matches the snow and ice around them, but a brown pelt in warmer weather blends in with their woodland environs. Some reptiles and fish can alter their surface appearance instantly as they move from place to place. The green anole lizard changes from green to brown as it travels among leaves and branches, whereas the flounder and other types of flatfish are able to match not just the color but also the silty or mottled sandy texture of the ocean floor beneath them.

Most animals, though, cannot change their appearance so easily. Because background matching works only for a specific setting and often requires animals to remain motionless for long periods, a somewhat more effective strategy involves having a camouflage that works on many backgrounds, blending in with all, but not perfectly matching any of them.

Disruptive coloration uses a pattern such as stripes or spots to disrupt the body's outline. The pattern breaks up the contour of the animal's body, confusing observers and making it difficult to distinguish an individual shape. Colors with more contrast, like a tiger's stripes, tend to increase the disruptive effect. This type of camouflage works well for animals that travel in herds. It helps zebras blend in not so much with their background as with each other. Their major predator, the lion, sees a mass of moving stripes and has trouble targeting a specific animal. A single zebra, on the other hand, may use background matching when hiding in tall grass, where its black and white stripes merge with the green and yellow

---

[1]British: hypothesises

stalks. The different colors of the grasses and zebra are no help to a lion, which is color-blind.[1]

Animals with countershading typically have a dark backside and a light belly, which affect an onlooker's perception of their three-dimensional appearance and help decrease their visibility in sunlight. Countershading also can create a more uniformly dark appearance, presenting an apparent lack of depth. Caterpillars make good use of this effect, which gives them a flat look that blends in with tree bark.

Countershading is useful to birds and marine animals that are typically seen against a light environment from below and against dark surroundings from above. Predatory birds like hawks take advantage of it to conceal themselves from the small birds and rodents they hunt. While in flight, a dark back absorbs the sunlight above them and a light underside reflects the light below, diminishing telltale shadows that might give them away. On the ground or in a tree, their mottled brown feathers blend in with branches and leaves. Penguins also use countershading. Their white chests and black backs stand out on land but disappear in water where penguins spend most of their time. They are almost invisible to an observer looking down into dark water, while a creature in deeper water looking up sees a splash of white that looks like a beam of sunlight.

Mimicry, or masquerading, works not by hiding a creature but by making it appear to be something else. Walking stick insects are virtually indistinguishable from twigs, and katydids look so much like green leaves that leaf-eating insects have been observed trying to chew on them.

A type of mimicry known as *aposematism* involves masquerading as an animal that is undesirable or even dangerous. Predators bypass the foul-tasting monarch butterfly, but they also avoid the tasty look-alike viceroy butterfly. Coral snake impersonators, like the harmless scarlet snake, have the same red, black, and yellow bands but in a different order: black, yellow, red, yellow on the coral snake and red, black, yellow, black on the scarlet snake. Different types of moths use aposematism to scare off predators; some species have a big spot on each wing to mimic the eyes of a large animal, while the hawk moth caterpillar has a pattern on its rear that looks like a snake head.

Some predators use what is known as aggressive mimicry to disguise themselves as something harmless so they can catch prey off guard. Small animals are not afraid of turkey vultures, which are scavengers, not predators. So when the similar zone-tailed hawk flies with a group of turkey vultures, it has an easy time locating and zeroing in on its living prey.

No single type of camouflage works best in all situations, and many animals use more than one technique to enhance their ability to avoid detection by predator and prey alike.

---

[1]British: colour-blind

Questions 28–36

Complete the summary below. Choose **NO MORE THAN THREE WORDS** *from the passage for each answer.*
Write your answers on lines 28–36 on your answer sheet.

Camouflage helps animals hide from both **28** ....

Animals pass on their **29** .... through their genes.

There are four different types of camouflage. In background matching, an

animal's appearance helps it **30** .... with its environment.

The arctic fox and snowshoe hare are examples of animals that

31 .... with the seasons. However, not all animals can

easily change their appearance. Many use a different strategy, having

camouflage that helps them disguise themselves on a variety of

32 .... Animals with disruptive coloration have

marking such as **33** .... that make it difficult for a

predator to discern the shape of the body. Therefore, the predator has

a hard time targeting one animal out of a group. Although zebras are

black and white, they can hide in tall grass because their major predator is

34 .... **35** .... is a type of

camouflage that helps hide animals that are seen from above or below. Penguins,

for example, have **36** .... , which help them blend in

with the dark water from the point of view of an observer standing above.

Questions 37–40

Do the following statements agree with the information in the passage? On lines 37–40 on your answer sheet, write:

TRUE   *if the statement agrees with the information*
FALSE   *if the statement contradicts the information*
NOT GIVEN *if there is no information on this*

37 The walking stick insect looks like a small stick.

38 The viceroy butterfly is similar in appearance to the monarch butterfly.

39 The scarlet snake is extremely poisonous.

40 The hawk moth caterpillar is brightly colored.

ANSWER SHEET
Academic Module
Practice Test 5

Writing Answer Sheet

TASK 1

_____
_____
_____
_____
_____
_____
_____
_____
_____
_____
_____
_____
_____
_____
_____
_____
_____
_____
_____
_____
_____
_____
_____
_____

ANSWER SHEET
Academic Module
Practice Test 5

-2-

ANSWER SHEET
Academic Module
Practice Test 5

-3-

TASK 2

_____

_____

_____

_____

_____

_____

_____

_____

_____

_____

_____

_____

_____

_____

_____

_____

_____

_____

_____

_____

ANSWER SHEET
Academic Module
Practice Test 5

-4-

ACADEMIC MODULE TEST 5

Candidate Name _____

International English Language Testing System

ACADEMIC WRITING

Time: 1 hour

INSTRUCTIONS TO CANDIDATES

Do not open this booklet until you are told to do so.

Write your name in the space at the top of this page.

All answers must be written on the separate answer booklet provided.

Do not remove this booklet from the examination room.

INFORMATION FOR CANDIDATES

There are **2** tasks on this question paper.

You must do **both** tasks.

Underlength answers will be penalized.[1]

---

[1]British: penalised

Writing Task 1

You should spend about 20 minutes on this task.

The following diagrams show a current map of Peyton Park and a plan for proposed changes.

Summarize[1] the information by selecting and reporting the main features, and make comparisons where relevant.

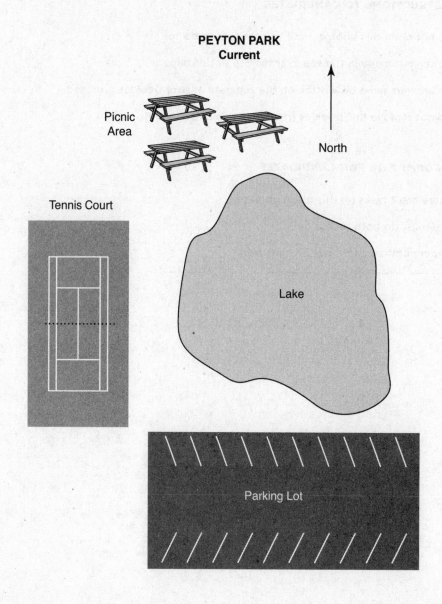

PEYTON PARK
Current

North

Picnic Area

Tennis Court

Lake

Parking Lot

---

[1]British: Summarise

Proposed

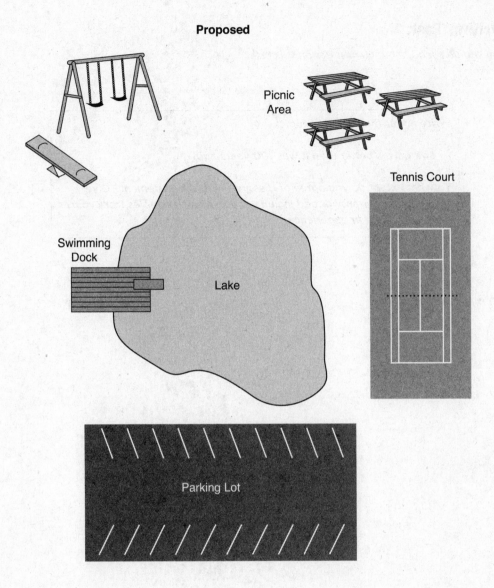

Picnic Area

Tennis Court

Swimming Dock

Lake

Parking Lot

Write at least 150 words.

Writing Task 2

You should spend about 40 minutes on this task.

Write about the following topic:

Life now is better than it was 100 years ago.

To what extent do you agree or disagree with this statement? Give reasons for your answer and include any relevant examples from your own knowledge or experience.

Write at least 250 words.

SPEAKING

Examiner questions:

Part 1

Computers

How much time do you spend using a computer?

Do you use a computer more for work, study, or personal reasons?

What different kinds of things do you do on the computer?

What are some things you like and dislike about using computers?

Parks

Describe a park in your neighborhood or city

What are some things people can do there?

Do you enjoy spending time there? Why or why not?

Are parks important? Why or why not?

Part 2

You will have one to two minutes to talk about this topic.

You will have one minute to prepare what you are going to say.

Tell about your favorite[1] subject you studied in school.

You should say:

What the subject was

In which grade or grades you studied it

What kinds of things you learned about it and explain what you
liked about it

Part 3

Change in Education

What school subjects were offered in the past that are not offered now?

What school subjects should be offered in the future that are not offered now?

Importance of Education to Society

Do you think the main purpose of education is to accumulate knowledge or to prepare
for a job?

How important is it to have an educated society?

What consequences are there for a society when people have a poor education?

_____

[1]British: favourite

ANSWER KEY
Practice Test 5

Listening

1. June
2. Karla
3. 257
4. vegetarian
5. B
6. A
7. C
8. A
9. D
10. E
11. B
12. E
13. A
14. F
15. C
16. swimming lessons
17. tennis competition
18. party/club party
19. B
20. C
21. B
22. C
23. F
24. G
25. I
26. 1895
27. new wing
28. local artists
29. art history
30. concerts/concert series
31. C
32. C
33. B
34. A
35. A
36. a (gardener's) calendar
37. served tomatoes
38. in public
39. tomato recipes/recipes
40. raw tomatoes

Reading

1. A
2. C
3. C
4. C
5. D
6. C
7. A
8. B
9. C
10. D
11. B
12. D
13. D
14. B
15. Not Given
16. False
17. True
18. True
19. True
20. False
21. True
22. False
23. True
24. C
25. A
26. C
27. B
28. predators and prey
29. protective coloring
30. blend in
31. alter their coloring
32. backgrounds
33. stripes or spots
34. color-blind
35. countershading
36. black backs
37. True
38. True
39. False
40. Not Given

ANSWER EXPLANATIONS

ACADEMIC MODULE—PRACTICE TEST 5

Listening

1. *June.* The speakers discuss the month of the River Valley tour, and the man says, "It actually takes place the first week of June."

2. *Karla.* The woman spells her first name, "That's Karla with a K, not a C. K-A-R-L-A."

3. *257.* The woman gives her P.O. box number, "It's P. O. Box 257, Manchester."

4. *vegetarian.* The speakers discuss dietary restrictions, and the woman says, "Well, yes, I'm a vegetarian."

5. **(B)** The man says he needs a 30 percent deposit. Choice (A) is the size of the recommended tip. Choice (C) sounds similar to $750, the total cost of the trip.

6. **(A)** The man explains that Karla will need to pay the deposit in two weeks. Choice (B) is confused with how long before a tour the deposit must be paid. Choice (C) is when the tour begins.

7. **(C)** The man explains that a van will carry the luggage from hotel to hotel. Choice (A) is not mentioned. Choice (B) is what the woman asks.

8. **(A)** The man recommends, "so you should bring a raincoat. . . ."

9. **(D)** The man says, "you should definitely have a water bottle."

10. **(E)** The man says, "A camera would be a good idea, too. . . ."

11. **(B)** The guide points out the new paint and says, "Both of the pools needed painting. . . ."

12. **(E)** The guide says, "We've expanded both the men's and women's locker rooms. . . ." *Expanded* means the same as *enlarged*.

13. **(A)** The guide says, "Here you'll notice the new floor."

14. **(F)** The guide says, "We replaced all the nets and the ball-throwing machine." Nets and a ball-throwing machine are types of *equipment*.

15. **(C)** The guide says, "here we are at the club store in its new location."

16. *swimming lessons.* The guide says, "Now that the pools are ready for use again, swimming lessons will begin tomorrow, for both adults and children."

17. *tennis competition.* The guide says, "If you're a tennis player, you'll be interested to hear about the tennis competition coming up on Wednesday."

18. *party/club party.* The guide says, "you're invited to our club party, coming up next weekend."

19. **(B)** The guide says, "The entire renovation project was finished in just nine months." Choice (A) is confused with the fact that the work took three months less than planned. Choice (C) is the number of months originally planned for the work.

20. **(C)** The guide says, "next year we plan to install an outdoor pool. . . ." Choices (A) and (B) are things the club already has.

21. **(B)** Dr. Johnson explains, "You'll spend some time working in here so you can learn what the administrative duties involve. . . ."

22. **(C)** Dr. Johnson says, "you'll all have a chance to lead some tours. . . ." *Lead* means the same as *guide*.

23. **(F)** Dr. Johnson tells the students that they will spend some time working in the Research Department.

24. **(G)** Dr. Johnson says, "Also, as an extension of your research work, you'll probably contribute to some of the museum's brochures." In this context, *contribute* means *do some writing*.

25. **(I)** Dr. Johnson says, "We've planned a reception for the first day of your internship, and you'll have the chance to meet several local artists then."

26. *1895.* Dr. Johnson explains, "The main part of the museum was built in 1895 with a combination of public and private funds."

27. *new wing.* Dr. Johnson says, "The new wing was built sixty years later with a donation from the Rhinebeck family."

28. *local artists.* Dr. Johnson describes the museum's collections, "In the main part of the museum, we have a gallery devoted to works by local artists, our sculpture collection, and a small collection of classical European art."

29. *art history.* Dr. Johnson says, "In our Adult Education program, we offer a series of art history classes. . . ."

30. *concerts/concert series.* Dr. Johnson says, "We offer a weekly concert series during the fall and winter. . . ."

31. **(C)** The speaker says, "The tomato originated in the highlands of Peru." Choice (A) is mentioned as a place where tomatoes were later cultivated. Choice (B) is confused with the mention of Spanish explorers.

32. **(C)** The speaker says, "The Aztec tomato was not the large red vegetable we know today. Rather, it was small and yellow." Choice (A) is the color of tomatoes today. Choice (B) is plausible but is not mentioned.

33. **(B)** The speaker says, "The actual word *tomato* comes from the Aztec name for the vegetable, meaning "plump thing.'" Choice (A) is the meaning of the Italian name for *tomato*. Choice (C) is the way the speaker describes tomatoes.

34. **(A)** The speaker says, "The tomato arrived in Europe in the 1500s and quickly became a popular food in Spain and Italy." Choice (B) is what the British did with tomatoes. Choice (C) is not mentioned.

35. **(A)** The speaker says, "It was grown as an ornamental plant in Britain in the 1600s, but it wasn't eaten because it was thought to be poisonous." Choice (B) is what the Italians did. Choice (C) is not mentioned and would have happened later.

36. *a (gardener's) calendar.* The speaker says, "In 1806, a gardener's calendar mentioned that tomatoes could be used to improve the flavor of soups and other foods."

37. *served tomatoes.* The speaker says, "Thomas Jefferson. . . .first served tomatoes to visitors at his home in Virginia in 1809."

38. *in public.* The speaker says, "To prove his point, he ate one kilo of ripe red tomatoes in public."

39. *tomato recipes/recipes.* The speaker says, "By the 1830s, American newspapers and magazines were publishing thousands of tomato recipes."

40. *raw tomatoes.* The speaker says, "It wasn't until a century later, in the 1930s, that it became popular for people to eat raw tomatoes."

Reading

PASSAGE 1

1. **(A)** Paragraph 1: "paraffin wax, which is derived from petroleum." This means it is a by-product of petroleum. Choice (B) is where crude oil is found, not paraffin. Choice (C) is confused with the explanation of the wax coming from decayed vegetable matter.

2. **(C)** Paragraph 2: "At that time, paraffin was derived by a process of distilling bituminous schist, now known as shale oil." Choice (A) is what paraffin is derived from now. Choice (B) is confused with the explanation of petroleum coming from "decayed vegetable matter."

3. **(C)** According to paragraph 2, James Young was an industrial chemist, a type of scientist. Choice (A) is confused with a use for paraffin. Choice (B) is confused with the material James Young worked with.

4. **(C)** According to paragraph 6, tallow was made from the fat of cattle and sheep.

5. **(D)** According to paragraph 7, the "Bayberry shrubs. . .grow. . .in salt-laden, coastal soil unsuitable for other horticulture. . . ." A *shrub* is a bush, and *coastal* means "near the sea."

6. **(C)** According to paragraph 6, tallow was melted and then strained, or filtered, to remove impurities.

7. **(A)** Paragraph 2: "Paraffin, however, was not discovered until the early 1800s." The 1800s are the nineteenth century.

8. **(B)** Paragraph 3: "beeswax candles emit no smoke when burning. . . ."

9. **(C)** Paragraph 6: "Tallow candles needed to be stored in tightly closed containers, usually made of tin or wood, to keep out rodents and other animals that might eat them." Mice and rats are types of rodents.

10. **(D)** Paragraph 7: "In winter, the female plants bear clusters of blue–gray berries, which lend their color to the wax."

11. **(B)** Paragraph 5: "Many of the early settlers brought honeybee hives with them from Europe."

12. **(D)** According to paragraph 8, bayberry candles "were often saved for special occasions, particularly Christmas and New Year's Eve."

13. **(D)** According to paragraph 7, bayberry candles have "a pleasing scent." *Scent* means the same as *aroma*.

14. **(B)** According to paragraph 5, honey and beeswax were used for bartering. *Bartering* means the same as *trading*.

PASSAGE 2

15. *Not Given.* The passage does not mention when people began drinking coffee.

16. *False.* Paragraph 2: "Many of the world's people, including children, ingest it in some form daily."

17. *True.* Paragraph 4 discusses the effect of caffeine on nerve cells.

18. *True.* Paragraph 4 explains how caffeine contributes to increased heart rate.

19. *True.* Paragraph 5: "Caffeine. . . .is, after all, a mildly habit-forming stimulant. . . ." *Habit-forming* means the same as *addictive.*

20. *False.* Paragraph 6 explains how caffeine may help lower the incidence of Alzheimer's disease.

21. *True.* Paragraph 7 explains how caffeine may help lower the incidence of non-melanoma skin cancers.

22. *False.* Paragraph 7 explains how caffeine may help decrease, not increase, the incidence of endometrial cancer.

23. *True.* Paragraph 8: "As a component of numerous over-the-counter diet pills and pain relievers, caffeine increases their effectiveness and helps the body absorb them more quickly."

24. **(C)** Paragraph 8: "By constricting blood vessels in the brain, it can alleviate headaches. . . ." Choice (A) refers to a disease that caffeine can make worse. Choice (B) is a condition that caffeine may help to prevent, but caffeine is not mentioned as a treatment for it.

25. **(A)** Paragraph 9: "Studies of runners and cyclists have shown that caffeine can improve their stamina. . . ." *Endurance* means the same as *stamina.* Choice (B) is plausible but is not mentioned. Choice (C) is mentioned in the paragraph but not in reference to athletes.

26. **(C)** According to paragraph 10, withdrawal symptoms last only one or two days. Choices (A) and (B) are plausible but not mentioned.

27. **(B)** Paragraph 10: "most doctors agree that the equivalent of three cups of coffee a day does not harm healthy people." Choice (A) is incorrect because there is no recommendation by doctors mentioned. Choice (C) contradicts the information given.

PASSAGE 3

28. *predators and prey.* Paragraph 1: "Animals that use camouflage to conceal themselves from their enemies, predator and prey alike, provide a classic example of natural selection at work."

29. *protective coloring.* Paragraph 1: "Creatures with some type of protective coloring pass along the genes responsible. . . ."

30. *blend in.* Paragraph 2: "all sorts of wildlife use background matching. . .to blend in with their surroundings."

31. *alter their coloring.* Paragraph 2: "Some have the ability to alter their coloring as their environment changes seasonally. . . ."

32. *backgrounds.* Paragraph 3: "a somewhat more effective strategy involves having a camouflage that works on many backgrounds. . . ."

33. *stripes or spots.* Paragraph 4: "Disruptive coloration uses a pattern such as stripes or spots to disrupt the body's outline."

34. *color-blind.* Paragraph 4: "The different colors of the grasses and zebra are no help to the lion, which is color-blind."

35. *countershading.* Paragraph 6: "Countershading is useful to birds and marine animals that are typically seen against a light environment from below and against dark surroundings from above."

36. *black backs.* Paragraph 6: "Their white chests and black backs stand out on land but disappear in water where penguins spend most of their time. They are almost invisible to an observer looking down into dark water. . . ."

37. *True.* Paragraph 7: "Walking stick insects are virtually indistinguishable from twigs. . . ."

38. *True.* "Paragraph 8: "Predators bypass the foul-tasting monarch butterfly, but they also avoid the tasty look-alike viceroy butterfly."

39. *False.* Paragraph 8: "Coral snake impersonators, like the harmless scarlet snake, have the same red, black, and yellow bands but in a different order. . . ."

40. *Not Given.* Paragraph 8 mentions the shape of a pattern on the hawk moth caterpillar but does not mention its coloring.

Writing

These are models. Your answers will vary. See page 2 in the Introduction to see the criteria for scoring.

WRITING TASK 1

The maps show what Peyton Park looks like now and what it will look like after the proposed changes are made.

On both maps, there is a lake at the center of the park. Both maps also show a parking lot to the south of the lake. Now Peyton Park has tennis courts to the west of the lake and a picnic area to the north of the lake. The picnic area is also close to the tennis courts.

When the proposed changes are made, some things will be moved, and some new things will be added. The tennis courts will be moved to the east end of the lake. The picnic area will also be moved. It will still be near the tennis courts, but to the northeast of the lake. A swimming dock will be added at the west end of the lake. There will be a playground to the north of the lake, where the picnic area is now.

WRITING TASK 2

The way we live now is different in many aspects from the way people lived 100 years ago. Technology has changed how we earn our livings and carry out our daily lives. Our lives have improved in many important ways over the past 100 years. At the same time, there are certain positive things that have been lost.

Technology has improved our lives in many ways. We have machinery, electronic devices, and appliances that make our work and daily chores easier. Advances in communications technology make it easier to be in contact with colleagues, personal friends, and relatives everywhere. We have many types of transportation that make it easy to travel anywhere, even around the world, for both business and personal reasons. Finally, because of advances in medicine, fewer people die of common diseases that were fatal not long ago. For all these reasons, we can say that life now is better than it was a century ago.

On the other hand, there are other, less material, aspects of our lives that have not necessarily improved. For example, while it is true that technology makes communication with distant loved ones easier, at the same time families are breaking up. Family members no longer tend to live near one another as was common in the past. This means a loss of important social and emotional support. In addition, because we have so many electronic devices, such as personal computers, cell phones, and so on, people tend to pay more attention to these devices than they do to their actual face-to-face personal relationships.

It is easy to see that in a material sense, life is much better for many people now than it was just 100 years ago. However, even though our material existence has greatly improved, our social and emotional lives have suffered. This is a challenge for people living in the twenty-first century.

Speaking

These are models. Your answers will vary. See page 2 in the Introduction to see the criteria for scoring.

PART 1

How much time do you spend using a computer?
I spend several hours every day using a computer because it's an important part of my work. I try to stay away from the computer on weekends, but I'm not always successful at that because there are always so many things I want to do with it. Maybe I spend too much time on the computer. I don't know. It's a little bit addictive.

Do you use a computer more for work, study, or personal reasons?
The reason I'm on the computer so much is because I use it at work. Most of my work involves creating documents for the company. Because of that, the computer has become a habit for me, so I also end up using it a lot for personal reasons. So, I guess I could say the main reason I use it is for work, but it's a big part of my personal life, too.

What different kinds of things do you do on the computer?
Besides creating documents at work, I use e-mail a lot to communicate with my work colleagues and also with my friends and relatives. I also keep a lot of personal records on the computer, like the family budget, photographs, and things like that. And I have to admit that I spend a lot of time playing computer games. That helps me relax when I'm working on a big project.

What are some things you like and dislike about using computers?
Nobody can deny that computers make so many things convenient. I couldn't do my job without a computer, and e-mail makes communications so much easier. Everything I do on

the computer is a lot easier than it would be without the computer. On the other hand, as I said before, a computer can be addictive. Sometimes I end up spending an entire Saturday afternoon doing things on the computer, instead of spending time with my family or going outside and getting exercise. It takes some discipline, I think, to keep from overusing the computer.

Describe a park in your neighborhood or city.
There's a small park at the end of my street. It has a fountain in the middle and a few benches where you can sit and relax. It also has a small garden. Some of the local neighbors plant flowers there every year.

What are some things people can do there?
It's a small park, so there's not much to do there. It's mostly there for looking pretty. You can sit on the benches and watch the water in the fountain. That's relaxing. You can enjoy the flowers. It's right next to the bus stop, so you can wait for the bus there, too.

Do you enjoy spending time there? Why or why not?
Yes, I like to go there when the weather is nice. After being inside all day at work, I like to go to the park on my way home. It's a way to be outside for a little while. Sometimes I run into friends there. I've gotten to know some of my neighbors by spending time in the park, so that's an advantage.

Are parks important? Why or why not?
Parks are very important in the city. Without parks, there wouldn't be any nice outdoor places to spend time in. Parks add beauty to the city because they're places where we can see trees and flowers. Larger parks also provide places for outdoor sports. Without parks, it would be difficult to do any outdoor activities in a city.

PART 2

When I was in school, my favorite subject was history. I liked all kinds of history, and I still do. I studied it every year I was in high school, from ninth through twelfth grade. I learned a lot of things. I learned about the important events in the history of my country and about the important people. I learned about all kinds of people—politicians, inventors, soldiers, and even common everyday people who contributed to our history. I learned these things about other countries, too. I like history a lot because I like to imagine and understand what life was like at different times. People have lived under different conditions during different periods of history, and they've had different kinds of interests, motivations, and needs. In each period of history, the conditions of that time shaped the events. I think it's interesting to learn about these things and important to understand them. We are who we are today because of what our ancestors did. I'm still interested in history, and I still read about it often.

PART 3

What school subjects were offered in the past that are not offered now?
My parents told me that when they were in school, the girls studied home economics and the boys studied shop. The girls learned how to cook and sew and the boys learned how to build and fix things. We don't have subjects like those in school now. To me it seems funny to spend school time on things like that. I think those are things you can learn at home, if

you are interested in them, but they aren't academic things, they aren't things for school, in my opinion.

What school subjects should be offered in the future that are not offered now?
That's an interesting question because we can't predict the future. But the thing that is always changing is technology, so whatever schools teach in the future, it will have to be related to the technology of the future. Maybe students will study at home alone by using the computer and the Internet. Maybe they will learn the same or similar subjects as we learn now, but they will learn them in a different way, on the Internet or something like that.

Do you think the main purpose of education is to accumulate knowledge or to prepare for a job?
I think both things are important. When you are younger, you need to learn basic skills. First you learn to read and write and use a computer. Then you learn to think and analyze and interpret. These are things you need for all areas of life, for your future job but also for everything else you might do in life. Then when you are a little older, in high school or college, you start focusing on skills you might need for a specific type of job. So, education prepares you for life, all aspects of it.

How important is it to have an educated society?
It is very important to have an educated society. If some people are highly educated and others are poorly educated, then there is not equal participation in society. People who have more education are also more likely to have more money and more political power than people who have less education. So if you want to have an equal society, everyone needs to be equally educated. I know that is an ideal, but it is something to work for.

What consequences are there for a society when people have a poor education?
As I said before, people who have less education also probably have less money and less political power. If a lot of people are poorly educated, then there will be a lot of people with no jobs or poorly paid jobs. There will be a lot of people with bad health. There will not be an educated, healthy workforce to contribute to the economy. There are consequences for everyone when a large percentage of a country is not well educated.

Academic Module

PRACTICE TEST 6

ANSWER SHEET
Academic Module
Practice Test 6

	✓ ✗			✓ ✗
1	1	21		21
2	2	22		22
3	3	23		23
4	4	24		24
5	5	25		25
6	6	26		26
7	7	27		27
8	8	28		28
9	9	29		29
10	10	30		30
11	11	31		31
12	12	32		32
13	13	33		33
14	14	34		34
15	15	35		35
16	16	36		36
17	17	37		37
18	18	38		38
19	19	39		39
20	20	40		40
		Listening Total		

ACADEMIC MODULE TEST 6

ACADEMIC MODULE TEST 6

Candidate Name _____

International English Language Testing System

LISTENING

Time: Approx. 30 minutes

INSTRUCTIONS TO CANDIDATES

Do not open this booklet until you are told to do so.

Write your name in the space at the top of this page.

You should answer all questions.

All the recordings will be played ONCE only.

Write all your answers on the Question Paper.

At the end of the test, you will be given ten minutes to transfer your answers to an Answer Sheet.

Do not remove this booklet from the examination room.

INFORMATION FOR CANDIDATES

There are **40** questions on this question paper.

The test is divided as follows:

Section 1	Questions 1–10
Section 2	Questions 11–20
Section 3	Questions 21–30
Section 4	Questions 31–40

SECTION 1

Questions 1–5

TIP

If you do not
have access
to the MP3
files on the
enclosed
disk, please
refer to the
audioscripts
starting on
page 421 when
prompted to
listen to an
audio passage.

Complete the information below.

*Write **NO MORE THAN TWO WORDS AND/OR A NUMBER** for each answer.*

City Library

Head Librarian   ***Example*** .... Mrs. Phillips ....

Hours   **1** .... to 4:30

Books

Ground floor[1]   **2** ....

Second floor   Adult collection

Third floor   **3** ....

Book carts

Brown cart   books to re-shelve

Black cart   books to **4** ....

White cart   books to **5** ....

Questions 6–10

Complete the library schedule below.

*Write **NO MORE THAN ONE WORD AND/OR A NUMBER** for each answer.*

Activity	Location	Day and Time
Story Time	Children's Room	**6** .... at 11:00
7	Reference Room	Saturday at **8** ....
Lecture Series	**9** .... Room	Friday at **10** ....

---

[1] In the United States the ground floor is considered the first floor; the next floor up is the second floor.

SECTION 2

Questions 11–15

*Choose **FIVE** letters, **A–I**.*
*Which **FIVE** activities are available at Golden Lake Resort?*

A   swimming

B   boating

C   waterskiing

D   fishing

E   tennis

F   golf

G   horseback riding

H   biking

I   arts and crafts

Questions 16–20

Complete the schedule below.
*Write **NO MORE THAN ONE WORD** for each answer.*

Night	Activity
Sunday	16 ....
Monday	Dessert Night
Tuesday	17 .... Night
Wednesday	18 ....
Thursday	19 ....
Friday	Talent Show
Saturday	20 ....

SECTION 3

Questions 21–23

*Choose **THREE** letters, **A–F**.*

*Which **THREE** things are the students required to submit to their professor?*

A   a written summary

B   notes

C   a case study

D   charts and graphs

E   a list of resources used

F   a video

Questions 24 and 25

Answer the questions below.

*Write **NO MORE THAN THREE WORDS** for each answer.*

24   What two sources of information will the students use when preparing their presentation?

   ....

25   What will the students show during their presentation?

   ....

Questions 26–30

*Choose the correct letter, **A**, **B**, or **C**.*

26 Only rescue birds that are

   A all alone.

   B obviously hurt.

   C sitting on the ground.

27 Protect yourself by wearing

   A gloves.

   B a hat.

   C protective glasses.

28 Put the bird in a

   A cage.

   B box.

   C bag.

29 Keep the bird calm by

   A petting it.

   B talking to it.

   C leaving it alone.

30 When transporting the bird,

   A talk softly.

   B play music.

   C drive very slowly.

 SECTION 4

Questions 31–32

*Choose the correct letter, **A**, **B**, or **C**.*

31 The Great Barrier Reef consists of about .... individual coral reefs.

   A 400

   B 900

   C 3,000

32 The larger islands in the Great Barrier Reef are covered with

   A sand.

   B plants.

   C coral.

Questions 33–38

Complete the notes below.
Write **NO MORE THAN TWO WORDS** for each answer.

Great Barrier Reef

Habitats

Habitats include reefs, salt marshes, and **33** ....

Types of plants

Reef habitat: **34** ....

Islands: mostly **35** .... at the northern end

                          mostly herbaceous at the southern end

Types of animals

Salt marsh: **36** ....

Sea grass beds: **37** ....

Islands: **38** ....

Questions 39 and 40

Answer the questions below.
Write **NO MORE THAN THREE WORDS** for each answer.

39 What causes coral bleaching?

....

40 What has been one response to this problem?

....

Take ten minutes to transfer your answers onto the Answer Sheet on page 217.

ANSWER SHEET
Academic Module
Practice Test 6

IELTS Reading Answer Sheet

#		✓ ✗
1		1
2		2
3		3
4		4
5		5
6		6
7		7
8		8
9		9
10		10
11		11
12		12
13		13
14		14
15		15
16		16
17		17
18		18
19		19
20		20

#		✓ ✗
21		21
22		22
23		23
24		24
25		25
26		26
27		27
28		28
29		29
30		30
31		31
32		32
33		33
34		34
35		35
36		36
37		37
38		38
39		39
40		40
Reading Total		

ACADEMIC MODULE TEST 6

Candidate Name _____

International English Language Testing System

ACADEMIC READING

Time: 1 hour

INSTRUCTIONS TO CANDIDATES

Do not open this booklet until you are told to do so.

Write your name in the space at the top of this page.

Start at the beginning of the test and work through it.

You should answer all questions.

If you cannot do a particular question, leave it and go on to the next. You can return to it later.

All answers must be written on the Answer Sheet.

Do not remove this booklet from the examination room.

INFORMATION FOR CANDIDATES

There are 40 questions on this question paper.

The test is divided as follows:

Reading Passage 1	Questions 1–14
Reading Passage 2	Questions 15–27
Reading Passage 3	Questions 28–40

Reading Passage 1

*You should spend about 20 minutes on **Questions 1–14**, which are based on Reading Passage 1 below.*

Pollination

Plants have evolved a wide variety of methods to reproduce themselves. Some plants reproduce asexually by splitting off new roots or bulbs (e.g., garlic, lilies) or even branches, stems, or leaves (e.g., mangroves, spider plants). Plants that reproduce asexually are essentially reproducing clones of themselves. This is a simple and direct method of reproduction, producing new plants more quickly and with less energy than plants using sexual reproduction. The majority of plants, however, reproduce sexually. The advantages from an evolutionary perspective include more genetic variety and better dispersal than the colonies of clones formed by asexual reproduction. In flowering plants, pollen (male) grains are moved from the anther to the stigma, where the pollen fertilizes[1] the ovaries (female), resulting in seeds.

A few flowering plants such as peas, beans, and tomatoes pollinate themselves, but more commonly, pollination occurs between separate plants, either through pollen being borne by the wind (most conifers and many grasses) or by pollinators, animal species that plants rely on to help move the pollen from one plant to the ovaries of another. Most pollinators are insects, but some species of bird and bats also play an important role.

Plants have evolved a variety of methods to entice pollinators to do their work. Many produce nectar, a sugary substance that pollinators use as food. A well-known example is the honeybee, which collects nectar as well as pollen for food. When a bee enters one flower, it brushes against the anther, and pollen grains are picked up by the surface of its body. When the bee enters a second flower and brushes against the stigma, some of that pollen comes in contact with the ovaries of the second plant, thus fertilizing it, resulting in seeds that contain genetic material from the male gametes of the first plant combined with the female reproductive organs of the second plant. Most bees, butterflies, and moths, as well as certain species of bats and birds, are attracted to nectar-producing flowers.

Flowering plants have evolved a variety of methods for signaling[2] their usefulness to pollinators or for otherwise making their work easier. Butterflies are attracted to flowers that are open during the day, are bright—typically red, yellow, or orange—and have a "landing platform." In contrast, many moths are active at night and thus are attracted to flowers that are pale or white, have a strong fragrance, but also have broad areas to land on. Both butterflies and moths have long tongues and have coevolved with plants that have developed deep sources of nectar that are available only to certain species. Hummingbirds are also attracted by color[3] especially by bright reds, and flowers that attract these tiny birds also have

[1]British: fertilises.
[2]British: signalling
[3]British: colour

strong stems and are designed for pollen to be brushed on the hummingbirds' heads as they sip nectar.

Bees do not see red; thus, flowers that attract bees tend to be blue, yellow, purple, or other colors. Many bee attractors also have nectar guides, which are spots near the center[1] of each flower that reflect ultraviolet light, making it easier for the bees to find the nectar. Bees are also attracted to flowers with a mintlike or sweet smell. Snapdragons not only attract bees visually, they are adapted to appeal to certain bee species: snapdragons have a landing platform that, if the bee is the correct weight, opens—allowing access to the nectar and pollen.

Pollinators play a major role in agriculture. While many staple crops such as rice, corn, canola, and wheat are self-pollinating or pollinated by the wind, farmers are dependent on pollinator species for many fruit, vegetable, nut, and seed crops. Over 30 percent of the world's crops require the work of pollinator species. Bees are the most common agricultural pollinators, with crops including fruit trees such as apples and cherries; vegetables such as squash, beans, tomatoes, and eggplant; flowering shrubs and annual and perennial flowers; forage crops such as clover and alfalfa; and fiber[2] crops such as cotton. Other pollinators include midges (cocoa), wasps (figs), moths (yucca, papaya), butterflies (asters, daisies, marigolds), and even a few species of bats (agave, palms, durians) and hummingbirds (fuchsia).

Recent declines in honeybees and in other pollinator species around the world have raised concerns about future food production, and many scientists have called for increased study of the role of pollinators, the agricultural and environmental changes involved in the declines, as well as the economic and environmental effects and ways to prevent further declines.

[1]British: centre
[2]British: fibre

Questions 1–5

Complete the summary using the list of words and phrases below.
*Write the correct letter, **A–I**, on lines 1–5 on your answer sheet.*

A	pollen
B	flowering plants
C	roots
D	grains
E	spider plants
F	wind
G	copies
H	fertilization
I	time

The reproduction of plants occurs in different ways. Some plants send out new

parts such as **1** .... or bulbs. These grow into new plants, which

are actually **2** .... of the original plant. The advantage of this

form of reproduction is that it does not require a lot of **3** .... or

energy. Many **4** .... reproduce themselves by forming seeds

through the process of pollination. Some plants pollinate themselves. Others rely

on the **5** .... or animals to carry the pollen from plant to plant.

Questions 6–14

Do the following statements agree with the information given in the passage? On lines 6–14 on your answer sheet, write:

TRUE	*if the statement agrees with the information*
FALSE	*if the statement contradicts the information*
NOT GIVEN	*if there is no information on this*

6　Honeybees eat both nectar and pollen.

7　If an attractive flower is very small, a butterfly will land on its leaves.

8　Moths are attracted by scent.

9　Certain flowers are shaped to be pollinated by hummingbirds.

10　Special markings on a flower help bees to locate the nectar.

11　Bees rarely respond to scent.

12　Most grain crops are pollinated by insects.

13　Close to one third of the world's harvest depends on animals for pollination.

14　Farmers in certain parts of the world have suffered economically because of the decline in the honeybee population.

Reading Passage 2

*You should spend about 20 minutes on **Questions 15–27**, which are based on Reading Passage 2 below.*

Paleolithic[1] Cave Art

Students of art history tend to be familiar with the images of horses and bison discovered in the famous cave art site in Lascaux, France, in 1940. Less well known but vitally important to understanding Ice Age art and culture is the art discovered by three cave explorers in the Chauvet Cave near Vallon-Pont-d'Arc in southern France in 1994.

The Chauvet Cave hosts one of the largest groups of Paleolithic drawings yet discovered on one site, as well as the fossilized[2] remains of a number of now-extinct animals. The art found in the Chauvet Cave differs from that found in most other European cave art sites, which primarily feature prey animals such as horses, bison, wild cattle, and reindeer. The Chauvet paintings include many animals that humans would have feared—panthers, bears, lions, hyenas, and rhinoceroses. While the Chauvet paintings also include many species that would have been hunted by the artists—horses, aurochs, bison, and extinct species of moose and deer—the presence of non-prey animals calls into question a common theory that the primary purpose of cave art was to magically ensure plentiful game. Perhaps the discovery of the Chauvet art points to a shift in emphasis from the hunters' predators to the hunters' prey over time, but more evidence is needed.

Carbon-14 dating has established three of the paintings (one bison and two rhinoceroses) as being 31,000 years old. This discovery pushes the common understanding of the date range for European cave art much further back than what had been assumed. It has also clearly disproved theories that earlier cave art was cruder and more primitive because these older images are equally sophisticated in execution.

In addition to the hundreds of animal paintings, the Chauvet Cave also has an image of a being, referred to as the Sorcerer, with the body of a human and the head of a bison. There is also part of an image of a woman. In addition, explorers found the skull of a cave bear placed on a squared-off altarlike rock. The cave had been untouched for thousands of years due to a rock slide that had sealed off the cave; the floor of the cave contains the footprints of humans and cave bears, and fire pits, stone tools, remnants of torches, and bones from meals. After scientists collected data and recorded images, the site was placed off-limits to prevent the damage that has occurred at many other caves known for their rock art.

Ice Age paintings in certain European caves have been extremely well preserved and have reached iconic status because of their beauty and the artists' skill in execution. As a result, many people assume that the art of early hunt-

---

[1]British: Palaeolithic
[2]British: fossilised

ers and gatherers was limited to cave paintings. While the artwork in the deep caves has been the best preserved, artwork was also done on the walls of rock shelters and on rock faces out in open light. Paleolithic artists not only painted with pigments but also created engravings by scratching designs into rock with pointed tools, as well as creating low-relief sculptures. Often the artists seemed to have seen a suggestion of an animal's shape in a rock, and then added detail through incising lines, incorporating clay, or applying pigment. In addition to animal images, most sites also have geometrical designs, including dots and quadrangles. Archeologists[1] have also discovered small sculpted figures from the same time period.

Images of hands, created either by wetting the palm of the hand with paint and pressing the hand onto rock or by applying paint around the hand, perhaps by spitting pigment from the mouth, are common. However, full images of humans are rare in the European caves. Images combining human and animal elements such as the Chauvet Cave Sorcerer have been found in various sites as have partial images of women, but portrayals of a full human are few and far between, and they tend to be simple abstract depictions. Most of the animal images, on the other hand, are detailed, realistic portrayals of an individual animal species, not simply an abstract symbol meant to depict an animal such as a horse or bison.

Questions 15–21

*Choose the correct letter. Write the correct letter, **A**, **B**, or **C**, on lines 15–21 on your answer sheet.*

15 As compared with the Chauvet Cave, the cave art site in Lascaux is

   A more well known.
   B less important.
   C more difficult to explore.

16 The art discovered in the Chauvet Cave differs from other European cave art because

   A it does not include images of horses and bison.
   B it shows images of now-extinct animals.
   C it includes images of predatory animals.

17 According to the passage, a common belief about the function of cave art is that

   A it was meant to bring animals to be hunted.
   B it was intended to drive away predatory animals.
   C it was used to warn others about the presence of fearsome animals.

---

[1]British: Archaeologists

18 As compared with other European cave art sites, the art in the Chauvet Cave is

    A cruder and more primitive.

    B significantly older.

    C more sophisticated in subject matter.

19 Images found in the Chauvet Cave include

    A a crude map.

    B a part-human, part-animal being.

    C a complete drawing of a woman.

20 In addition to art, other discoveries in the Chauvet Cave include

    A implements made of stone.

    B human bones.

    C bison pelts.

21 No humans had visited the Chauvet Cave for thousands of years because

    A cave bears lived inside it.

    B it was declared off limits.

    C the entrance was blocked by rocks.

Questions 22–27

Complete the sentences below.

*Choose **NO MORE THAN TWO WORDS** from the passage for each answer. Write your answers on lines 22–27 on your answer sheet.*

22 People often believe that Paleolithic art consisted only of.................................

23 Ice Age artists used pointed tools to make............................. and sculptures on rocks.

24 As well as pictures of animals,............................. are common in most sites.

25 Pictures of............................. were sometimes made by wetting the palm with paint.

26 It is unusual to see an image of a............................. in European cave art.

27 Rather than being symbolic; paintings of animals are............................. images.

Reading Passage 3

*You should spend about 20 minutes on **Questions 28–40**, which are based on Reading Passage 3 below.*

The Braille System

A

About 200 years ago, a curious three-year-old boy playing in his father's shop had an accident that ended up changing the lives of hundreds of thousands of people. The little boy was Louis Braille, and his father was a harness maker in Coupvray, France, a small town near Paris. Louis poked his eye with one of the sharp tools on his father's workbench. The injury and the ensuing infection, which spread through both eyes, caused him to lose his vision. Only a dozen years later, at the age of fifteen, Braille developed a system of raised dots on paper that made it possible for blind people to read and write. While he was not the first person to toy with the idea of tactile reading—that is, reading by feeling shapes on a flat surface—his system surpassed others thanks to its simplicity, ease of use, and adaptability.

B

During the first few years after his accident, Braille attended a local school with sighted children, where he learned by the only means available to him—listening and memorizing.[1] He was a gifted student and at the age of ten earned a scholarship to attend the Royal Institution for Blind Youth in Paris. He later became a teacher at the Institution and remained there until his death in 1852 at the age of forty-three. The Institution relied largely on oral instruction, but pupils had access to a few books specially designed for blind students by Valentin Haüy, the school's founder. Haüy had developed a method for pressing shapes of letters onto wet paper and then letting them dry, providing pages with raised characters that students could "read" by running their fingertips across the thick paper. The books were big and cumbersome and took a long time to produce—and to read. In addition, they addressed only part of the blind students' communication dilemma—the ability to read. For full literacy, students also needed to be able to write.

C

A man named Charles Barbier, who had invented a system known as night writing for soldiers to send messages in the dark, provided the inspiration Braille needed for his reading method. Barbier visited the Royal Institution for Blind Youth in 1821 to demonstrate his technique, which used rectangular cells with raised dots. The cells, thirty-six in all, represented sounds rather than individual letters of the alphabet and consisted of a template of twelve dots in six rows of two. Braille saw the system's benefits right away and then zeroed in on its drawbacks. He thought it should be based on the alphabet—the way sighted people read—and not on phonetics. It also needed a way to designate punctuation marks, accents, num-

---

[1]British: memorising

bers, and other symbols; and, for the user to be able to read with ease, a cell had to be small enough to fit beneath one's fingertip.

D

For the next three years, Braille fine-tuned his system and in 1824 came up with a version that worked to his satisfaction: a six-dot cell (three rows of two) that allowed for sixty-three possible combinations of dots, enough for all twenty-six letters of the Roman alphabet plus accents, capital letters, punctuation marks, and numbers. For example, a cell with one dot at the top left (position one) represents the letter *a*, whereas a cell with one dot at the bottom right (position six) means the next symbol is a capital letter. The numbers zero to nine are coded the same as the letters *a* to *j*, except they are preceded by a cell with dots in positions three through six (bottom left dot and all three dots in the right column). Users could read an individual cell with a single touch of the fingertip, and they scanned dots from left to right as in normal reading. What's more, the Braille system made it possible to write by punching dots into paper (from right to left because the reverse side is read).

E

Originally, Braille symbols were written with a slate and stylus—the equivalent of paper-and-pencil writing, using the slate to hold the paper and the stylus to prick holes in it. In 1892, a Braille writing machine was invented; used like a typewriter, it has six keys and a space bar. Today, writing Braille is no more difficult or time-consuming than producing a printed document. You need only to hook up a standard computer to a machine that will emboss the text in Braille. Braille's fellow students quickly learned his system; for the first time, they could take notes in class and write papers, not to mention pass notes back and forth to one another. Yet the system was not widely used in Braille's lifetime. It did not become the official communication system for blind people in France until 1854, two years after he died.

F

The system remains in use today, only slightly altered from the original version. It has incorporated symbols for math, science, and music and has been adapted to dozens of languages, including many with non-Roman alphabets, such as Chinese and Japanese. Braille symbols often show up in public places, such as on elevator buttons, and their helpfulness in labeling household items like canned goods is undisputed. Nevertheless, knowledge of Braille has declined in recent years as technology has provided innovations, such as recorded books and computers with synthetic speech, that make it less necessary to read the old-fashioned way. Many now deem Braille an obsolete system, but its devotees still consider it a form of literacy as basic as the three R's.

Questions 28–36

*Reading Passage 3 has six paragraphs, **A–F**. Which paragraph contains the following information? Write the correct letter, **A–F**, on lines 28–36 on your answer sheet. You may use any letter more than once.*

28 a description of the Braille system of representing letters and numbers

29 Louis Braille's early education

30 how people write in Braille

31 reasons why Braille is used less now than in the past

32 when the Braille system was officially accepted in France

33 a reading system for the blind used when Louis Braille was a child

34 how Braille is read

35 the reason why Louis Braille was blind

36 a description of the method on which Louis Braille based his system

Questions 37–40

Do the following statements agree with the information given in the passage? On lines 37–40 on your answer sheet, write:

TRUE	*if the statement agrees with the information*
FALSE	*if the statement contradicts the information*
NOT GIVEN	*if there is no information on this*

37 Braille symbols represent letters and numbers only.

38 Braille is used in a variety of languages.

39 Braille readers can read faster than sighted readers.

40 Modern technology has made Braille less important.

ANSWER SHEET
Academic Module
Practice Test 6

Writing Answer Sheet

TASK 1

-2-

_____

_____

_____

_____

_____

_____

_____

_____

_____

_____

_____

_____

_____

_____

_____

_____

_____

_____

_____

_____

_____

-3-

TASK 2

_____
_____
_____
_____
_____
_____
_____
_____
_____
_____
_____
_____
_____
_____
_____
_____
_____
_____
_____
_____
_____
_____

-4-

ACADEMIC MODULE TEST 6

Candidate Name _____

International English Language Testing System

ACADEMIC WRITING

Time: 1 hour

INSTRUCTIONS TO CANDIDATES

Do not open this booklet until you are told to do so.

Write your name in the space at the top of this page.

All answers must be written on the separate answer booklet provided.

Do not remove this booklet from the examination room.

INFORMATION FOR CANDIDATES

There are **2** tasks on this question paper.

You must do **both** tasks.

Underlength answers will be penalized.[1]

---

[1]British: penalised

Writing Task 1

You should spend about 20 minutes on this task.

> The graphs below show unemployment rates and average earnings
> according to level of education.
>
> Summarize[1] the information by selecting and reporting the main features,
> and make comparisons where relevant.

Unemployment and Average Earnings by Educational Level—2016

Unemployment Rate by Education Level

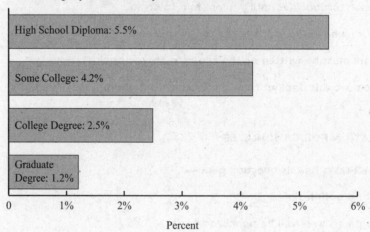

Average Weekly Earning by Education Level

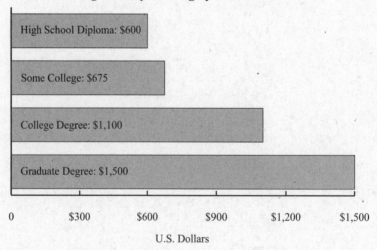

Write at least 150 words.

---

[1]British: Summarise

Writing Task 2

You should spend about 40 minutes on this task.

Write about the following topic:

> Some people think that young people should choose their professions themselves. Others believe that their parents should choose for them.

Discuss both these views and give your own opinion.

Write at least 250 words.

SPEAKING

Examiner questions:

Part 1

Shopping

How often do you go shopping?

What kinds of shops are there in your neighborhood[1]?

What kinds of things do you usually shop for?

Do you enjoy shopping? Why or why not?

Food

What are some of your favorite[2] foods? Why?

Who does the cooking at your house?

Do you prefer eating at home or in restaurants? Why?

What kinds of restaurants do you enjoy eating in?

Part 2

You will have one to two minutes to talk about this topic.

You will have one minute to prepare what you are going to say.

> Tell about a place you would like to visit.
>
> You should say:
>
> The name of the place and where it is
> What kind of a place it is
> What things you would do there and explain why you want to go there

[1]British: neighbourhood
[2]British: favourite

Part 3

Travel Destinations

Where do people from your country travel to most frequently?

What are some popular places to visit in your country? Why are they popular?

Reasons for Travel

What are some reasons that people travel?

Do you think parents should make a point of taking their children to see a variety of different places? Why or why not?

Effects of Tourism

Why should governments invest in tourism?

How can tourism negatively affect societies?

Listening

1. 8:30
2. reference books
3. children's books
4. be repaired/repair
5. be sold/sell
6. Thursday
7. (family) movies
8. 2:30
9. meeting
10. 6:30
11. A
12. B
13. D
14. G
15. I
16. film/movie
17. discussion
18. lectures
19. games
20. dance
21. A
22. C
23. E
24. interviews, journal articles
25. photos (of birds)
26. B
27. A
28. B
29. C
30. A
31. C
32. B
33. deep ocean
34. seaweed
35. woody
36. crocodiles
37. turtles
38. frogs
39. rising sea temperatures
40. shading the reef/shading certain areas

Reading

1. C
2. G
3. I
4. B
5. F
6. True
7. Not Given
8. True
9. True
10. True
11. False
12. False
13. True
14. Not Given
15. A
16. C
17. A
18. B
19. B
20. A
21. C
22. cave paintings
23. engravings
24. geometrical designs
25. hands
26. (full) human
27. detailed, realistic
28. D
29. B
30. E
31. F
32. E
33. B
34. D
35. A
36. C
37. False
38. True
39. Not Given
40. True

ACADEMIC MODULE—PRACTICE TEST 6

Listening

1. *8:30.* The librarian says, "the library opens at eight-thirty in the morning. . . ."

2. *reference books.* The man says, "It looks like here on the ground floor is where the reference books are," and on the next line the librarian agrees with him.

3. *children's books.* The librarian says, "Children's books are up one more flight on the third floor."

4. *be repaired/repair.* The speakers discuss the books in the black cart, and the librarian says, "They're all books that need to be repaired."

5. *be sold/sell.* The speakers discuss the books in the white cart. The man asks, "So they're all ready to sell?" and the librarian says "Yes."

6. *Thursday.* The librarian says, "Story Time . . . takes place in the Children's Room on Thursday mornings at eleven."

7. *(family) movies.* The librarian explains, "we had to switch Family Movies to the weekend—Saturday afternoon."

8. *2:30.* The librarian says, "The movie always starts at two thirty in the Reference Room."

9. *meeting.* The librarian tells the man, "one of your duties will be to set up the Meeting Room on the first floor for the lecture."

10. *6:30.* The librarian says, "The lecture starts at 6:30. . . ."

11. **(A)** The man says, "We have a pleasant beach for swimming."

12. **(B)** The man says, "We also have canoes and sailboats available, and many of our guests enjoy boating on the lake."

13. **(D)** The man says, "you'll often see guests fishing from our dock or from the canoes."

14. **(G)** The man says, "We've made an arrangement with a local stable, so now we're going to have horseback riding available for our guests. We've created several riding trails around the lake."

15. **(I)** The man says, "some of our very talented staff members offer arts and crafts classes, for all ages."

16. *film/movie.* The man says, "Every Sunday we show a film. . . ."

17. *discussion.* The man says, "Our discussion night is on Tuesday."

18. *lectures.* The man says, "Then on Wednesdays we have lectures."

19. *games.* The man says, "Thursday nights are totally different because that's when we play games."

20. *dance.* The man says, "And we end every week with big fun, with a dance on Saturday night."

21. **(A)** Student 2 says, "We have to give the professor a written summary of the information we've gathered on our topic. . . ."

22. **(C)** Student 1 says, "The other written thing we have to turn in is a case study of the rehabilitation of one bird."

23. **(E)** Student 1 says, "But we do have to turn in a list of the resources we used."

24. *interviews, journal articles.* In discussing the sources, Student 2 mentions interviews with wildlife rehabilitators and Student 1 mentions journal articles.

25. *photos (of birds).* Student 1 says, "But we have lots of photos of rehabilitated birds. We can show those."

26. **(B)** Student 2 says, "we should emphasize that people should only attempt to rescue a bird that's clearly injured." Choices (A) and (C) refer to how people might find a bird that does not need rescuing.

27. **(A)** Student 1 says, "the rescuer needs to wear protective gloves. . . ." Choices (B) and (C) are both plausible but are not mentioned.

28. **(B)** Student 2 says, "let's tell people to put the injured bird in a box . . . with good air circulation." Choice (A) is something that is not necessary. Choice (C) is something that should not be used.

29. **(C)** Student 1 says, "the best way to help the bird stay calm is not by petting it or talking to it, but by leaving it completely alone." Choices (A) and (B) are the things that people should not do.

30. **(A)** Student 1 says, "Yes, it's better just to speak quietly while you have the bird in the car." Choice (B) is something that people should not do. Choice (C) is not mentioned.

31. **(C)** The speaker says, "The approximately three thousand individual reefs that make up the Great Barrier Reef system. . . ."

32. **(B)** The speaker says, ". . . large continental islands covered with vegetation. . . ."

33. *deep ocean.* The speaker says, "Other types of habitat in the area range from the shallow waters of coastal salt marshes to deep ocean habitat."

34. *seaweed.* The speaker says, "Plant life in the reef habitat includes 500 different species of seaweed."

35. *woody.* The speaker says, "Those at the northern end support over 300 plant species, most of which tend to be woody. . . ."

36. *crocodiles.* The speaker says, "Many types of reptiles can also be found living among and near the reefs, including crocodiles and several species of marine turtles. The former find their home in the saltwater marshes along the coastal areas, while the latter are attracted to sea grass beds."

37. *turtles.* See answer above.

38. *frogs.* The speaker says, "At least seven species of frogs, for example, inhabit the reef's islands."

39. *rising sea temperatures.* The speaker says, "Rising sea temperatures have led to an effect called coral bleaching. . . ."

40. *shading the reef/shading certain areas.* The speaker says, "One proposed solution involves shading the reef in certain areas to help keep the surrounding water temperatures down."

Reading

PASSAGE 1

1. **(C)** Paragraph 1: "Some plants reproduce asexually by splitting off new roots or bulbs ... or even branches, stems, or leaves."

2. **(G)** According to paragraph 1, these plants make clones, or copies, of themselves.

3. **(I)** Paragraph 1: "This is a simple and direct method of reproduction, producing new plants more quickly and with less energy than plants using sexual reproduction."

4. **(B)** Paragraph 1: "In flowering plants, pollen ... fertilizes the ovaries ... resulting in seeds."

5. **(F)** Paragraph 2: "more commonly, pollination occurs between separate plants, either through pollen being borne by the wind ... or by pollinators. ..."

6. *True.* Paragraph 3: "the honeybee, which collects nectar as well as pollen for food."

7. *Not Given.* Paragraph 4 mentions a butterfly's need for a "landing platform" but does not mention what a butterfly does if there is no place to land on a flower.

8. *True.* Paragraph 4: "many moths are active at night and thus are attracted to flowers that are pale or white, have a strong fragrance. ..."

9. *True.* Paragraph 4: "flowers that attract these tiny birds also have strong stems and are designed for pollen to be brushed on the hummingbirds' heads as they sip nectar."

10. *True.* Paragraph 5: "Many bee attractors also have nectar guides, which are spots near the center of each flower that reflect ultraviolet light, making it easier for the bees to find the nectar."

11. *False.* Paragraph 5: "Bees are also attracted to flowers with a mintlike or sweet smell."

12. *False.* Paragraph 6: "While many staple crops such as rice, corn, canola, and wheat are self-pollinating or pollinated by the wind. ..."

13. *True.* Paragraph 6: "Over 30 percent of the world's crops require the work of pollinator species."

14. *Not Given.* Paragraph 7 mentions the decline of the honeybee population and concern for effects that may have, but it does not mention any specific economic effects.

PASSAGE 2

15. **(A)** Paragraph 1 explains that the Chauvet Cave is less well known than the cave art site in Lascaux. Choices (B) and (C) are plausible but incorrect.

16. **(C)** Paragraph 2 explains that most European cave art sites show images of prey animals but that the Chauvet Cave also has images of animals that people feared. Choice (A) is contradicted by the information in the passage. Choice (B) refers to animal remains found in the cave.

17. **(A)** Paragraph 2: "a common theory that the primary purpose of cave art was to magically ensure plentiful game." Choice (B) is the opposite of the correct answer. Choice (C) refers to images found in the cave art, but these are not mentioned as the function of cave art.

18. **(B)** Paragraph 3 explains that some of the images in the Chauvet Cave are much older than people had assumed most European cave art is. Choice (A) refers to a theory about

cave art that has been disproved. Choice (C) confuses the meaning of the last sentence of the paragraph.

19. **(B)** Paragraph 4: "the Chauvet Cave also has an image of a being, referred to as the Sorcerer, with the body of a human and the head of a bison." Choice (A) is not mentioned. Choice (C) is incorrect because only an incomplete image of a woman's body is mentioned.

20. **(A)** Paragraph 4: "the floor of the cave contains the footprints of humans and cave bears, and fire pits, stone tools. . . ." *Implements made of stone* means "stone tools." Choice (B) is confused with the "bones from meals," which must have been animal bones. Choice (C) is confused with the image of the bison's head.

21. **(C)** Paragraph 4: "The cave had been untouched for thousands of years due to a rock slide which had sealed off the cave. . . ." Choice (A) is confused with the evidence of cave bears found when scientists visited the cave. Choice (B) occurred after humans had visited the cave.

22. *cave paintings.* Paragraph 5: "many people assume that the art of early hunters and gatherers was limited to cave paintings."

23. *engravings.* Paragraph 5: Paleolithic artists not only painted with pigments but also created engravings by scratching designs into rock with pointed tools, as well as creating low-relief sculptures."

24. *geometrical designs.* Paragraph 5: "In addition to animal images, most sites also have geometrical designs, including dots and quadrangles."

25. *hands.* Paragraph 6: "Images of hands, created . . . by wetting the palm of the hand with paint . . . are common."

26. *(full) human.* Paragraph 6: "full images of humans are rare in the European caves."

27. *detailed, realistic.* Paragraph 6: "Most of the animal images, on the other hand, are detailed, realistic portrayals of an individual animal species. . . ."

PASSAGE 3

28. **(D)** This paragraph gives some examples of how letters and numbers are represented by dots in the Braille system.

29. **(B)** This paragraph briefly describes Braille's experiences at his local school up to age ten.

30. **(E)** This paragraph describes the Braille slate and stylus and the Braille writing machine, as well as the use of a computer.

31. **(F)** This paragraph mentions some examples of technology that makes reading with Braille unnecessary.

32. **(E)** This paragraph says that it did not become the official communication system for blind people in France until 1854, two years after Braille died.

33. **(B)** This paragraph describes the system developed by Valentin Haüy, which was used at the institution where Braille studied as a child.

34. **(D)** This paragraph describes how the Braille system of raised dots is read.

35. **(A)** This paragraph describes the injury to Braille's eyes when he was three years old.

36. **(C)** This paragraph describes the system developed by Charles Barbier, which inspired Braille's system.

37. *False.* Paragraph F: "The system . . . has incorporated symbols for math, science, and music."

38. *True.* Paragraph F: "has been adapted to dozens of languages, including many with non-Roman alphabets, such as Chinese and Japanese."

39. *Not Given.* There is no comparison made between the reading speed of Braille readers and sighted readers.

40. *True.* Paragraph F: "knowledge of Braille has declined in recent years as technology has provided innovations, such as recorded books and computers with synthetic speech."

Writing

These are models. Your answers will vary. See page 2 in the Introduction to see the criteria for scoring.

WRITING TASK 1

The graph compares unemployment rates and average weekly earnings across different educational levels in the year 2016. The information clearly illustrates that people with higher educational levels were better off economically than those with lower educational levels.

The first graph shows unemployment rates. There was a significant gap between those with the lowest educational level and those with the highest. In 2016, unemployment for workers with a high school diploma only was at 5.5 percent. This rate gradually decreased with each succeeding educational level. It was lowest among those with a graduate degree—only 1.2 percent.

The second graph shows average weekly earnings. Again, the differences between the lower and higher educational levels are significant. In 2016, workers with a high school diploma earned an average of just $600 a week. The level of earnings increased with each educational level. Workers with a college degree earned an average of $1,100 weekly, almost twice as much as the high school graduates. The workers with graduate degrees earned almost half again as much as the workers with college degrees. These graphs show that it pays to get an education.

WRITING TASK 2

In many families it has been traditional for parents to choose their children's professions. In other families, the children themselves decide what professions they are interested in pursuing. I can see the advantages to both situations. However, I think it is best to let the children decide for themselves.

Many parents around the world still follow the tradition of choosing their children's professions for them. Some parents want their children to follow in their footsteps. Other parents choose professions for their children that they believe will enable a comfortable lifestyle. Parents are, of course, older and more experienced than their children, and they know their children well. It is reasonable to expect that they can make good choices for their children.

On the other hand, by the time someone is old enough to start thinking about college and preparing for a profession, he or she is no longer really a child. He or she is old enough to know something about him- or herself, what things interest him or her, and what his or her strengths are. His or her future is his or her own to live, so he or she should be the one to make important decisions about it. In addition, the modern world changes rapidly. By the time a young person is ready to prepare for a profession, things are probably very different from the way they were when his or her parents were young. Because of this, in a certain sense, a young person may understand the world better than his or her parents do and so make better decisions for his or her future.

The tradition of parents choosing professions for their children is just that—a tradition. Young people of today are more independent. Of course, it is never a bad idea for a young person to ask his or her parents for advice, but the final decision about a profession should be made by the young person.

Speaking

These are models. Your answers will vary. See page 2 in the Introduction to see the criteria for scoring.

PART 1

How often do you go shopping?
I don't go shopping very often. Well, I generally stop at a store a few times a week to pick up something small, pens, maybe, or something like that, my everyday needs. But I don't make major shopping trips very often, maybe once a month, maybe even less than that. I just don't need to buy very many things.

What kinds of shops are there in your neighborhood?
My neighborhood is residential, so there are very few businesses. We have a small grocery store. It has a limited assortment of things for sale, and they're more expensive than at a supermarket, so we really just use that store for convenience. We use it when we need only one or two things and don't want to go all the way to the supermarket, which is farther away. We also have a drug-store and a small bookstore that sells newspapers and magazines as well as books. Those are all the shops we have. We usually have to go to another part of the city to go shopping.

What kinds of things do you usually shop for?
I don't have to shop for groceries or anything for the house because my mother does that, so I just have to buy the things I need. Once or twice a year I buy the clothes I need for school. Besides that, I like to buy things for my computer, and I have to buy the things I need for school, books and pens and things like that.

Do you enjoy shopping? Why or why not?
I don't think shopping is very interesting. If I need something, I buy it. If I don't need anything, there's no reason to go to the store. I know some people think of shopping like a hobby or a

sport, but I don't. I just think of it as a necessity. Well, sometimes I like to go to the store and look through the phones and electronics that are for sale, just because I like to look at them. Then sometimes I might buy something that maybe I hadn't been planning on buying. But most of the time I never think about shopping unless there's something I particularly need.

What are some of your favorite foods?
I like all different kinds of foods. I especially like to try foods from different countries. I like dishes that are served with rice and noodles and that have a lot of vegetables. I don't like meat very much. I almost never eat it. I don't like sweet things too much either.

Who does the cooking at your house?
My mother does almost all the cooking at my house. She's a very good cook, and I always enjoy the meals she prepares. Sometimes I do some of the cooking, or one of my brothers or sisters might cook a meal occasionally. My mother has taught all of us to cook, so we help her out in the kitchen from time to time. But she does most of the cooking.

Do you prefer eating at home or in restaurants? Why?
I like eating at home because, as I said, my mother always prepares delicious meals. And usually it's more convenient to eat at home. But I like eating in restaurants, too. The food is different, and it's really fun to get together with my friends at a restaurant. But it's also expensive to eat out, so I don't do it very often.

What kinds of restaurants do you enjoy eating in?
I like eating in restaurants that specialize in food from other countries. I like to try all different kinds of foods. My favorite thing to do is to go to a restaurant that has a style of cooking I haven't tried before and just choose something from the menu. Most of the time I end up with a dish I really like. It's a fun adventure to try different kinds of food. We have a lot of different restaurants in my city, so I have a lot of opportunities to try new kinds of foods.

PART 2

I've always wanted to go to the Great Barrier Reef, off the coast of Australia. It's a natural place, a place where you can see and learn about the natural world, specifically, about ocean life. I think it might be considered one of the wonders of the natural world. I would really like to have the opportunity to go diving there. I think it would be really fun and really interesting to go swimming among the coral reefs and see all the different kinds of animals that live there. There are thousands of species of animals and fish living there, as well as different kinds of coral. I'd like to go there because I'm interested in marine biology. I'm interested in learning about ocean life, and the Great Barrier Reef is one of the best places to observe it. Also, I've never been diving, and I would really like to learn how. I'm thinking about getting a degree in marine biology, so learning to dive at the Great Barrier Reef would probably be a good way to start!

PART 3

Where do people from your country travel to most frequently?
I would say that the beach is the place where people go the most. We have some very nice beaches on our coast and when the weather is warm, they are always filled with visitors from

all over the country. Almost every holiday people spend at least part of the time at the beach. People who travel abroad like to visit big cities such as New York or London or Paris. People say that they go to those cities for the culture, but I think the real reason is for the shopping.

What are some popular places to visit in your country? Why are they popular?
There are a lot of popular places to visit in my country. We have a lot of natural places that are interesting to see, we have historical sites, and we have some very nice beaches. One of my favorite places to visit is Mountain National Park. It's a popular place for tourists to visit, mostly because it's very beautiful. Also, it has something for everybody. There are some great hiking trails, there's fishing in the rivers, there's camping, and for people who like to take things easy, there's a road to the top of the mountain. You can drive to the top and see the spectacular views, or take a tour by bus. Then you can ride back to your hotel and be comfortable.

What are some reasons that people travel?
I think the biggest reason people travel is that change is relaxing. If you follow the same routine at school or at work every day, then when you have a vacation, you want to do something different. Being in a different place can take your mind off the problems or boredom of your daily life. You can empty your mind of all those things and just relax. People like to take all different kinds of vacations. Some people like to go to other countries and see a different way of life. Some like outdoor adventures. Some like to relax on the beach or at a resort. But the one thing all these different ways of traveling have in common is that they all involve a change of scene from the traveler's usual daily life.

Do you think parents should make a point of taking their children to see a variety of different places? Why or why not?
I think it's very important for parents to take their children traveling. Children should learn from an early age that life everywhere isn't the same as the life they know at home. That's one thing that's important to learn. The other thing is that traveling gives children the opportunity for different kinds of experiences. They can learn how to go camping, they can learn about art and history in museums, they can go on a boat and experience the ocean. Having different experiences like these is an important part of learning and growing up.

Why should governments invest in tourism?
Tourism can really help the economy of areas, especially poor areas. Bringing tourists to an area brings money in and creates jobs where maybe there weren't any before. Private investors might want to build hotels and restaurants and things like that for the tourists, but in order to do that, the government has to build roads and water systems and electric lines. Private investors can't develop an area for tourism without the help of the government.

How can tourism negatively affect societies?
Tourism can change the whole way of life in a place, especially if it is a small town. Crowds of tourists can change quiet and peaceful towns into noisy crowded places. If people are used to living a traditional way of life, tourism might change that because it gives people lots of contact with the outside world that they might not have had before. Also, tourism can harm the environment if new roads and buildings are constructed to accommodate tourists. So, tourism can bring money to an area, but it can also bring crowds, noise, new customs, and pollution, and these things really change the way of life in a place.

PART 2
General Training Module

The following practice tests include only the Reading and Writing sections for the General Training Module.

For the Listening and Speaking sections, go to the Academic Module, Practice Tests 1–6. The Listening and Speaking sections are the same for all test takers. See the charts on pages 1–2 for page numbers.

General Training Module

Reading and Writing

PRACTICE TEST 1

ANSWER SHEET
General Training Practice Test 1

IELTS Reading Answer Sheet

	✓ ✗			✓ ✗
1	✓1✗	21		✓21✗
2	▭2▭	22		▭22▭
3	▭3▭	23		▭23▭
4	▭4▭	24		▭24▭
5	▭5▭	25		▭25▭
6	▭6▭	26		▭26▭
7	▭7▭	27		▭27▭
8	▭8▭	28		▭28▭
9	▭9▭	29		▭29▭
10	▭10▭	30		▭30▭
11	▭11▭	31		▭31▭
12	▭12▭	32		▭32▭
13	▭13▭	33		▭33▭
14	▭14▭	34		▭34▭
15	▭15▭	35		▭35▭
16	▭16▭	36		▭36▭
17	▭17▭	37		▭37▭
18	▭18▭	38		▭38▭
19	▭19▭	39		▭39▭
20	▭20▭	40		▭40▭
		Reading Total		

GENERAL TRAINING MODEL TEST 1

Candidate Name _____

International English Language Testing System

GENERAL TRAINING READING

Time: 1 hour

INSTRUCTIONS TO CANDIDATES

Do not open this booklet until you are told to do so.

Write your name in the space at the top of this page.

Start at the beginning of the test and work through it.

You should answer all questions.

If you cannot do a particular question, leave it and go on to the next. You can return to it later.

All answers must be written on the Answer Sheet.

Do not remove this booklet from the examination room.

INFORMATION FOR CANDIDATES

There are **40** questions on this question paper.

The test is divided as follows:

Section 1	Questions 1–14
Section 2	Questions 15–27
Section 3	Questions 28–40

SECTION 1

*You are advised to spend 20 minutes on **Questions 1–14**.*
*Read the text below and answer **Questions 1–7**.*

Barchester Office Towers
Visitor Information

Welcome to Barchester Office Towers. All areas beyond the ground[1]-floor lobby are off-limits to visitors without a pass. Please approach the security desk near the back of the lobby to obtain your pass. You must present a photo ID. The security officer on duty will direct you to the office you are visiting. In addition, a building directory and map are located near the security desk.

To reach the rooftop parking area, take the elevator[2] to the fourth floor and then follow the signs. Also located on that floor is the City View Bistro, serving three meals daily.

Barchester Office Towers offers a number of business services for the convenience of tenants and visitors. The Copy Center[3] is located on the second floor. Photocopy and fax services are available here, and you can also purchase basic office and computer supplies. A small branch post office is located down the hall from the Copy Center. Mail pickup is twice a day, at 7:30 A.M. and 5:00 P.M. On the floor above, you will find a branch of the National Bank, where all banking services are offered.

The Barchester Café is located next to the National Bank. Here you can enjoy coffee, tea, and home-baked snacks. Most of the major daily papers, as well as business journals and magazines, are on sale at the café.

---

[1]In the United States, the ground floor is considered the first floor; the next floor up is the second floor, and so on.
[2]British: lift
[3]British: Centre

Questions 1–7

On which floor of the office complex can you do each of the following activities?
On lines 1–7 on your answer sheet, write:

> **A**   if you can do this on the ground floor
>
> **B**   if you can do this on the second floor
>
> **C**   if you can do this on the third floor
>
> **D**   if you can do this on the fourth floor

1 have lunch

2 cash a check

3 buy stamps

4 get permission to enter the building

5 buy a newspaper

6 buy pens for your office

7 find the location of any office in the building

Questions 8–14

*Read the text below and answer **Questions 8–14**.*

Spring Willow Farm Museum and Education Center

Spring Willow Farm is a fully operating farm designed to educate the public about farm operation, farm history, and issues facing farmers today.

Schedule

We are open to the pubic every day of the year, excluding holidays. The grounds are open year-round from 8:00 A.M. until 6:00 P.M. Visitors can access the buildings on most days between 10:00 A.M. and 5:00 P.M., with a reduced schedule during the winter months. Please call the farm or visit our website for a current schedule of events, classes, and opening times.

Visiting the Farm

Visitors are free to tour the farm on their own. Maps are available at the information desk in the Main Building. Guided tours are included in the cost of admission. Tours leave from the Main Building front entrance at 10:30 A.M. and 2:00 P.M. daily.

The ground floor of the Main Building contains exhibits explaining daily farm life in different periods of history, with displays showing farm implements, kitchen and other household utensils, photographs, and more. Also in the Main Building is the Farm Gift Shop. Available for sale are a variety of books on farming and farm life as well as reproductions of old photographs and historical farm implements.

In the cow barn, visitors can watch milking demonstrations every afternoon. The horse and goat barns are also open to visitors. Please note: Our animals are used to attention from people and enjoy being petted, but use caution. Please don't tease the animals, and please don't feed them.

Classes

Spring Willow Farm offers classes on various aspects of farming and farm history two evenings a week throughout the year. If you are interested in learning about the history of farming in our region or about current food policy and agricultural issues, take a look at the class schedule on our website. In addition, classes on special subjects related to farming can be arranged for your club or group. Please contact the Education Office for further information.

Do the following statements agree with the information given in the text about the Spring Willow Farm Museum and Education Center? On lines 8–14 on your answer sheet, write:

> **TRUE**   *if the statement agrees with the information*
> **FALSE**   *if the statement contradicts the information*
> **NOT GIVEN**   *if there is no information on this*

8 Spring Willow Farm is a training center for future farmers.

9 The farm buildings are closed to the public during the winter.

10 Visitors must pay to visit the farm.

11 The guided tours last two hours.

12 Visitors can purchase copies of old tools at the farm.

13 Visitors are allowed to touch the farm animals.

14 Farmers are offered a special discount on classes.

SECTION 2

*You are advised to spend 20 minutes on **Questions 15–27**.*

Questions 15–20

*The following passage has six sections, **A–F**. Choose the correct heading for sections **A–F** from the list of headings below. Write the correct number, **i–viii**, on lines 15–20 on your answer sheet. There are more headings than sections, so you will not use them all.*

15   Section A

16   Section B

17   Section C

18   Section D

19   Section E

20   Section F

LIST OF HEADINGS

i	Feeling Confident
ii	Solving Problems
iii	Room Arrangement
iv	Equipment
v	Defining Your Purpose
vi	Using Visuals
vii	Your Audience
viii	Speaking Well

How to Give an Effective Presentation

When planning an effective presentation, there are a number of things to keep in mind.

A

First ask yourself, "Why am I giving this presentation?" The point of your presentation may be to outline a project plan, report on work that has been done, solve a problem, provide training, or generate support for an idea. Once you are clear on the reason for your presentation, it will be easier to organize[1] your information.

B

If you are not used to giving presentations, you may feel nervous. There are a few things you can do to counteract this. The most important thing is to rehearse your presentation several times until you feel comfortable with it. Before you begin speaking, take a few deep breaths. This will help you relax. Stand up straight and look your audience in the eye. Most of all, don't try to be perfect. This is an impossible goal.

C

Even though you may be using a microphone, you still need to pay attention to your voice. Talk slowly and clearly. Pause often to give your audience time to absorb the information. Do not garble your words or talk so quickly that no one can follow you.

D

There is no better way to lose your audience than to stand at the front of the room and talk on and on but give them nothing to look at. Plan to use presentation software to show charts and graphs, photographs, maps, or other graphics that will make your ideas clearer. This is particularly important for numbers, but it is also useful for other kinds of information.

E

Before you begin your presentation, remember to check the microphone, computer, and any other special tools you may be using. Make sure everything is in working order before you start talking so that there will be no interruptions due to breakdowns.

F

Something that is often overlooked but that is very important for an effective presentation is the location setup. Make sure that the seating is placed so that it allows everyone to see your slides and hear your voice. The chairs should be comfortable, too.

---

[1]British: organise

Questions 21–27

*Read the text below and answer **Questions 21–27**.*

The Marcy Corporation

Information for New Employees

All new employees at the Marcy Corporation are required to attend an orientation session during their first month of employment. The next orientation session will be held on March 21 in the company conference room. Employee benefits, payment policies, employee responsibilities, and other personnel matters will be discussed. Employees are requested to read the employee manual and submit the signed statement prior to attending the orientation.

The Marcy Corporation Employee Manual has been provided to inform our employees about the company's procedures and policies. We ask each employee to take the time to read the manual carefully. After a thorough review of the manual, the statement below should be signed and returned to the employee's supervisor by the date noted below. Every effort has been made to present the information in the manual in a clear and concise manner. If there are any questions regarding the content of the manual, they should be submitted in writing to Human Resources.

....

Statement

I, _____, have read a copy of the Marcy Corporation Employee Manual and am familiar with its contents. By signing below, I certify that I understand and accept the information contained in the Marcy Corporation Employee Manual and agree to abide by the Marcy Corporation's policies.

_____

(Employee signature)

Please submit by: March 15

Questions 21–27

Complete the sentences below.

*Choose **NO MORE THAN THREE WORDS** from the text for each answer.*

Write your answers on lines 21–27 on your answer sheet.

21 All .... must participate in an orientation session.

22 The .... will take place in the company conference room.

23 The manual should be read before ....

24 The employee manual contains information about the company's ....

25 The signed statement should be submitted to ....

26 .... will answer questions about the content of the manual.

27 The signed statement is due by ....

SECTION 3

*You should spend 20 minutes on **Questions 28–40**, which are based on the Reading Passage below.*

Canoes Around the World

Many cultures throughout the world have developed some form of canoe—a long, slender, open boat powered by handheld paddles. In each case, the technologies and materials used to construct the canoe reflect the resources available to that particular culture. There are three basic types of canoe: the frame-and-bark canoe, the dugout, and the plank canoe. Developed by cultures on every continent since prehistoric times, canoes continue to be used today both for survival and for recreation.

The birch-bark canoe, an example of the frame-and-bark type of construction, was developed in the region that is now the northeastern United States and eastern Canada. Native Americans constructed birch-bark canoes by building a frame from spruce wood and then using roots to stitch pieces of birch bark over the frame. In areas where birch was not available, bark from elm or spruce trees was used instead. After the bark was sewn to the frame, the canoes were then sealed with a mixture of spruce gum and bear grease. These substances worked very well to make the boat watertight. Birch-bark canoes were lightweight and thus easily transported around waterfalls or from lake to lake. Most were designed to hold no more than two or three people and were used for lake and river travel. When Europeans opened up the fur trade in North America in the seventeenth century, the French traders used larger versions (30 to 40 feet in length) to transport furs in large quantities across the Great Lakes for shipment back to Europe.

The dugout—a canoe created from a single tree trunk—has been used in many areas throughout the world. Simple versions of hollowed-out logs were used by native peoples throughout much of North America. Coastal groups such as the Haida and Tlinglit in the Pacific Northwest developed large dugout crafts 60 feet or longer that could carry large numbers of people on the ocean for trade, warfare, fishing, whaling, and travel to ceremonial gatherings. First, the outer and inner bark around the entire circumference of a tall, straight tree, often a cedar or redwood, was removed. This process, called girdling, cuts off the flow of sap, thus killing the tree and making it easier to chop down. Then the tree was felled and cut to the appropriate length. The opening of the dugout was created by repeatedly burning the wood, then carving it out with tools. In early times, stone tools were used, but later metal tools came into use. Once the canoe was carved out, the boat builders filled it with water and brought the water to a boil using stones heated on a fire. This softened the wood and the weight of the water caused the walls of the canoe to bow outward, giving it more width than the original girth of the tree.

The ocean-going Chumash people of what is now southern California developed the *tomol*, or plank canoe. They created their canoes by cutting planks from redwood trees, carving and shaping them into a canoe without any frame. They lashed the planks together by drilling holes and tying them with cords. Pitch from pine trees and tar, also found locally, were used between the planks and over the entire hull for waterproofing.

The canoe played a major role in the spread of all the Pacific Island cultures. These cultures developed outrigger and double-hulled dugout canoes. Outriggers have one or more parallel floats attached to a dugout canoe with poles for increased stability in ocean waves. Double-hulled canoes have a platform between two parallel dugouts. These highly stable designs, combined with sails, enabled the Polynesians to go on epic ocean journeys and to inhabit far-flung islands. Several families (or as many as 200 people in the largest vessels), could sail in each of these double-hulled canoes with food, water, and domesticated plants and animals across huge expanses of ocean, and in this way the Polynesian people spread throughout the Pacific, establishing new communities on previously uninhabited islands.

In areas of dense rain forest throughout the world, including the Amazon basin, and parts of Africa and Asia, river travel with dugouts was, and in many cases still is, the primary means of transportation. In West Africa, large war canoes capable of transporting many fighters were carved from single trees.

Descendants of the ancient canoes are still widely used today. Traditional cultures around the world still use dugout canoes for fishing and transportation. Today's modern recreational canoes, while now often constructed with aluminum,[1] fiberglass,[2] wood, and canvas, plastic, and other synthetic materials, still retain the shape and basic design of the birch-bark canoes developed in the distant past. The catamaran sailboat, widely used in racing, is a direct descendant of the double-hulled sailing canoe used thousands of years ago by the Polynesian cultures.

---

[1]British: aluminium
[2]British: fibreglass

Questions 28–34

Look at the following descriptions, **Questions 28–34**, of the different types of canoes.
Match each description with the correct canoe, **A**, **B**, or **C**.
Write the correct letter, **A**, **B**, or **C**, on lines 28–34 on your answer sheet.

TYPES OF CANOES

A   birch-bark

B   dugout

C   plank

28   held together with rope

29   made from a hollowed-out log

30   made waterproof with gum and grease

31   constructed with the use of both fire and water

32   easy to carry over land

33   sealed with pitch and tar

34   made to carry just a few people

Polynesians turned dugout canoes into outrigger canoes by attaching

Questions 35–40

Complete the summary below.
Choose **NO MORE THAN TWO WORDS** from the text for each answer.
Write your answers on lines 35–40 on your answer sheet.

35 .... to them. Double-hulled canoes were made by

connecting two outrigger canoes with 36 .... Because

they could travel over 37 .... of ocean in these canoes,

Polynesians were able to inhabit islands all across the Pacific Ocean. In West

Africa, large war canoes were used to carry 38 .... Today,

39 .... canoes are made of modern materials such as

aluminum, fiberglass, and plastic. These modern canoes are similar in form to

40 .... canoes.

ANSWER SHEET
General Training
Practice Test 1

Writing Answer Sheet

TASK 1

_____

_____

_____

_____

_____

_____

_____

_____

_____

_____

_____

_____

_____

_____

_____

_____

_____

_____

ANSWER SHEET
General Training Practice Test 1

-2-

-3-

TASK 2

_____

_____

_____

_____

_____

_____

_____

_____

_____

_____

_____

_____

_____

_____

_____

_____

_____

_____

_____

ANSWER SHEET
General Training
Practice Test 1

-4-

GENERAL TRAINING MODEL TEST 1

Candidate Name _____

International English Language Testing System

GENERAL TRAINING WRITING

Time: 1 hour

INSTRUCTIONS TO CANDIDATES

Do not open this booklet until you are told to do so.

Write your name in the space at the top of this page.

All answers must be written on the separate answer booklet provided.

Do not remove this booklet from the examination room.

INFORMATION FOR CANDIDATES

There are **2** tasks on this question paper.

You must do **both** tasks.

Underlength answers will be penalized.[1]

---

[1]British: penalised

WRITING TASK 1

You should spend about 20 minutes on this task. You do NOT need to write any addresses.
Begin your letter as follows:

Dear ————————————————,

> You have been offered a job that will require you to move to a city that you have never visited before. You have a friend who lives there.
>
> **Write a letter to your friend. In your letter**
>
> ■ **explain your situation**
> ■ **say why you feel unsure about living in the city**
> ■ **ask some questions about life in the city**

Write at least 150 words.

WRITING TASK 2

You should spend about 40 minutes on this task.

> **Write about the following topic:**
>
> *In some countries, employees are generally given two weeks of paid vacation[1] time each year. In other countries, employees are given four or six weeks of paid vacation time.*
>
> *Considering the needs of both employee and employer, what do you think is a reasonable amount of paid vacation time for employees to have? Give reasons for your answer and include any relevant examples from your own knowledge or experience.*

Write at least 250 words.

---

[1]British: holiday; in the United States, holiday refers to a specific date on which a special event, such as Thanksgiving, is observed.

ANSWER KEY
Practice Test 1

Reading

1. D	16. i	28. C
2. C	17. viii	29. B
3. B	18. vi	30. A
4. A	19. iv	31. B
5. C	20. iii	32. A
6. B	21. new employees	33. C
7. A	22. (next) orientation	34. A
8. False	session	35. parallel floats
9. False	23. (attending) the	36. a platform
10. True	orientation	37. huge expanses
11. Not Given	24. procedures and policies	38. (many) fighters
12. True	25. the employee's	39. (modern) recreational
13. True	supervisor	40. birch-bark
14. Not Given	26. Human Resources	
15. v	27. March 15	

GENERAL TRAINING MODULE—PRACTICE TEST 1

Reading

1. **(D)** The City View Bistro is on the fourth floor and serves three meals a day.

2. **(C)** The National Bank is located on the third floor.

3. **(B)** The post office is down the hall from the Copy Center, which is on the second floor.

4. **(A)** The security desk, where visitor's passes are issued, is located on the ground floor lobby.

5. **(C)** Newspapers are available in the Barchester Café, located next to the bank on the third floor.

6. **(B)** Office supplies are for sale in the Copy Center on the second floor.

7. **(A)** A building directory and map are located near the security desk, in the ground floor lobby.

8. *False.* Paragraph 1: "Spring Willow Farm is designed to educate the public," that is, people in general. It is not a training center.

9. *False.* Paragraph 2: The farm has a reduced schedule during the winter. It is open for fewer hours, but it is open.

10. *True.* Paragraph 3: "Guided tours are included in the cost of admission."

11. *Not Given.* Guided tours are mentioned in paragraph 3, but their length is not.

12. *True.* Paragraph 4 mentions that reproductions of historical farm implements are for sale in the gift shop.

13. *True.* Paragraph 5 advises using caution when petting, that is, touching, the animals.

14. *Not Given.* Classes are discussed in the fifth paragraph but no discount is mentioned.

15. *v.* Section A lists the different reasons, or purposes, for a presentation.

16. *i.* Section B discusses ways to relax and overcome nervousness, that is, ways to feel confident when giving a presentation.

17. *viii.* Section C discusses talking and voice.

18. *vi.* Section D talks about using presentation software to give the audience something to look at.

19. *iv.* Section E talks about computers and microphones, that is, equipment.

20. *iii.* Section F talks about the seating arrangement.

21. *new employees.* Paragraph 1: "All new employees at the Marcy Corporation are required to attend an orientation session . . . ."

22. *(next) orientation session.* Paragraph 1: "The next orientation session will be held . . . in the company conference room."

23. *(attending) the orientation.* Paragraph 1: "Employees are requested to read the employee manual . . . prior to attending the orientation."

24. *procedures and policies.* Paragraph 2: "The Marcy Corporation Employee Manual has been provided to inform our employees about the company's procedures and policies."

25. *the employee's supervisor.* Paragraph 2: "the statement below should be signed and returned to the employee's supervisor . . . ."

26. *Human Resources.* Paragraph 2: "If there are any questions regarding the content of the manual, they should be submitted in writing to Human Resources."

27. *March 15.* The bottom of the form shows March 15 as the date to submit the statement.

28. **(C)** Paragraph 4: "They lashed the planks together by drilling holes and tying them with cords."

29. **(B)** Paragraph 3 describes how the dugout canoe is made from a single tree trunk, or log.

30. **(A)** Paragraph 2 explains that birch-bark canoes were: "sealed with a mixture of spruce gum and bear grease."

31. **(B)** Paragraph 3: "The opening of the dugout was created by repeatedly burning the wood, then carving it out with tools . . . the boat builders filled it with water and brought the water to a boil using stones heated on a fire . . . ."

32. **(A)** Paragraph 2: "Birch-bark canoes were lightweight and . . . easily transported around waterfalls or from lake to lake."

33. **(C)** Paragraph 4 says of plank canoes: "Pitch from pine trees and tar . . . were used between the planks and over the entire hull for waterproofing."

34. **(A)** Paragraph 2 says of birch-bark canoes: "Most were designed to hold no more than two or three people . . . ."

35. *parallel floats.* Paragraph 5: "Outriggers have one or more parallel floats attached to a dugout canoe with poles for increased stability in ocean waves."

36. *a platform.* Paragraph 5: "Double-hulled canoes have a platform between two parallel dugouts."

37. *huge expanses.* Paragraph 5: "across huge expanses of ocean . . . ."

38. *(many) fighters.* Paragraph 6: "capable of transporting many fighters . . . ."

39. *(modern) recreational.* Paragraph 7: "Today's modern recreational canoes, while now often constructed with aluminum, fiberglass, wood, and canvas, plastic, and other synthetic materials . . . ."

40. *birch-bark.* Paragraph 7: "still retain the shape and basic design of the birch-bark canoes developed in the distant past."

Writing

These are models. Your answers will vary. See page 2 in the Introduction to see the criteria for scoring.

WRITING TASK 1

Dear Chris,

I am writing to ask you for some information that will help me make a decision. I have recently been offered a job in Seattle. I am very much interested in the job, but, as you know, I have never even visited Seattle. I am not sure whether I would like living there. Since you have lived there for a while, I thought you could answer some questions for me.

One thing I am worried about is the weather. I have heard that it rains in Seattle all the time. Is this true? It sounds very depressing. I have also heard that Seattle is a growing city, and I am afraid it would feel very crowded to me. I have never lived in a big city before. Another thing I wonder about is leisure activities. I like going out dancing a lot. Are there good places to go dancing in Seattle? What about music? I would not want to live in a place where I could not go to concerts frequently.

Another important issue is housing. I have heard that Seattle is very expensive. Is it hard to find a nice apartment at a reasonable rent? What neighborhoods would you recommend?

I appreciate your taking the time to answer my questions, and I look forward to hearing from you. If I decide to accept the job in Seattle, then I hope we will be able to get together frequently.

Best wishes,
Miranda

WRITING TASK 2

I believe that two weeks of annual vacation time is a good amount for a company to offer employees, at least when they are first hired. There are several reasons this is a good practice. It saves the employer money, it minimizes disruption to normal work routines, and the possibility of earning more vacation time in the future can act as an incentive to the employee.

When an employee uses paid vacation time, he or she is not contributing to the company but is still being paid. This means the employer is paying out money without getting work in return. The shorter the vacation, the less the employer has to pay out. Of course, we could say that the cost to the employer is repaid when the employee returns from vacation rested and with renewed energy. For longer vacations, however, the loss of work is probably greater than the benefit to be gained when the employee returns with greater energy. Of course, something like this is difficult to measure, and each employer must evaluate his or her own particular situation.

An employee takes a vacation, but in most cases his or her work does not. Other people must carry out the worker's responsibilities while he or she is away. In many cases, companies hire temporary workers to cover for employees who are on vacation. This is an extra expense and an inconvenience. The longer the vacation, the greater the disruption to the normal work routine.

At many companies, employees are offered more vacation time after they have worked there for a certain amount of time. This benefit can be an incentive, encouraging employees to do well in their positions and remain at the company.

Generally, I feel that all new employees should be given two weeks of annual vacation time initially, with the possibility of earning more after working with the company for some time. I think a system like this is fair to both the employer and the employee.

General Training Module

Reading and Writing

PRACTICE TEST 2

ANSWER SHEET
General Training
Practice Test 2

IELTS Reading Answer Sheet

	✓ 1 ✗
1	
2	2
3	3
4	4
5	5
6	6
7	7
8	8
9	9
10	10
11	11
12	12
13	13
14	14
15	15
16	16
17	17
18	18
19	19
20	20

	✓ 21 ✗
21	
22	22
23	23
24	24
25	25
26	26
27	27
28	28
29	29
30	30
31	31
32	32
33	33
34	34
35	35
36	36
37	37
38	38
39	39
40	40
	Reading Total

GENERAL TRAINING MODEL TEST 2

Candidate Name _____

International English Language Testing System

GENERAL TRAINING READING

Time: 1 hour

INSTRUCTIONS TO CANDIDATES

Do not open this booklet until you are told to do so.

Write your name in the space at the top of this page.

Start at the beginning of the test and work through it.

You should answer all questions.

If you cannot do a particular question, leave it and go on to the next. You can return to it later.

All answers must be written on the Answer Sheet.

Do not remove this booklet from the examination room.

INFORMATION FOR CANDIDATES

There are **40** questions on this question paper.

The test is divided as follows:

Section 1	Questions 1–14
Section 2	Questions 15–27
Section 3	Questions 28–40

*You are advised to spend 20 minutes on **Questions 1–14**.*

Questions 1–4

*The following text has four sections A–D. Choose the correct heading for each section from the list of headings below. Write the correct number **i–vii** on lines 1–4 on your answer sheet. There are more headings than sections, so you will not use them all.*

1 Section A

2 Section B

3 Section C

4 Section D

LIST OF HEADINGS

i	Other Uses for Your Machine
ii	Baking Bread
iii	The Science of Bread Dough
iv	Customer Assistance
v	Ingredients for Bread
vi	Caring for Your Machine
vii	What's Included
viii	Recipes for Your Machine

Presto Bread Machine

Thank you for buying a Presto Bread Machine. You and your family will enjoy delicious homemade bread for years to come.

A

Your Presto Baking Machine is ready to use right out of the box. All you need to add are the ingredients. You may also wish to have on hand an extra measuring cup and several measuring spoons in different sizes. Your machine comes with a baking pan, a measuring cup, and a recipe booklet, which provides all the assistance you'll need to bake a variety of delicious breads that the whole family will enjoy.

B

Choose a recipe from the enclosed recipe booklet. Each recipe lists the ingredients in the order they are to be added to the machine. Liquid ingredients should be added to the machine before dry ingredients. Place all the ingredients in the removable pan, place the pan inside the machine, and close the lid. Push the *menu* button and the type of bread you are making—white, whole wheat, or raisin. If you are making rolls, select *dough*. Push the *start* button. Your bread will be ready in three hours for white or raisin bread or four hours for whole wheat bread. Dough takes two hours.

C

Your Presto Bread Machine comes equipped with a Presto bread pan that has been designed for optimal baking. The inside is coated with a special nonstick coating to keep the crust from adhering to the sides, ensuring a perfect loaf every time. To protect the nonstick coating, avoid the use of scouring pads and abrasive cleansers. Instead, wipe the pan gently with a cloth that has been wrung out in warm, soapy water. It is also important to pay attention to the inside of the machine as bits of dough may fall out of the pan and burn during baking. After each use, let the machine cool, then wipe the insides gently with a damp cloth.

D

Instructions for making different types of bread are clearly outlined in the recipe booklet. If you have questions about any of the recipes or require help with using your Presto Bread Machine, you may call our help line: 800-555-1212. You can also check the FAQ section on our website: *www.prestobread.com*. Also available on our website is a variety of international bread recipes. If you are dissatisfied with your Presto Bread Machine for any reason, please call us at the number above and we will replace it or send you a refund.

Questions 5–7

*Answer the questions below. Choose **NO MORE THAN THREE WORDS** from the text for each answer. Write your answers on lines 5–7 on your answer sheet.*

5 How long does it take to bake raisin bread? ....

6 How often should you clean the inside of the machine? ....

7 According to these instructions, where can you find bread recipes from around the world? ....

Read the text below and answer **Questions 8–14**.

Regional Share-Your-Ride

Information for Commuters

Regional Share-Your-Ride is a free service offered to all commuters in our area. We help you save costs on commuting by matching you up with other commuters who travel the same route. When you share your daily ride to work with other commuters, you save on transportation costs and help reduce traffic congestion and air pollution.

Carpool

Share your ride to work with one or more other commuters. You can choose to carpool daily or just a few days a week, whatever suits your schedule best.

Vanpool

Using your van to share your ride with four or more people will save you even more on commuting costs. Regional Share-Your-Ride is available to help you keep your van running smoothly and filled with riders. According to state law, vanpools are permitted to travel in special high-occupancy vehicle (HOV) lanes located on highways in urban areas throughout the region.

Matching

Log on to our website at *www.rsyrp.net*. Type in your location, destination, and work schedule. Our system will generate a list of other commuters whose route and schedule match yours. The website also has maps of the region to help you plan the most efficient route for your commute. These are available for free download.

Contact

Contact the commuters on the list, and arrange a ride-sharing schedule and route with them. You can also discuss how you want to share the responsibility of driving. When you have arranged a carpool or vanpool group, return to our website and register your group with us.

Benefits

Registered participants in Regional Share-Your-Ride can sign up to receive daily traffic and weather reports by e-mail. As a participant, you are also eligible for the Urgent Ride service, which provides you with free transportation to your house in case you or your carpool or vanpool driver has an emergency.

*Complete each sentence with the correct ending, **A–M**, below.*

*Write the correct letter, **A–M**, on lines 8–14 on your answer sheet.*

A	money on traveling[1] costs.
B	participating in the program for one month.
C	a free ride home.
D	a reduced-cost Regional Share-Your-Ride program membership.
E	wear and tear on their cars.
F	permission to use certain highway lanes.
G	rentals of cars and vans for commuting purposes.
H	after forming a carpool or vanpool group.
I	if interested in learning more about carpools.
J	information to commuters who want to share rides.
K	daily information on road conditions.
L	a trip to the hospital.
M	visiting the website.

---

8 Regional Share-Your-Ride provides

9 By using a carpool or vanpool, commuters can save

10 Commuters who travel by van receive

11 Commuters can get free maps by

12 Commuters should register with the program[2]

13 After signing up for the program, participants can receive by e-mail

14 In case of emergency, program participants can get

---

[1]British: travelling
[2]British: programme

SECTION 2

*You are advised to spend 20 minutes on **Questions 15–27**.*

Questions 15–20

*Read the text below and answer **Questions 15–20**.*

Job Interview Success

When you apply for a job, the impression you create during the interview is just as important as the skills and background you bring to the table. The following suggestions will help you prepare for a successful interview.

Before You Leave Home

Dress appropriately. This means the attire you choose should be the same as what you would wear for work once you are hired. Conservative colors[1] and styles always convey a more trustworthy image.

Rehearse the interview at home. Think of questions that you will probably be asked, and prepare answers for them. This will help you be calm when you are at the actual interview.

Don't be late for your interview. The best way to avoid this problem is to decide ahead of time how you want to get there. If by bus or subway, check the schedules the day before. If by car, plan your route carefully and figure out how long it will take. Careful planning will ensure that you will make a good impression by arriving on time.

During the Interview

Speak clearly. Look the interviewer in the eye when speaking and use clear, confident tones. Do not speak too quickly or nervously. Rather, pronounce your words carefully and pause when searching for ideas. Speaking with a firm, clear voice is one of the best ways to give an impression of self-assurance.

Ask questions. Do not be afraid to do this. It will not make you appear unprepared or stupid. On the contrary, asking the right questions shows that you are knowledgeable about the company and conveys the impression that you are interested and enthusiastic.

---

[1]British: colours

Complete the sentences below.

*Choose **NO MORE THAN THREE WORDS** from the text for each answer. Write your answers on lines 15–20 on your answer sheet.*

15 Wearing .... clothes makes a better impression during the job interview.

16 Practice answering questions ahead of time so that you feel .... during the interview.

17 If traveling to the interview by bus, make sure you know .... ahead of time.

18 You will be .... for the interview if you plan your trip beforehand.

19 Use your .... to convey an attitude of confidence.

20 Show what you know by asking ....

*Read the text below and answer **Questions 21–27**.*

Five Reasons Your Business Needs a Website

All businesses, large or small, need a website. Here are several reasons a website can help a company of any size improve its business.

A

A website is the most important tool a business has for maintaining contact with customers. The website gives customers a way to know what services or products you sell and how to contact you. By offering an e-newsletter sign-up on your website, customers can stay informed about events related to your business and your products, and you save on printing costs. A link to your blog keeps customers up-to-date on what is happening with your business, and keeps them coming back.

B

A website allows you to expand your customer base beyond your immediate community, and even to other countries. Anyone in the world can have access to your services and products through your website, at no extra cost.

C

No matter what the size of your business, it is not hard to afford a website. It is easy to set up, and it does not have to break your budget. There are templates available if you want to create a website yourself. Or, you can hire a Web designer for a more professional look. Depending on what you need, using the services of a professional does not necessarily cost huge amounts of money. The hosting fees you pay to keep your website up and running are minimal.

D

You can save on expenses by keeping your website simple. Even just a few pages can be enough to provide your customers with the necessary information to keep them interested in what your business has to offer. A large website with lots of pages is not always necessary. The most essential facts to include in any website—your business name and location, your products, and your contact information—can be contained on just one page.

E

Your website can be a place for your customers to buy your products. You may still do most of your selling at your physical place of business, but the website is another opportunity to sell, and you can reach more customers this way, too.

The text contains five sections, A–E. In which section can information about the following be found? Write the correct letter, A–E, on lines 21–27 on your answer sheet. You may use any letter more than once.

21 finding international customers

22 the cost of maintaining a website

23 ways to communicate with customers

24 selling your products online

25 the size of your website

26 website design

27 the most important information to include

SECTION 3

*You are advised to spend 20 minutes on **Questions 28–40**, which are based on the Reading Passage below.*

Phases of the Moon

Traveling a distance of approximately 382,400 kilometers, the moon takes just over twenty-nine days to complete its orbit around the Earth. During this lunar cycle, many different phases of the moon are visible from Earth, even though the moon itself never changes shape. The cyclic period of the moon is determined by the extent to which the sun illuminates the moon on the side that is facing Earth. Just like Earth, the moon is sphere shaped, and thus always half illuminated by the sun. However, because the moon and the Earth are in synchronous rotation, we can see only the near side of the moon. The side we do not see is called the far side, or the *dark side*, a term that is often misunderstood. The dark side refers to the mysteriousness of this unseen side, not the amount of light it receives. Both the near and the far sides of the moon receive approximately the same amount of sunlight. Though we see a slightly different moon from Earth each day, its repetitive cycle is both predictable and functional.

There are eight phases of the moon, each with a unique name that signifies how much of the moon is visible from Earth. In the early phases, the moon is said to be *waxing*, or gradually getting larger. The first phase is called *new moon*. In this phase, the moon is lined up between the Earth and the sun. The illuminated side of the moon is facing the sun, not the Earth, so from Earth, there appears to be no moon at all. As the moon begins to move slowly eastward away from the sun, it becomes slightly more visible.

After new moon, the *waxing crescent* phase begins. During this phase, the moon appears to be less than half illuminated. *First quarter* occurs when one-half of the moon is visible. It is called first quarter, not because of its size, but because it represents the end of the first quarter of the moon's cycle. The next phase is called *waxing gibbous* and represents a moon that is larger than half a sphere, but not quite a whole. This phase is followed by *full moon*, which occurs when the moon's illuminated side is directly facing Earth.

As the moon begins to get smaller again, it is said to be *waning*. The phases in the second half of the cycle appear the same as the first, except that the opposite half of the near side of the moon is illuminated, thus the moon appears to be shrinking rather than growing. *Waning gibbous* is followed by *last quarter*, when one-half of the moon is visible, and finally *waning crescent*. In the Northern Hemisphere, when the moon is waxing, the light of the moon increases from right to left. The opposite occurs in the Southern Hemisphere.

Like the sun, the moon is an accurate tool for measuring time. A complete cycle of the moon is called a *lunation*. A full cycle of the moon typically lasts just under one calendar month, therefore, the phase of the moon that starts a month usually repeats just before the month is through. When two full moons occur in one calendar month the second one is called a *blue moon*. This phenomenon occurs about once every 2.7 years. Within one cycle, the moon's "age" is calculated from the last day of the new moon. For example, the moon is approximately fifteen days old during the full moon phase.

The moon can also be used to calculate the time of day. Just like the sun, the moon rises and sets each day and is visible on the Earth's horizon. At new moon, the moon and sun rise and set at almost the same time. As the moon begins to wax, or move farther in its orbit, it rises approximately one hour later each day. By full moon, the moon rises at about the same time the sun sets and sets when the sun rises. Therefore, the moon is out in the daytime as often as it is at night even though it is not always as easy to see in the daylight. The Islamic calendar is based on the phases of the moon. The beginning of each new month in the Islamic calendar begins when the waxing crescent first appears in the night sky.

The primary phases of the moon, which include new moon, first quarter, full moon, and last quarter are published in almanacs for each month. The phases can also be found on many calendars in the Western world. Despite the world's fascination with the moon, its phases are not entirely unique. The planets Venus and Mercury have similar phases; however, unlike the moon, these planets can never be on the opposite side of the Earth from the sun. To see the equivalent of the "full moon" phase of these planets, we would need to have the capacity to see through the sun.

Questions 28 and 29

Write the correct letter, A, B, or C, on lines 28 and 29 on your answer sheet.

28 It takes the moon approximately twenty-nine days to

    A orbit the sun.
    B travel 382,400 kilometers.
    C complete one phase.

29 The dark side of the moon

    A receives no light from the sun.
    B faces the Earth during the day.
    C is never visible from the Earth.

Questions 30–33

*Label the diagram below. Choose **NO MORE THAN TWO WORDS** from the reading passage for each answer. Write your answers on lines 30–33 on your answer sheet.*

The Primary Phases of the Moon

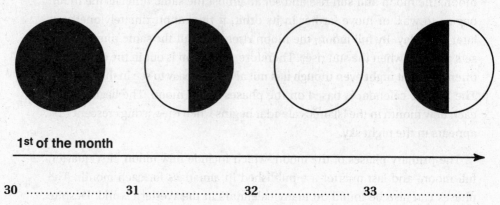

1st of the month

30 .... 31 .... 32 .... 33 ....

Questions 34–40

Do the following statements agree with the information given in the passage? On lines 34–40 on your answer sheet, write:

YES	*if the statement agrees with the views of the writer*
NO	*if the statement disagrees with the views of the writer*
NOT GIVEN	*if there is no information on this in the passage*

34 A lunation takes a little more than one month to complete.

35 The term *blue moon* refers to the color of the moon at certain times of the year.

36 It takes about fifteen days for the moon to move from new moon to full moon.

37 At certain times of the month, the moon rises at the same time as the sun.

38 There are twelve months on the Islamic calendar.

39 Some planets have phases similar to the moon's phases.

40 The moons of Venus and Mercury are visible from Earth.

Writing Answer Sheet

TASK 1

_____

_____

_____

_____

_____

_____

_____

_____

_____

_____

_____

_____

_____

_____

_____

_____

_____

_____

_____

-2-

GENERAL TRAINING MODULE TEST 2

-3-

TASK 2

_____
_____
_____
_____
_____
_____
_____
_____
_____
_____
_____
_____
_____
_____
_____
_____
_____
_____
_____
_____
_____
_____

GENERAL TRAINING MODULE TEST 2

-4-

GENERAL TRAINING MODEL TEST 2

Candidate Name _____

International English Language Testing System

GENERAL TRAINING WRITING

Time: 1 hour

INSTRUCTIONS TO CANDIDATES

Do not open this booklet until you are told to do so.

Write your name in the space at the top of this page.

All answers must be written on the separate answer booklet provided.

Do not remove this booklet from the examination room.

INFORMATION FOR CANDIDATES

There are **2** tasks on this question paper.

You must do **both** tasks.

Underlength answers will be penalized.[1]

---

[1]British: penalised

WRITING TASK 1

You should spend about 20 minutes on this task. You do NOT need to write any addresses. Begin your letter as follows:

Dear _____,

> Your next-door neighbor[1] likes to listen to music late at night. Because of the loud music, you often lose sleep.
>
> **Write a letter to the building manager. In your letter**
>
> - describe the situation
> - explain the problems it is causing you
> - offer at least one solution

Write at least 150 words.

WRITING TASK 2

You should spend about 40 minutes on this task.

> Write about the following topic:
>
> The use of cell phones (mobile phones) has increased rapidly in the twenty-first century. Additionally, cell phones can now be used for many purposes besides making phone calls.
>
> What are the advantages and disadvantages of cell phones? Give reasons for your answer and include any relevant examples from your own knowledge or experience.

Write at least 250 words.

---

[1]British: neighbour

Reading

1. vii
2. ii
3. vi
4. iv
5. three hours
6. after each use
7. on the website
8. J
9. A
10. F
11. M
12. H
13. K
14. C
15. conservative
16. calm
17. the schedule(s)
18. on time
19. voice
20. (the right) questions
21. B
22. C
23. A
24. E
25. D
26. C
27. D
28. B
29. C
30. new moon
31. first quarter
32. full moon
33. last quarter
34. No
35. No
36. Yes
37. Yes
38. Not Given
39. Yes
40. Not Given

GENERAL TRAINING MODULE—PRACTICE TEST 2

Reading

1. *vii.* Section A is about how to start using the machine and what items the machine comes with.

2. *ii.* Section B explains how to use the machine to bake bread.

3. *vi.* Section C is about cleaning, or caring for, the bread machine.

4. *iv.* Section D is about the help available to customers who have bought a bread machine.

5. *three hours.* Section B: "Your bread will be ready in three hours for white or raisin bread. . . ."

6. *after each use.* Section C: "It is important to clean the inside of the machine after each use."

7. *on the website.* Section D: "Also available on the website is a variety of international bread recipes."

8. **(J)** The program provides lists of commuters who are looking to share rides as well as maps to help plan efficient commuting routes.

9. **(A)** Paragraph 1: "When you share your daily ride to work with other commuters, you save on transportation costs and help reduce traffic congestion and air pollution."

10. **(F)** Paragraph 3: "According to state law, vanpools are permitted to travel in special high-occupancy vehicle (HOV) lanes. . . ."

11. **(M)** Paragraph 4: "The website also has maps. . .to help you plan the most efficient route for your commute. . .available for free download."

12. **(H)** Paragraph 5: "When you have arranged a carpool or vanpool group, return to our website and register your group with us."

13. **(K)** Paragraph 6: "Registered participants in Regional Share-Your-Ride can sign up to receive daily traffic and weather reports by e-mail."

14. **(C)** Paragraph 6: "As a participant, you are also eligible for the Urgent Ride service, which provides you with free transportation to your house in case you or your carpool or vanpool driver has an emergency."

15. *conservative.* Paragraph 2, about clothes to wear to the interview, suggests "conservative colors and styles."

16. *calm.* Paragraph 3 advises that rehearsing the interview at home "will help you be calm when you are at the actual interview."

17. *the schedule(s).* Paragraph 4: "check the schedules the day before."

18. *on time.* Paragraph 4: "Careful planning will ensure that you will make a good impression by arriving on time."

19. *voice.* Paragraph 5: "Speaking with a firm, clear voice is one of the best ways to give an impression of self-assurance."

20. *(the right) questions.* Paragraph 6: "asking the right questions shows that you are knowledgeable about the company and conveys the impression that you are interested and enthusiastic."

21. **(B)** "A website allows you to expand your customer base beyond your immediate community, and even to other countries."

22. **(C)** "The hosting fees you pay to keep your website up and running are minimal."

23. **(A)** This section talks about using newsletters and blogs to keep customers informed.

24. **(E)** This section talks about the website as a place where customers can buy products.

25. **(D)** This section mentions that a large website is not necessary and that just a few pages can be enough.

26. **(C)** This section talks about using either a template or a professional to design your website.

27. **(D)** This section mentions "the most essential facts to include in any website."

28. **(B)** Paragraph 1 explains that the moon travels 382,400 kilometers in its orbit around Earth. Choice (A) is incorrect because the moon orbits the Earth, not the sun. Choice (C) is incorrect because paragraph 1 explains that the moon goes through many different phases during its twenty-nine-day cycle.

29. **(C)** Paragraph 1: "we can see only the near side of the moon. The side we do not see is called the far side, or the dark side. . . ." Choice (A) is incorrect because the dark, or far, side of the moon receives as much sunlight as the near side does. Choice (B) is incorrect because the dark side of the moon is the side that we do not see.

30. *new moon.* Paragraph 2 explains that during the new moon phase there appears to be no moon at all.

31. *first quarter.* Paragraph 3: "First quarter occurs when one half of the moon is visible."

32. *full moon.* Paragraph 3: "This phase is followed by full moon, which occurs when the moon's illuminated side is directly facing Earth."

33. *last quarter.* Paragraph 4: "last quarter, when one half of the moon is visible."

34. *No.* Paragraph 5: "A full cycle of the moon typically lasts just under one calendar month. . . ."

35. *No.* Paragraph 5: "When two full moons occur in one calendar month the second one is called a blue moon."

36. *Yes.* Paragraph 5: "Within one cycle, the moon's "age" is calculated from the last day of the new moon . . . the moon is approximately fifteen days old during the full moon phase."

37. *Yes.* Paragraph 6: "At new moon, the moon and sun rise and set at almost the same time."

38. *Not Given.* The Islamic Calendar is mentioned, but the number of months in it is not.

39. *Yes.* Paragraph 7: "The planets Venus and Mercury have similar phases. . . ."

40. *Not Given.* The planets Venus and Mercury are mentioned, but their moons are not.

Writing

These are models. Your answers will vary. See page 2 in the Introduction to see the criteria for scoring.

WRITING TASK 1

Dear Mr. Wilson,

I have been living in this apartment building for five years now, and I have always been a responsible tenant. I am especially careful to be respectful of my neighbors in this building. I would like to bring your attention to a problem I am having with one of my neighbors.

Last month, Mrs. Johnson moved into apartment 3B, right next door to me. She enjoys listening to music late at night, often after midnight. The music is very loud and I can easily hear it in my bedroom. It makes it very difficult for me to fall asleep. I have to get up at 5:30 A.M. in order to get to work on time, so this is a serious problem for me.

Since Mrs. Johnson is new to the building, perhaps she isn't aware of the building rules about noise at night. I wonder if you would speak to her and remind her of this. Also, maybe you could post a notice in the lobby about the noise rule for all the tenants to see.

Thank you for your help.

Sincerely,
Mark Jones

WRITING TASK 2

Cell phones have become very common in this century, and they have many uses. They make life convenient in many ways but, like anything else, they also have disadvantages.

The main advantage of cell phones is convenience. Cell phones make it easy to communicate with anyone at any time, whether for personal or professional reasons. The communication can be by phone call, text message, or e-mail. In addition, with most cell phones, it's easy to access the Internet for any reason no matter where you are. Depending on the kind of cell phone you use, you can also do a lot of other things with it. You can use software that helps you find the best prices when you are shopping, for example, or that gives you access to the latest news reports. These are just two examples of the things cell phones can be used for. They make life easier in many ways.

On the other hand, cell phones have their disadvantages. One common concern is that they reduce face-to-face communication. People are becoming more accustomed to communicating by cell phone and less accustomed to actually spending time with each other. It is still too soon to know what effects this will have on our society. Parents also worry about their children who spend too much time texting, playing games, and doing other things with their cell phones. This can distract children from their homework and other responsibilities. There are also health concerns and the possibility that exposure to cell phones can lead to brain cancer.

Cell phones have brought many advantages to our lives, but they also have their drawbacks. People need to consider the possible disadvantages when they pick up their phone for any reason.

General Training Module

Reading and Writing

PRACTICE TEST 3

ANSWER SHEET
General Training
Practice Test 3

IELTS Reading Answer Sheet

#		✓ ✗
1		✓ 1 ✗
2		2
3		3
4		4
5		5
6		6
7		7
8		8
9		9
10		10
11		11
12		12
13		13
14		14
15		15
16		16
17		17
18		18
19		19
20		20

#		✓ ✗
21		✓ 21 ✗
22		22
23		23
24		24
25		25
26		26
27		27
28		28
29		29
30		30
31		31
32		32
33		33
34		34
35		35
36		36
37		37
38		38
39		39
40		40
	Reading Total	

GENERAL TRAINING MODEL TEST 3

Candidate Name _____

International English Language Testing System

GENERAL TRAINING READING

Time: 1 hour

INSTRUCTIONS TO CANDIDATES

Do not open this booklet until you are told to do so.

Write your name in the space at the top of this page.

Start at the beginning of the test and work through it.

You should answer all questions.

If you cannot do a particular question, leave it and go on to the next. You can return to it later.

All answers must be written on the Answer Sheet.

Do not remove this booklet from the examination room.

INFORMATION FOR CANDIDATES

There are 40 questions on this question paper.

The test is divided as follows:

Section 1	Questions 1–14
Section 2	Questions 15–27
Section 3	Questions 28–40

SECTION 1

*You are advised to spend 20 minutes on **Questions 1–14**.*

Questions 1–8

*Read the text below and answer **Questions 1–8**.*

AREA HOTELS

A

Rosewood Hotel. Spend your vacation with us. We offer luxury suites, an Olympic-sized pool, a state-of-the-art fitness center,[1] and a beauty spa. Leave business cares behind while you relax in luxury at the Rosewood. You'll never want to leave! Call 800-555-0942 for reservations.

B

The Woodside Motel is the place to stay while visiting our city. After a day of sightseeing, relax in the comfort of your luxury room. All our rooms have king-sized beds, free movies, and minibars. Our outdoor playground and indoor recreation room mean the little ones will never be bored. Babysitting service available. Enjoy your next family vacation at the Woodside Motel.

C

The Columbus Hotel is conveniently located in the heart of the city's theater[2] district and close to the city's finest restaurants and clubs. Enjoy the spectacular view of the city skyline from the Columbus Rooftop Restaurant. Host your next conference or banquet with us. We have a selection of reception rooms and banquet rooms suitable for conferences and parties. Call 245-555-0982 to speak to our banquet coordinator, 245-555-0987 for dinner reservations at the Rooftop Restaurant, and 245-555-0862 to reserve a room.

D

Next time you're in town, stay at the City View Suites. Whether you're here to shop, play, or work, City View's location can't be beat. We're close to all major bus lines and right next to the city's business district. All rooms include kitchenettes. Call 492-555-5932 for reservations. Don't forget to ask about our special weekly and monthly rates.

E

Sunflower Motel offers reasonable rates, a convenient location, and cable TV in every room. Pets are welcome (extra charge applies). Special weekend rates. Call 488-555-0821 for reservations.

---

[1]British: centre
[2]British: theatre

*Look at the five hotel advertisements, **A–E**. Which hotel is appropriate for each of the following people? Write the correct letter, **A–E**, on lines 1–8 on your answer sheet. You may use any letter more than once.*

Which hotel is most appropriate for a person who

1 plans to stay for over a month?

2 is traveling[1] with children?

3 always travels with a dog?

4 plans to go out for entertainment in the evenings?

5 is on a business trip?

6 likes to exercise every day?

7 is looking for a place to hold a wedding reception?

8 prefers cooking to eating in restaurants?

---

[1]British: travelling

Questions 9–14

*Read the text below and answer **Questions 9–14**.*

Welcome to the Riverdale City Pool

The following information is provided for your convenience.

A

The Riverdale City Pool is for everybody's enjoyment. To make sure that all pool users have a pleasant experience, please observe the following:

- All children under twelve must be accompanied by an adult.
- Running and shouting in the pool area are not allowed.
- Diving is permitted only in the designated area at the deep end of the adult pool.
- Please shower before entering the pool.

Thank you for your cooperation.

B

The pool is open for the summer season from May 15 through September 15. Hours are Monday–Thursday, noon until 7:30 P.M.; Friday, noon until 9:30 P.M.; Saturday and Sunday, 9:30 A.M. until 9:30 P.M. During the week, the pool will be open for classes only from 8:30 until 11:30 A.M. Three trained lifeguards will be on duty at all times that the pool is open.

C

The pool garage will be closed from June 1 to August 31 for renovations. We are sorry for any inconvenience this may cause. Pool users can leave their cars in the area behind the pool office during this time. A bicycle rack is also located there. There is no fee for using this area.

D

For Riverdale residents, charges for using the pool are $5 per individual per visit, $250 for an individual season pass, and $500 for a family season pass. For nonresidents, the charge is $7 per individual per visit. Season passes are not available to pool users who are not residents of Riverdale.

E

This summer we are offering swimming lessons for children, teens, and adults, as well as diving lessons and water aerobics. Morning lessons are from 9:30 to 10:30 and afternoon lessons are from 2:00 to 4:00. Fees start at $75 a week. The Riverdale swim team will continue this season as well. Please visit the pool office for a complete schedule of this summer's lessons and swimming meets.

F

The new snack bar is now open. The hours are 11:30–5:00 daily. It serves a variety of inexpensive drinks and snacks, including cold and hot sandwiches, ice cream treats, and homemade cookies. All items purchased at the snack bar as well as snacks, drinks, and lunches brought from home must be consumed in the picnic area.

Do the following statements agree with the information given in the text about the Riverdale City Pool? On lines 9–14 on your answer sheet, write

> **TRUE** if the statement agrees with the information
> **FALSE** if the statement contradicts the information
> **NOT GIVEN** if there is no information on this

9 Children under twelve are allowed to use the pool.

10 The pool is open to the general public on weekday mornings.

11 Pool users can park in the garage during the entire pool season.

12 People who don't live in Riverdale are not allowed to use the pool.

13 The Riverdale swim team practices every weekend.

14 Food is sold at the pool.

SECTION 2

*You are advised to spend 20 minutes on **Questions 15–27**.*

Questions 15–20

*Read the information below and answer **Questions 15–20**.*

Lakeville College
Employee Benefits

Vacations[1]

All employees are entitled to a minimum of two weeks paid vacation time annually. The actual days to be used as vacation are subject to approval by the individual employee's supervisor.

Insurance

All employees are eligible for any of the health insurance plans offered by the college. Information on the various plans are available from Human Resources. This benefit is extended to members of the employee's immediate family. Part-time employees may apply for this benefit but will pay a higher percentage of the premium.

Use of College Facilities

All employees, full and part time, may use any of the college facilities, including the library, gym, swimming pool, and tennis courts, free of charge. A faculty or staff ID card must be shown when requesting access to these facilities. Immediate family members are also entitled to this benefit, but must obtain an ID card from Human Resources before using college facilities.

Parking

Free parking is available on campus for all college employees; however, a parking sticker must be obtained from Human Resources. The sticker must be displayed on the windshield[2] at all times when parked on campus. The sticker is valid for parking in specially designated employee parking areas as well as in any parking space marked "Visitor." Student parking areas are reserved for student parking only.

Taking Classes

Employees may take classes in any department at the college. Show your faculty or staff ID when registering for the class. Employees may enroll[3] in up to three classes per year free of charge. Any additional classes beyond that must be paid for at the full tuition rate. In addition, any employee wishing to pursue a degree must apply for and be accepted into the program of his or her choice before being considered a degree candidate. In this case, student service fees will apply.

---

[1]British: holiday; in the United States, *holiday* refers to a specific date on which a special event, such as Thanksgiving, is observed.
[2]British: windscreen
[3]British: enrol

*Write the correct letter, **A**, **B**, or **C**, on lines 15–20 on your answer sheet.*

15 How much annual vacation time are employees allowed?

    A No more than two weeks
    B Exactly two weeks
    C At least two weeks

16 Who is qualified for health insurance benefits?

    A Full-time employees only
    B All employees and their spouses and children
    C All employees, but not their family members

17 What must an employee's family member do in order to use the library?

    A Get an ID card
    B Apply for a job at Human Resources
    C Pay a fee

18 Where can employees park their cars?

    A In the employee parking areas only
    B Anywhere on campus
    C In both employee and visitor parking areas

19 If an employee takes one class in a year, how much will he or she have to pay?

    A Nothing
    B The full tuition rate
    C A student service fee

20 What is required of employees who want to study for a degree?

    A Permission of their supervisors
    B Application for admission into a program
    C Payment of full tuition

Questions 21–27

*Read the text below and answer **Questions 21–27**.*

Long Mountain Learning Center
Writing Courses

A

The Art of Correspondence

Have you always wished you could write more elegantly? This course will help you develop your own style when writing letters of friendship, condolence, congratulations, and so on.

Mondays, 5–7 P.M.

B

Client Communication

The success of any business depends on clear communications with clients. This course will show you the essentials of letter, e-mail, and fax writing to help you enhance those all-important business relationships with clients.

Tuesdays, 1–3 P.M.

C

Rules of Communication

Do you wonder where to place commas or when to use exclamation points? Do you know when it is appropriate to use apostrophes and when it is not? This course will clear up any confusion you may have about the rules for using commas, periods, semicolons, and so on, and it will help you to make your writing clear and correct.

Wednesdays, 9:30–10:30 A.M.

D

Fiction Workshop

This course is for writers who are currently working on a novel or short story. Class time will be spent reading and critiquing classmates' work.

Saturdays, 9:30–11:30 A.M.

E

What Do You Mean?

Finding the exact words to express your ideas is an art in itself. In this course, you will learn about words, what they mean, how to avoid confusing similar words, and how to choose just the right words in your writing.

Thursdays, 7:30–9:30 P.M.

F

Write It Right

Writing a research paper involves more than gathering information. Knowing how to organize[1] your information, express your ideas clearly, and document your sources are essential. This course is specifically designed for students preparing to enter college.

Tuesdays, 3:30–5:00 P.M.

G

Express Your Opinion

The Letters to the Editor column in your local paper is a public forum for expressing opinions on matters of interest to all citizens. In this course, you will learn how to develop and eloquently express your opinions and improve your chances of getting your letter published.

Fridays, 8:45–10:00 P.M.

H

Report It

Have you always dreamed[2] of being a correspondent for a newspaper or magazine? This course will cover the basics of gathering news and turning it into interesting newspaper and magazine articles.

Wednesdays, 1–3 P.M.

I

Retelling Old Favorites[3]

Do you remember the traditional folktales and fairy tales that you loved as a child? In this course, you will rewrite some of your favorite old tales in new ways that will delight the youngsters in your life.

Tuesdays, 5–7 P.M.

J

Writing to Sell

In this course, you will learn to write advertisements that will attract more clients to your product or business. Previous business writing experience is required.

Thursdays, 9:30–11:30 A.M.

K

Selling for Poets

Don't let anyone tell you there aren't any good markets for poetry. In fact, there are hundreds of places, both online and in print, that publish poetry and pay good money for it, too. Find out about how to sell your poetry in this course.

---

[1]British: organise
[2]British: dreamt
[3]British: Favourites

Look at the descriptions of the writing courses, A–K. For which descriptions are the following statements true? Write the correct letter, A–K, on lines 21–27 on your answer sheet.

21 This course helps you with academic writing.

22 This course shows you how to write personal letters.

23 This course helps you improve your vocabulary.

24 This course is about writing stories for children.

25 This course teaches you about journalism.

26 This course teaches you how to use punctuation.

27 This course is about business marketing.

SECTION 3

*You are advised to spend 20 minutes on **Questions 28–40**, which are based on the reading passage below.*

Questions 28–34

*The following passage has seven paragraphs, **A–G**. Choose the most suitable heading for each paragraph from the list of headings below. Write the correct numbers, **i–x**, on lines 28–34 on your answer sheet. There are more headings than paragraphs, so you will not use them all.*

28 Paragraph A

29 Paragraph B

30 Paragraph C

31 Paragraph D

32 Paragraph E

33 Paragraph F

34 Paragraph G

LIST OF HEADINGS

i	The Neoclassical Architectural Style
ii	Choosing a Location
iii	Naming the President's House
iv	First Ladies and Interior Design
v	A Designer Is Chosen
vi	Reconstruction of the President's House
vii	The President's House Burns Down
viii	Funding the Construction
ix	Renovation and Modernization[1]
x	Completion of the First President's House

---

[1]British: Modernisation

The Construction of the White House

A

Located at 1600 Pennsylvania Avenue in Washington, DC, the White House was originally designed by James Hoban, an Irish-born American architect. In 1792, after defeating eight other entrants, Hoban won a contest to design a mansion for the president of the United States. President George Washington oversaw the original construction, which began on October 13, 1792. Prior to the design contest, engineer Pierre Charles L'Enfant had worked with President Washington to design the capital city. L'Enfant's vision of the president's house was four times larger than the mansion Hoban built. Labor[1] and material expenses required Hoban to build the house on a much smaller scale, with only two main floors instead of three. In addition, rather than using the expensive imported stone of his original plan, the majority of the brick he used was made right on site. Hoban employed builders and craftsmen from overseas as well as local slaves and laborers. The total expenditure for the project was $232,372. This was just a fraction of what L'Enfant's proposed palace would have cost.

B

James Hoban's design was a near copy of a residence in James Gibbs's *Book of Architecture*, published in 1728. Neoclassicism, influenced by the Greco–Roman style, was the popular choice for architects throughout Europe during that time. When Napoleon became emperor, he employed the best architects he knew to transform Paris into a classical Roman capital. Roman triumphal arches and Corinthian columns adorned all of Paris's major structures. Architects in Germany built monuments, halls, and theaters inspired by classic Greek structures such as the Acropolis in Athens. The popularity of the neoclassical style grew internationally, spreading as far as America. Though the architectural styles were borrowed from classical designs, each country added a unique flair in order to achieve a sense of nationalism in its capital.

C

The house that James Hoban designed was not completed until after the second president of the United States took office. Despite the unfinished interior, President John Adams and his family moved from the temporary capital in Philadelphia, Pennsylvania, into the president's house on November 1, 1800. Throughout his term, Adams lived in the mansion with half-finished walls, no heating, and no running water. The interior of the building was completed in 1801 during Thomas Jefferson's term. Before Jefferson moved in, he hired architect Benjamin Latrobe to install coal-burning fireplaces and two water closets. Latrobe also created two terraces on the east and west sides of the building and installed a furnace that relied on kettles and pipes in the basement.

---

[1]British: Labour

D

Just over twenty years after the construction of the president's house began, the building was burned down during the War of 1812. After British troops torched the house on August 25, 1814, rumors[1] surfaced as to whether the capital would be moved inland. However, the Battle of New Orleans, an encounter in which the Americans came out victorious over Britain, evoked a sense of nationalism in the country's heart. The victory inspired the rebuilding of the president's house, a task that was once again handed over to James Hoban.

E

Hoban worked on the rebuilding for two years before President James Monroe moved into the unfinished home and purchased a number of furnishings. Benjamin Latrobe, who later built the Capitol building, designed large porticos for the house with columns that supported the roof. In 1824, his south portico was completed with a double staircase leading up to the new porch. The north portico was completed in 1830 during the presidency of Andrew Jackson. Though these columns give the White House its distinguishing features today, there was some criticism at the time that they overshadowed the intricate stone carvings on the house. During Jackson's term, running water was installed, though a furnace and gas lighting were not introduced until the 1840s.

F

Major renovations on the president's house continued through the 1800s, including modern innovations such as the telephone and electric wiring. A hot water system, a greenhouse, a private bath, and a number of conservatories were also added. The conservatories, including the rose and orchid houses, were removed in 1902, when construction began on the West Wing. The president's Oval Office was added to the West Wing at the order of President Taft in 1909. Each succeeding president and first lady contributed to the interior and its furnishings. Inspectors ordered a full renovation of the White House after the building almost collapsed while a balcony was being added for Harry Truman in the late 1940s. During the temporary closure, all of the modern conveniences, including central air-conditioning, were added. The last major modification to the White House was the removal of over forty layers of paint from the exterior walls in 1978.

G

For over 100 years, the White House was only a nickname associated with the presidents' home. This term was likely related to the whitewashed exterior that stonemasons completed in 1798. The home was either referred to as the "President's House" or the "Executive Mansion" until Theodore Roosevelt formally established it as the White House soon after taking office in 1901.

---

[1]British: rumours

Questions 35–40

*Choose the correct letters, **A–C**, and write them on lines 35–40 on your answer sheet.*

35 Pierre Charles L'Enfant was

    A an importer of stone.

    B the designer of the capital city.

    C the winner of a contest to build the president's house.

36 The influential *Book of Architecture* was written by

    A James Hoban.

    B James Gibb.

    C Napoleon.

37 The first president to live in the original president's house was

    A John Adams.

    B Thomas Jefferson.

    C George Washington.

38 After the White House burned down

    A the capital was moved inland.

    B James Hoban lost his reputation.

    C the house was rebuilt.

39 Air-conditioning was added to the president's house

    A at the same time it was undergoing structural renovation.

    B while it was closed during its last big modification.

    C because inspectors ordered it.

40 In 1901

    A the White House was officially named the "Executive Mansion."

    B stonemasons finally completed the exterior of the building.

    C Theodore Roosevelt became president.

ANSWER SHEET
General Training Practice Test 3

Writing Answer Sheet

TASK 1

_____

_____

_____

_____

_____

_____

_____

_____

_____

_____

_____

_____

_____

_____

_____

_____

_____

ANSWER SHEET
General Training
Practice Test 3

-2-

ANSWER SHEET
General Training
Practice Test 3

-3-

TASK 2

ANSWER SHEET
General Training
Practice Test 3

-4-

GENERAL TRAINING MODEL TEST 3

Candidate Name _____

International English Language Testing System

GENERAL TRAINING WRITING

Time: 1 hour

INSTRUCTIONS TO CANDIDATES

Do not open this booklet until you are told to do so.

Write your name in the space at the top of this page.

All answers must be written on the separate answer booklet provided.

Do not remove this booklet from the examination room.

INFORMATION FOR CANDIDATES

There are **2** tasks on this question paper.

You must do **both** tasks.

Underlength answers will be penalized.[1]

---

[1]British: penalised

WRITING TASK 1

You should spend about 20 minutes on this task. You do NOT need to write any addresses. Begin your letter as follows:

Dear _____,

> While your friend was away on vacation, you stayed in his apartment. While you were there, you dropped an expensive bowl and broke it.
>
> Write a letter to your friend. In your letter
>
> - explain what happened
> - apologize[1] for the accident
> - tell your friend what you plan to do about the bowl

Write at least 150 words.

WRITING TASK 2

You should spend about 40 minutes on this task.

> Write about the following topic:
>
> Some people choose a career according to the social status and salary it will give them. Others choose a career according to whether they will enjoy the work.
>
> Which do you think is the best way to choose a career? Give reasons for your answer and include any relevant examples from your own knowledge or experience.

Write at least 250 words.

---

[1]British: apologise

ANSWER KEY
Practice Test 3

Reading

1. D	15. C	29. i
2. B	16. B	30. x
3. E	17. A	31. vii
4. C	18. C	32. vi
5. D	19. A	33. ix
6. A	20. B	34. iii
7. C	21. F	35. B
8. D	22. A	36. B
9. True	23. E	37. A
10. False	24. I	38. C
11. False	25. H	39. A
12. False	26. C	40. C
13. Not Given	27. J	
14. True	28. v	

GENERAL TRAINING MODULE—PRACTICE TEST 3

Reading

1. **(D)** This hotel has suites with small kitchens and special weekly and monthly rates.

2. **(B)** This hotel has a playground, recreation room, and babysitting service.

3. **(E)** This hotel welcomes pets.

4. **(C)** This hotel is near theaters, restaurants, and clubs.

5. **(D)** This hotel is near the business district.

6. **(A)** This hotel has a large swimming pool and a fitness room.

7. **(C)** This hotel has reception and banquet rooms for rent.

8. **(D)** This hotel has suites with kitchenettes.

9. *True.* According to section A, children under twelve are allowed when accompanied by an adult.

10. *False.* According to section B, the pool doesn't open until noon Monday–Friday. It is open in the morning for classes only.

11. *False.* According to section C, the garage will be closed June 1–August 31.

12. *False.* Section D mentions a $7 fee for nonresidents.

13. *Not Given.* The swim team is mentioned in section E but its practice schedule is not.

14. *True.* Section F gives information about the snack bar.

15. **(C)** Paragraph 1 explains that all employees have "a minimum of two weeks." *Minimum* means *at least*. Choices (A) and (B) are incorrect because they do not correctly interpret the meaning of *minimum.*

16. **(B)** Paragraph 2: "All employees are eligible for any of the health insurance plans offered by the college . . . . This benefit is extended to members of the employee's immediate family." Choice (A) is incorrect because the benefit is for "all employees." This includes part-time employees. Choice (C) is incorrect because the benefit is also for "members of the employee's immediate family."

17. **(A)** Paragraph 3: "Immediate family members are also entitled to this benefit, but must obtain an ID card from Human Resources . . . ." Choice (B) is confused with the mention of Human Resources, where the ID cards are available. Choice (C) is incorrect because use of college facilities is "free of charge."

18. **(C)** Paragraph 4 explains that the parking sticker is valid in employee and visitor parking areas but not in student parking areas. Choices (A) and (B) are contradicted by the information in the paragraph.

19. **(A)** Paragraph 5: "up to three classes per year free of charge." Choices (B) and (C) are contradicted by the information in the paragraph.

20. **(B)** Paragraph 5: "In addition, any employee wishing to pursue a degree must apply for and be accepted into the program of his or her . . . ." Choice (A) is not mentioned. Choice (C) is incorrect because an employee in a degree program might choose to take only three classes per year, which would be free of charge.

21. **(F)** Course F is about writing research papers and is for students who will enter college.

22. **(A)** Course A is about writing letters of friendship, condolence, and congratulations, which are examples of personal letters.

23. **(E)** Course E is about words, that is, vocabulary.

24. **(I)** Course I is about rewriting traditional tales (stories) for youngsters (children).

25. **(H)** Course H is about writing news articles for newspapers and magazines, which is journalism.

26. **(C)** Course C is about commas, periods, semicolons, and so on, that is, punctuation.

27. **(J)** Course J is about writing advertisements for businesses.

28. *v.* Paragraph A is about James Hoban, the man who won the design contest.

29. *i.* Paragraph B discusses the influence of neoclassical architecture on eighteenth-century design.

30. *x.* Paragraph C describes how the building was completed during the term of Thomas Jefferson.

31. *vii.* Paragraph D describes the burning of the president's house during the War of 1812.

32. *vi.* Paragraph E describes the rebuilding of the president's house.

33. *ix.* Paragraph F talks about improvements made to the building over the years.

34. *iii.* Paragraph G tells how the building came to be called the "White House."

35. **(B)** Paragraph A: "engineer Pierre Charles L'Enfant had worked with President Washington to design the capital city." Choice (A) refers to the material used to build the White House. Choice (C) is James Hoban, not Pierre L'Enfant.

36. **(B)** Paragraph B: "James Hoban's design was a near copy of a residence in James Gibbs's *Book of Architecture*, published in 1728." Choice (A) is the person who was inspired by the book. Choice (C) is mentioned as a person who influenced European architecture.

37. **(A)** Paragraph C: "The house that James Hoban designed was not completed until after the second president of the United States took office." Choice (B) is the man who was president when the interior of the building was completed. Choice (C) is the president who oversaw the original construction, but he did not live in the building.

38. **(C)** Paragraph D: "The victory inspired the rebuilding of the president's house, a task that once again was handed over to James Hoban. Choice (A) was the subject of rumors. Choice (B) is incorrect because James Hoban would not have been asked to rebuild the house if his reputation had been ruined.

39. **(A)** In the 1940s, the balcony collapsed so inspectors ordered structural renovations to the house. During the renovations, modern conveniences, including air-conditioning, were installed. Choice (B) is incorrect because the last major modification occurred in 1978 and air-conditioning was installed in the 1940s. Choice (C) is incorrect because structural renovation, not the installation of modern conveniences, is what the inspectors ordered.

40. **(C)** According to paragraph G, Theodore Roosevelt took office in 1901. Choice (A) was the name of the building before 1901. Choice (B) happened in 1798.

Writing

These are models. Your answers will vary. See page 2 in the Introduction to see the criteria for scoring.

WRITING TASK 1

Dear Diego,

   Thank you very much for letting me use your apartment while you were away. I tried to leave everything just as I found it. You will, unfortunately, find one thing missing. I wanted to do you a favor by cleaning the living room. While I was dusting that beautiful bowl you keep on the coffee table, it fell out of my hands and broke.

   I am terribly sorry about breaking your bowl. I know that it was a present from your grandmother and that it means a lot to you. Things like that are irreplaceable. I think, however, that the bowl can be fixed. It broke into just three large pieces. I have a friend who is an expert on valuable china, and I have given her the bowl to repair. You should have it back in a few days, and I think it will look as good as new.

   I hope this solution is satisfactory to you. Again, I am so very sorry this happened. I will bring you the bowl soon.

Your friend,
Michael

WRITING TASK 2

If I had to choose between a high salary and a high level of enjoyment when deciding on a career, I think I would have to choose the high salary. Earning money is the major reason why we work. If we choose a career only on the basis of enjoyment, we might not earn enough money. Once we have a comfortable level of earning, then we can use our free time to pursue our personal interests.

   We work to support ourselves and our families. We need to pay for a place to live, food to eat, and clothes to wear. If we have children or other relatives who depend on us, we need to provide these things for them, too. Even just the basic necessities of life cost money, and the prices are always going up.

   If we do not make earning an adequate salary a top priority, we might not be able to afford to buy the things we need. We might not be able to provide our dependents with adequate food, clothing, and shelter. We might enjoy our work, but if we and our relatives cannot eat, that does not really matter.

   When we earn enough money to support ourselves and our families, then we can pursue our own interests in our free time. If we are not earning enough money, we spend a lot of time and energy worrying about it. When we do earn enough money, we feel secure. We can focus our energy on playing sports, playing music, painting pictures, or whatever activities we enjoy.

   Earning an adequate salary means that we can provide the necessities of life for ourselves and our relatives. It gives us the security we need to enjoy the other things that interest us.

General Training Module

Reading and Writing

PRACTICE TEST 4

ANSWER SHEET
General Training
Practice Test 4

IELTS Reading Answer Sheet

#		✓ ✗
1		⊡ 1 ⊡
2		⊡ 2 ⊡
3		⊡ 3 ⊡
4		⊡ 4 ⊡
5		⊡ 5 ⊡
6		⊡ 6 ⊡
7		⊡ 7 ⊡
8		⊡ 8 ⊡
9		⊡ 9 ⊡
10		⊡ 10 ⊡
11		⊡ 11 ⊡
12		⊡ 12 ⊡
13		⊡ 13 ⊡
14		⊡ 14 ⊡
15		⊡ 15 ⊡
16		⊡ 16 ⊡
17		⊡ 17 ⊡
18		⊡ 18 ⊡
19		⊡ 19 ⊡
20		⊡ 20 ⊡

#		✓ ✗
21		⊡ 21 ⊡
22		⊡ 22 ⊡
23		⊡ 23 ⊡
24		⊡ 24 ⊡
25		⊡ 25 ⊡
26		⊡ 26 ⊡
27		⊡ 27 ⊡
28		⊡ 28 ⊡
29		⊡ 29 ⊡
30		⊡ 30 ⊡
31		⊡ 31 ⊡
32		⊡ 32 ⊡
33		⊡ 33 ⊡
34		⊡ 34 ⊡
35		⊡ 35 ⊡
36		⊡ 36 ⊡
37		⊡ 37 ⊡
38		⊡ 38 ⊡
39		⊡ 39 ⊡
40		⊡ 40 ⊡
	Reading Total	

GENERAL TRAINING MODEL TEST 4

Candidate Name _____

International English Language Testing System

GENERAL TRAINING READING

Time: 1 hour

INSTRUCTIONS TO CANDIDATES

Do not open this booklet until you are told to do so.

Write your name in the space at the top of this page.

Start at the beginning of the test and work through it.

You should answer all questions.

If you cannot do a particular question, leave it and go on to the next. You can return to it later.

All answers must be written on the Answer Sheet.

Do not remove this booklet from the examination room.

INFORMATION FOR CANDIDATES

There are **40** questions on this question paper.

The test is divided as follows:

Section 1	Questions 1–14
Section 2	Questions 15–27
Section 3	Questions 28–40

SECTION 1

*You are advised to spend 20 minutes on **Questions 1–14**.*

Questions 1–7

*Read the text below and answer **Questions 1–7**.*

Volunteer Opportunities for Redux, Inc. Employees

You can give back to the community through the company's Volunteer Program. By signing up for the program, you can spend up to five hours a month of company time volunteering in an approved community program. This program is open to all Redux, Inc. employees. The following opportunities are currently available:

A

Nursing home residents are usually unable to get out to see plays, movies, and concerts. They count on your generosity to bring entertainment to them. Do you like to perform? Do you have a special talent that's just waiting for an audience? An appreciative audience is guaranteed if you can give just one afternoon a week to share your special talent with these special people.

B

The Citizen's Park Cleanup Committee needs more help. Committee members spend the last Saturday of each month at a different city park, picking up trash, repairing equipment, pulling weeds, and planting flowers.

C

Mayfield Elementary School needs people to help with their afterschool program. Volunteers will tutor children in reading and math. Must be able to commit to one afternoon a week for the entire school year.

D

The Mayfield Free Clinic is open every weekend and is looking for people willing to spend two days a month assisting the clinic staff. Volunteers will complete patient intake forms, educate the patients about clinic services, and provide assistance contacting other medical providers.

E

The Mayfield Shelter serves hot dinners to the homeless every evening. The shelter needs volunteers to help with preparing and serving meals. If you can volunteer one evening a week, the shelter needs you.

Look at the volunteer opportunities, A–E. Which volunteer opportunity is appropriate for each of the following people? Write the correct letter, A–E, on lines 1–7 on your answer sheet. You may use any letter more than once.

Which opportunity is most appropriate for a person who

1 is only free in the evening?

2 is interested in health care?

3 plays the guitar and sings?

4 enjoys spending time outdoors?

5 likes to cook?

6 only has one day a month free?

7 enjoys young children?

Read the text below and answer **Questions 8–14**.

Summer Classes at the Community Center[1]

The Community Center is offering adult summer classes again this year. The schedule includes classes in basic computer skills, martial arts, painting and drawing, and dance.

Registration

There are two ways to register for classes:

1. Go to our website: *www.cc.org/classes/winterschedule*. Click on "Class Descriptions" to see a full listing of the classes that are available this winter. Decide which class or classes you are interested in.

   Then click on "Register Now" and a registration form will appear.* Complete the form and calculate the amount of money you owe. This will include the cost of your classes plus a $15 registration fee. Any materials fees will be payable to the instructor on the first day of class. In addition, if your address is outside of the city, you will pay a nonresident fee of $25 per class.

   Fill in your credit card information and click "Send Now." You will receive registration confirmation by e-mail.

2. If you do not have access to a computer, you can call the Community Center at 872-555-5068 to request a class catalog[2] and registration form. Select your classes from the catalog, complete the form, and return it by mail with your check or credit card information.

Withdrawal Policy

Full refunds, minus the $25 registration fee, will be given for any withdrawals made up to one week before the class begins. Withdrawals made before the start of the second class will receive a 50 percent refund, minus the registration fee. No refunds will be made after the start of the second class.

Classes offered by the Community Center are for adults only. You must be eighteen years of age or older to participate. Classes for children and teens are available through the City Department of Recreation.

---

[1]British: Centre
[2]British: catalogue

Do the following statements agree with the information given in the text? On lines 8–14 on your answer sheet, write:

> **TRUE**   *if the statement agrees with the information*
> **FALSE**   *if the statement contradicts the information*
> **NOT GIVEN**   *if there is no information on this*

8   You must visit a website in order to sign up for classes.

9   A registration fee is required for all classes.

10 Dance classes cost less than computer classes.

11 People who live outside of the city pay an extra fee.

12 You are allowed to register for only two classes at a time.

13 You will not get your money back if you withdraw after the second class.

14 Classes at the Community Center are for people of all ages.

*You are advised to spend 20 minutes on **Questions 15–27**.*

Questions 15–20

*Read the text below and answer **Questions 15–20**.*

The Murgatroyde Corporation Employee Manual
Chapter 8: Professional Development Requirements

All employees of the Murgatroyde Corporation are required to attend fifteen hours of professional development workshops or classes in each calendar year. While there are many opportunities provided by the company, professional development hours can also be earned externally at local training centers, colleges, and other locations.

Listings of upcoming professional development opportunities offered by the company are posted on the company website and updated frequently. Employees can register for these workshops online. Before signing up for a particular workshop, employees should check with their supervisors to make sure they can be excused from their duties on the date of the workshop.

Employees who wish to receive professional development credit for attending workshops or courses offered elsewhere should provide their supervisor with materials describing the opportunity. The supervisor will determine whether the workshop or course is pertinent to the employee's work. After obtaining the supervisor's approval, the employee can apply to the Human Resources Office for tuition reimbursement if tuition is to be paid.

Employees attending any workshop offered by the company will receive a certificate of attendance. The number of professional development hours earned will be reported to the Human Resources Office by the workshop organizer.[1] In order to receive professional development credit for a course or workshop offered outside the company, the employee must have the workshop organizer complete a company Proof of Attendance form, and the employee must then submit the form to the Human Resources Office within one month of the end date of the course. Timely submission of this form is required in order for credit to be granted. There will be no exceptions.

---

[1]British: organiser

Complete the sentences below.
*Choose **NO MORE THAN THREE WORDS** from the text for each answer.*
Write your answers on lines 15–20 on your answer sheet.

15 Employees can choose from professional development workshops and classes offered
.... or at local training centers or colleges.

16 Employees can find out which workshops will be offered by looking at
....

17 It is the responsibility of .... to decide whether a
workshop is relevant.

18 Employees can request .... from Human Resources to pay for a class
or workshop.

19 The workshop presenter will let the Human Resources Office know how many
.... the employee should be credited with.

20 Professional development credit will be granted for workshops taken outside of
the company if a special form is filled out by ....

*Read the text below and answer **Questions 21–27**.*

Developing a Dress Code for Your Company

Whether your workplace has a formal or relaxed atmosphere, it is important to provide guidelines about how you expect your employees to dress while on the job. You need a dress code. This doesn't mean that you should permit only formal business attire or that you need to have strict regulations, but you do need to set the right tone and let your employees know that you expect them to act professionally and respectfully at all times.

Of course, any particular business will develop guidelines pertinent to its own circumstances. However, there are some general things that all employers should take into consideration when deciding the level of formality to require. In businesses where the staff spends a large portion of work time interacting with clients and customers, then a more formal dress code is appropriate. At the most formal end of the scale, this would include business suits with ties and formal shoes for men, and business suits or dresses and formal shoes for women. Formal business attire also means that hair styles should be simple and conservative, and facial hair should be kept neat and trimmed.

If interactions with clients and customers are not frequent, or if the nature of a particular business doesn't require a certain level of formality, then a more casual dress code may be in order. Depending on the company, a business casual dress code might permit khaki or corduroy pants, sweaters in place of jackets, and polo shirts in place of dress shirts with ties. Even if a company dress code is on the casual side, it is important, maybe even more so, to make it clear that there is still a dress code and that certain types of attire are not permissible. Most company dress codes, whether formal or casual, do not allow items such as T-shirts, sandals, or jeans. In addition to the regular dress code, Casual Fridays—one day a week when employees are allowed to dress more casually than normal—have become popular. However, the company still needs to provide clear guidelines as to what is and is not allowed on these days.

Contrary to popular belief, companies that require employees to wear uniforms also should have dress codes. Such dress codes specify whether all parts of the uniform are required at all times (i.e., a jacket or hat) and whether there are additional required accessories, for example, a name badge.

Questions 21–27

Do the following statements agree with the information given in the text about dress codes? On lines 21–27 on your answer sheet, write:

TRUE	*if the statement agrees with the information*
FALSE	*if the statement contradicts the information*
NOT GIVEN	*if there is no information on this*

21 Dress codes should include strict regulations.

22 It is a good idea for employees to wear business suits or dresses when meeting with clients.

23 Formal dress codes generally don't permit beards and mustaches.

24 A casual dress code might allow sweaters to be worn instead of jackets.

25 Most company dress codes mention certain clothing that is not permitted.

26 The majority of companies with formal dress codes have Casual Fridays.

27 Companies where employees use uniforms don't need dress codes

*You are advised to spend 20 minutes on **Questions 28–40**, which are based on the Reading Passage below.*

Seasonal Affective Disorder

A

When fall[1] days shorten and winter is around the corner, many people start to feel sluggish, moody, antisocial, or irritable. Like bears, they may feel as though they want to hibernate for the winter. But these symptoms may be more than the winter blues; they could indicate seasonal affective disorder (SAD). This is a form of depression that appears in the early fall and lasts through the first month or so of spring. It is triggered by the shortened daylight of the colder months and then dissipates as the days get longer and the warmer months approach.

B

Because a decrease in the number of daylight hours is a significant contributor, geographic location is an important factor in the incidence of the disorder. Residents of Canada and the northern United States, for example, are eight times more likely to suffer from SAD than are residents of sunny regions of the southern United States and Mexico. SAD is also more common in countries in arctic latitudes, such as Finland, where the rate of SAD is nearly 10 percent. It is seldom found in countries within 30 degrees of the equator, where there are long, constant hours of sunlight throughout the year.

C

As with other forms of depression, serious SAD may be accompanied by suicidal thoughts. One study of suicides in Japan examined a multitude of variables for each suicide, including hours of sunlight in the latitude, temperature, and economic factors, among others. Researchers found that yearly total sunshine was the only individual variable that correlated to a significant difference in the suicide rate. Thus, the study suggested that one's latitude can have a significant effect on mental health and even on tendencies toward suicidal thoughts.

D

SAD usually begins in adults between the ages of eighteen and thirty, and it is four times more prevalent in women than men. The disorder also tends to run in families. Some people suffer debilitating symptoms that interfere with interpersonal relationships and careers. Others with SAD experience mild symptoms. For people with this milder version of SAD, the winter may bring increased sadness or irritability, but they remain fully functional.

E

SAD's symptoms include many that are common in other forms of depression. SAD sufferers, like people who suffer from depression, experience fatigue, decreased levels of energy, and difficulty concentrating. Increased appetite, espe-

---

[1]British: autumn

cially a craving for carbohydrates, and weight gain, as well as an increased need for sleep and a desire to be alone are other common symptoms of depression that are seen among SAD sufferers as well.

F

The exact mechanism causing SAD is not known, but some researchers theorize[1] that SAD is related to hormonal changes. One theory is that reduced sunlight during fall and winter leads to reduced production of serotonin, a neurotransmitter with a calming effect, in the brain. Low levels of serotonin are associated with many forms of depression and can manifest in symptoms such as fatigue, carbohydrate craving, and weight gain. Because high-carbohydrate foods, such as chips, pretzels, and cookies,[2] boost serotonin, experts believe they have a soothing effect on the body and mind.

G

Others believe SAD is caused by the hormone melatonin, which is related to the body's circadian rhythms and can cause drowsiness. Plentiful light decreases the secretion of melatonin in the brain. However, during shorter and darker days more melatonin is produced, causing lethargy and other symptoms of depression.

H

The most common treatment for SAD is light therapy, in which patients expose themselves to full-spectrum lights, usually twenty times brighter than normal room lights, for fifteen to sixty minutes a day. Light helps to decrease the amount of melatonin and boost the serotonin in the brain. Thus, light therapy has an antidepressant effect. Sometimes, light therapy is used in combination with antidepressant medication and individual psychotherapy.

I

Experts also recommend some lifestyle changes that help to prevent SAD. People who have a tendency to suffer from SAD are encouraged to go outside every day during the winter months and to exercise regularly. Eating a well-balanced diet with plenty of vitamins and minerals is also important. Social support is extremely important for those with depression, so maintaining an active social life and regular activities is also recommended. For patients who use a light box, it is recommended to start using it in the early fall, before SAD symptoms appear.

J

Although some aspects of SAD are still being researched, experts agree that people who think they are suffering from SAD should see a doctor immediately. They do not advise using light therapy or any other treatment without the supervision of a physician.

---

[1]British: theorise
[2]British: biscuits

Questions 28–31

The text has ten paragraphs, **A–J**. Which paragraph contains the following information?
Write the correct letter, **A–J**, on lines 28–31 on your answer sheet.

28 a reason why certain types of food may alleviate the symptoms of SAD

29 descriptions of people who tend to suffer from SAD

30 parts of the world where SAD is common

31 a study showing a relationship between sunlight and mental health

Questions 32–36

Choose **FIVE** letters, **A–H**. Write the correct letter on lines 32–36 on your answer sheet.
Which **FIVE** of the following symptoms of SAD are mentioned in the passage?

A uncontrollable crying

B feeling tired frequently

C eating more than usual

D high levels of anxiety

E increased weight

F unhappy feelings

G having a bad temper

H inability to sleep

Questions 37–40

Choose **FOUR** letters, **A–G**. Write the correct letter on lines 37–40 on your answer sheet.
Which **FOUR** of the following treatments for SAD are mentioned in the passage?

A taking medicine

B writing in a journal

C attending a support group

D using a light box

E spending time outdoors

F traveling[1] to a sunny location

G talking with a therapist

---

[1]British: travelling

Writing Answer Sheet

TASK 1

_____

_____

_____

_____

_____

_____

_____

_____

_____

_____

_____

_____

_____

_____

_____

_____

_____

_____

_____

_____

_____

_____

GENERAL TRAINING MODULE TEST 4

-2-

-3-

TASK 2

_____
_____
_____
_____
_____
_____
_____
_____
_____
_____
_____
_____
_____
_____
_____
_____
_____
_____
_____
_____

GENERAL TRAINING MODULE TEST 4

-4-

GENERAL TRAINING MODEL TEST 4

Candidate Name _____

International English Language Testing System

GENERAL TRAINING WRITING

Time: 1 hour

INSTRUCTIONS TO CANDIDATES

Do not open this booklet until you are told to do so.

Write your name in the space at the top of this page.

All answers must be written on the separate answer booklet provided.

Do not remove this booklet from the examination room.

INFORMATION FOR CANDIDATES

There are **2** tasks on this question paper.

You must do **both** tasks.

Underlength answers will be penalized.[1]

---

[1]British: penalised

WRITING TASK 1

You should spend about 20 minutes on this task. You do NOT need to write any addresses. Begin your letter as follows:

Dear _____,

> You recently spent a vacation at the home of some friends who live in a different city.
>
> Write a letter to your friends. In your letter
>
> - thank your friends for letting you stay with them
> - describe some things you enjoyed about your vacation
> - invite your friends to visit you

Write at least 150 words.

WRITING TASK 2

You should spend about 40 minutes on this task.

> Write about the following topic:
>
> Learning to play team sports is an important part of a child's education.
>
> Do you agree or disagree? Give reasons for your answer and include any relevant examples from your own knowledge or experience.

Write at least 250 words.

Reading

1. E
2. D
3. A
4. B
5. E
6. B
7. C
8. False
9. True
10. Not Given
11. True
12. Not Given
13. True
14. False

15. by the company
16. the company website
17. the supervisor
18. tuition reimbursement
19. professional development hours
20. the workshop organizer
21. False
22. True
23. False
24. True
25. True
26. Not Given
27. False

28. F
29. D
30. B
31. C
32. B
33. C
34. E
35. F
36. G
37. A
38. D
39. E
40. G

GENERAL TRAINING MODULE—PRACTICE TEST 4

Reading

1. **(E)** This opportunity asks for one evening a week.

2. **(D)** This opportunity is at a health clinic, assisting with patients.

3. **(A)** This opportunity is for people who can provide entertainment (for example, playing music and singing) for nursing home residents.

4. **(B)** This opportunity takes place outside in a park.

5. **(E)** This opportunity involves preparing food.

6. **(B)** This opportunity takes place once a month, on the last Saturday of the month.

7. **(C)** This opportunity involves working with elementary school children.

8. *False.* You may either visit the website or call the Community Center to register.

9. *True.* In Part 1: "calculate the amount of money you owe. This will include the cost of your classes plus a $15 registration fee."

10. *Not Given.* Differences in the costs of the different classes is not mentioned.

11. *True.* In Part 1: "In addition, if your address is outside of the city, you will have to pay a nonresident fee of $25 per class."

12. *Not Given.* There is no mention of a limit on classes.

13. *True.* In Part 2: "No refunds will be made after the start of the second class."

14. *False.* In Part 2: "Classes offered by the Community Center are for adults only."

15. *by the company.*

16. *the company website.*

17. *the supervisor.*

18. *tuition reimbursement.*

19. *professional development hours.*

20. *the workshop organizer.*

21. *False.* Paragraph 1 states that a dress code doesn't mean that strict regulations are required.

22. *True.* Paragraph 2 states, "In businesses where the staff spends a large portion of work time interacting with clients and customers, then a more formal dress code is appropriate." The paragraph goes on to explain that a formal dress code means business suits or dresses.

23. *False.* Paragraph 2 states, "Formal business attire also means that ... facial hair should be kept neat and trimmed." This implies that facial hair (beards and mustaches) are permitted.

24. *True.* Paragraph 3 states, "... a business casual dress code might permit ... sweaters in place of jackets ..."

25. *True.* Paragraph 3 states, "Most company dress codes, whether formal or casual, do not allow items such as T-shirts, sandals, or jeans."

26. *Not Given.* Paragraph 3 mentions Casual Fridays but does not mention whether or not companies with formal dress codes have them.

27. *False.* Paragraph 4 states, ". . . companies that require employees to wear uniforms also need dress codes."

28. **(F)** Paragraph F: "Because high-carbohydrate foods, such as chips, pretzels, and cookies, boost serotonin, experts believe they have a soothing effect on the body and mind."

29. **(D)** Paragraph D: "SAD usually begins in adults between the ages of eighteen and thirty, and it is four times more prevalent in women than men. The disorder also tends to run in families."

30. **(B)** Paragraph B: "Residents of Canada and the northern United States, for example, are eight times more likely to suffer from SAD . . . ."

31. **(C)** Paragraph C: "One study of suicides in Japan examined a multitude of variables for each suicide, including hours of sunlight in the latitude, temperature, and economic factors, among others."

32. **(B)** Paragraph E: "SAD sufferers, like people who suffer from depression, experience fatigue, . . . as well as an increased need for sleep . . . ." *Fatigue* means *feeling tired frequently.*

33. **(C)** Paragraph E: "Increased appetite, especially a craving for carbohydrates, and weight gain . . . are seen among SAD sufferers as well."

34. **(E)** Paragraph E: "Increased appetite, especially a craving for carbohydrates, and weight gain . . . are seen among SAD sufferers as well."

35. **(F)** Paragraph F: "Low levels of serotonin are associated with many forms of depression . . . ."

36. **(G)** Paragraph D: "may bring increased sadness or irritability . . . ." *Irritability* means *bad temper.*

37. **(A)** Paragraph H: "Sometimes, light therapy is used in combination with antidepressant medication and individual psychotherapy."

38. **(D)** Paragraph H: "Sometimes, light therapy is used in combination with antidepressant medication and individual psychotherapy."

39. **(E)** Paragraph I: "People who have a tendency to suffer from SAD are encouraged to go outside every day during the winter months and to exercise regularly."

40. **(G)** Paragraph H: "Sometimes, light therapy is used in combination with antidepressant medication and individual psychotherapy." *Psychotherapy* means *talking with a therapist.*

Writing

These are models. Your answers will vary. See page 2 in the Introduction to see the criteria for scoring.

WRITING TASK 1

Dear Fred and Mary,

I am writing to thank you for your kind hospitality during my recent visit to your city. You made my vacation a really pleasant one. I thoroughly enjoyed the time we spent together, as well as seeing all the interesting sights in your city. I especially enjoyed the evening we went to the theater. The play was very interesting, and the actors were so talented. It was also very kind of you to provide the tickets. I also want to thank you for recommending that I visit the art museum and the gardens in Essex Park. I found so many things to interest me in both those places.

I would like to return your hospitality and invite you to visit me sometime next summer. There are a lot of interesting things to see and do here that I know you would enjoy, and it would be great to spend more time with you. Just let me know what dates are convenient for you. I look forward to hearing from you.

Your friend,
Jonathan

WRITING TASK 2

Playing team sports offers many benefits to children. However, I do not believe that all children need to learn to play these sports. I feel that there are other ways to get the same benefits and that team sports do not offer advantages to children who do not enjoy playing them.

Team sports offer a lot of good things to children who enjoy playing them. In the first place, children get a lot of exercise, which is important for their physical and mental health. In addition, they learn important skills such as teamwork, dealing with defeat, and winning graciously. Last but not least, they can have a lot of fun. However, team sports are not the only way to gain these benefits. Many children enjoy individual activities such as hiking or biking. Sports such as these are as healthy and as much fun for children as team sports. Team sports are also not the only way to learn to work with others. Children have opportunities to work on teams at school and with clubs or organizations.

Not all children enjoy playing team sports. For these children, being forced to play such sports can be a very disagreeable experience. They learn to associate physical exercise and teamwork with unpleasantness. After having bad experiences with team sports, children can easily be discouraged from learning to enjoy any form of physical exercise or to value being part of a group or team.

Team sports have a lot to offer, but they are not for everybody. There is no point in forcing them on children who do not like them. Children should be encouraged to work hard at being the best they can be in whatever they enjoy. That is the most beneficial type of learning situation for any child.

General Training Module

Reading and Writing

PRACTICE TEST 5

General Training Module

Reading and Writing

PRACTICE TEST 5

ANSWER SHEET
General Training
Practice Test 5

IELTS Reading Answer Sheet

#		✓ ✗	#		✓ ✗
1		✓ 1 ✗	21		✓ 21 ✗
2		2	22		22
3		3	23		23
4		4	24		24
5		5	25		25
6		6	26		26
7		7	27		27
8		8	28		28
9		9	29		29
10		10	30		30
11		11	31		31
12		12	32		32
13		13	33		33
14		14	34		34
15		15	35		35
16		16	36		36
17		17	37		37
18		18	38		38
19		19	39		39
20		20	40		40
				Reading Total	

GENERAL TRAINING MODEL TEST 5

Candidate Name _____

International English Language Testing System

GENERAL TRAINING READING

Time: 1 hour

INSTRUCTIONS TO CANDIDATES

Do not open this booklet until you are told to do so.

Write your name in the space at the top of this page.

Start at the beginning of the test and work through it.

You should answer all questions.

If you cannot do a particular question, leave it and go on to the next. You can return to it later.

All answers must be written on the Answer Sheet.

Do not remove this booklet from the examination room.

INFORMATION FOR CANDIDATES

There are **40** questions on this question paper.

The test is divided as follows:

Section 1	Questions 1–14
Section 2	Questions 15–27
Section 3	Questions 28–40

SECTION 1

*You are advised to spend 20 minutes on **Questions 1–14**.*

Questions 1–7

*Read the text below and answer **Questions 1–7**.*

Techno Institute of Training
Information for Students

Welcome to the Techno Institute of Training. Please read the following information carefully.

All texts and manuals required in our classes are available for sale in the Main Office, Room 105. Please see the receptionist to purchase your reading materials. You must have all materials when you arrive at your first class meeting, so please plan to get them ahead of time.

If for any reason you need to withdraw from a class that you are enrolled in, please note the following policies. Tuition will be fully refunded if you withdraw from the class before the second class meeting. Withdrawals made after the second class meeting but before the third will receive a refund of 50 percent of the tuition. Refunds cannot be made after the third class meeting. To withdraw from a class, please visit the Registrar's Office in Room 103.

Tickets to our Friday night lecture series are available to all students free of charge. If you are interested in attending a lecture, please get your ticket from the Student Activities Office, Room 107. Each student is allowed only one free ticket per lecture. Also, visit the Student Activities Office to see a schedule of local field trips, student social hours, and other upcoming events.

The Counseling[1] Office, Room 109, is open Monday through Thursday from 3:00 to 9:00 P.M. Assistance is available for choosing classes, making future educational plans, and searching for employment.

Changes in your class schedule may be made during the first week of the semester only. Class change forms are available in the Counseling Office. You must obtain the instructor's signature to change classes.

---

[1]British: Counselling

*The passage mentions several different rooms at the school. Which room would you visit in the following circumstances? Write the correct letter, **A–D** on lines 1–7 on your answer sheet. You may use any letter more than once.*

> | | |
> |---|---|
> | A | Room 103 |
> | B | Room 105 |
> | C | Room 107 |
> | D | Room 109 |

1 You are looking for a job.

2 You want to attend a lecture.

3 You have decided not to take a class and you want your money back.

4 You have decided not to take a class and you want to take another class instead.

5 You need to buy books for your classes.

6 You are looking for opportunities to socialize with other students.

7 You are trying to decide which classes to take.

Questions 8–14

*Read the text below and answer **Questions 8–14**.*

Department of Motor Vehicles
Applying for a Driver's License[1]

The Department of Motor Vehicles (DMV) is located on the fourth floor of City Hall. Business hours are Monday through Thursday 9:00 A.M. to 5:30 P.M. and Friday 12 noon to 8:30 P.M. Closed on holidays.

New Drivers

The fee for a first-time driver's license is $100, payable by check or credit card. You must take both a written test and a road test. Study manuals for the written test are available at the General Information desk in Room 400. Call the General Information desk at 473-555-7839 to make an appointment to take your tests. When you arrive for your appointment, you will take the written test first and then the road test. If you fail the written test, a thirty-day wait is required before taking the test again. You will not be permitted to take the road test until you have passed the written test. If you fail the road test, you must show a certificate of completion of a driver's education course given by an accredited institution before retaking the test. Driving courses are offered by the DMV. Ask for a course schedule at the General Information desk.

First-time applicants are required to present a valid form of identification with a photograph such as a passport, student identification card, work identification card, or military registration card when applying for a license. Citizens of other countries are asked to present a current visa in addition to one of the above-mentioned forms of identification.

License Renewals

You must renew a license no more than six months after the expiration date to avoid having to retake the written and road tests. You can renew your current driver's license in person or online. Bring your license and $65 cash or a check made out to the Department of Motor Vehicles to Room 405 during business hours. Credit cards are also accepted. License renewals can be made online at the DMV website. A credit card is required for online payment.

---

[1]British: Licence

*Complete each sentence with the correct ending, **A–L**, from the box below. Write the correct letter, **A–L**, on lines 8–14 on your answer sheet.*

> A present their passport.
> B wait a month before retaking the test.   9
> C sign up for a course at the DMV.
> D make an appointment before 9 A.M.
> E show a valid visa.   11
> F retake the written and road tests.   9 14
> G visit the office on Friday.   8
> H visit the DMV website.   12
> I show a work or student ID card.   13
> J take a driver's education course.   10
> K pay $100.
> L get a study manual from the DMV.

8 People who work during the day can

9 People who fail the written test must

10 People who fail the road test must

11 People from other countries have to

12 People who want to renew their license can

13 People who apply for their first license must

14 People whose license has been invalid for a year have to

SECTION 2

*You are advised to spend 20 minutes on **Questions 15–27**.*

Questions 15–20

*The following reading passage has six sections, **A–F**. Choose the correct heading for each section from the list of headings below. Write the correct number, **i–viii**, on lines 15–20 on your answer sheet. There are more headings than sections, so you will not use them all.*

15   Section A

16   Section B

17   Section C

18   Section D

19   Section E

20   Section F

LIST OF HEADINGS

i	Find Places for Everything
ii	Organize[1] Your Mail
iii	Empty Your Desk
iv	Follow a Schedule
v	Consult a Professional
vi	Why Is it Important?
vii	Categorize[2] Supplies and Papers
viii	Make It a Habit

---

[1]British: Organise
[2]British: Categorise

Organizing Your Desk

Follow these easy steps to a clutter-free desk:

A

The best way to begin is with a clean slate. Remove everything from the top of the desk—office supplies, documents, computer, printer—everything. Then move on to the drawers. Take out everything, then wipe down all surfaces with a damp cloth. Now all is clean and you are ready to start anew.

B

Next, take all those supplies and materials and sort through them. Group similar items together. For example, you might have a pile for small supplies such as paper clips and rubber bands, one for filing materials such as folders and labels, one for paperwork pertaining to current projects and another for paperwork to be filed, and so on. Group the items in a way that makes sense to you and the way you work.

C

Now, create an appropriate place for each group of items. A few items can be kept on the desktop, such as a pencil holder or a mail tray, but try to keep the desktop as clear as possible. Office supply stores sell a variety of trays, boxes, and other containers that are handy for storing everything from paper clips to large documents. They will help you keep both the drawers and the desktop organized.

D

Now you have completed the most important steps. Everything on your desk is organized. How will you keep it that way? The best way is to follow a routine. After you have finished using the paper clips or the scissors, put them back in their place. As soon as mail arrives on your desk, attend to it instead of letting it pile up. By developing regular practices like these, you will find it much easier to keep your desk organized.

E

Even when you have become accustomed to the routine of putting everything back in its place after use, you may still find that over time the organization starts to break down. This is why it is a good idea to develop a schedule. If you spend a short while reorganizing your desk at the end of every week or every month, you can keep the clutter from becoming overwhelming.

F

It is worth the small amount of time and effort it takes to keep your desk organized. Why? Psychologists tell us that an organized work space leads to more efficient and productive work.

Questions 21–27

*Read the text below and answer **Questions 21–27**.*

Telecommuting

Telecommuting, defined as working from home at least part of the time, is an increasingly common way to work. It has many benefits for employees. The fact that a telecommuter does not have to spend time each day traveling[1] to and from work is one obvious advantage. Working from home can mean significant savings in time and money that was formerly spent on daily travel. The telecommuter no longer has to spend part of his or her salary just to get to work in order to earn that salary. Not having to deal with traffic, bus schedules, or other logistics of travel also saves the telecommuter a good deal of unnecessary stress. As a result, the telecommuter can approach work with more energy and more positive feelings. There can also be a similar positive effect on the telecommuter's personal life, as there will be more energy and time left to devote to family.

Telecommuting is not for everyone. It works best for people who are able to manage their own time and work independently. Unfortunately, even the most independent worker can start to feel isolated over time. This can be managed, however, by creating a schedule that balances work hours spent at home with work hours spent at the office. Many telecommuters, for example, go into the office periodically in order to attend staff meetings or work with colleagues. Another issue many telecommuters face is the distractions of home life. It can be hard to concentrate on work when family members are demanding attention. Therefore, it is important for telecommuters to establish a work plan that is satisfactory to all members of the family. In addition, some telecommuters find that spending their workday at home results in higher costs for electricity and heating. They may also have new expenses, such as paying for an Internet connection, that they did not have before.

---

[1]British: travelling

Questions 21–24

*Choose **FOUR** letters, **A–G**. Write the correct letter on lines 21–24 on your answer sheet.*
*Which **FOUR** of the following advantages of telecommuting are mentioned in the passage?*

A   reduced travel expenses

B   salary increases

C   a better employer–employee relationship

D   more time to spend with the family

E   a more relaxed life

F   more time for personal business

G   an improved attitude toward work

Questions 25–27

*Choose **THREE** letters, **A–E**. Write the correct letter on lines 25–27 on your answer sheet.*
*Which **THREE** of the following disadvantages of telecommuting are mentioned in the passage?*

A   feeling lonely

B   missed staff meetings

C   interruptions of work

D   problems with colleagues

E   more expenses at home

SECTION 3

You are advised to spend 20 minutes on **Questions 28–40**, *which are based on the Reading Passage below.*

The Power of Earthquakes

Earthquakes have inspired both fear and curiosity in people throughout history. While ancient peoples used myths to explain earthquakes, modern scientists have developed the theory of plate tectonics. According to this theory, the Earth's surface is broken into many pieces that can move against each other, causing tremors at the Earth's surface. To better understand these events, scientists have developed sophisticated equipment to measure, record, and even begin to predict future earthquakes. While the scientists of today may understand a great deal more than our ancestors did, they also recognize that there is still much to learn about the destructive powers held deep within the Earth.

Before scientific explanations were established, many cultures explained earthquakes by attributing them to the movements of mythical creatures, such as frogs, turtles, and even flea-infested dogs. Japanese mythology tells of a great catfish guarded by the deity Kashima. When Kashima let his guard down, the catfish thrashed about, causing the Earth to tremble. In India, myths tell of the Earth being held upon the shoulders of an elephant that shook its head when tired. The Greeks believed that the shaking of the Earth was the rumbling of the god Poseidon's horses traveling through the skies or across the Earth. Or it was caused by Poseidon pounding his trident on the ground. The number and variety of these mythological explanations for earthquakes show how important it has always been to people everywhere to understand what causes the mysterious shakings of the Earth.

Beginning in the early 1960s, many in the scientific community began espousing the theory of plate tectonics, which explains that the surface of the Earth, the crust, is broken into many pieces called tectonic plates. Some of these plates are extremely large, such as the Eurasian Plate, on which sits most of Europe and Asia. Others are smaller, such as the Caribbean Plate, which is mostly underwater in the Caribbean Sea. These plates float on the Earth's mantle, a bed of molten rock called magma. Deeper forces inside the Earth's core heat this magma and cause it to flow underneath the plates, pushing the plates. The tension created at the boundaries of opposing plates can often become strong enough to snap them past each other, sometimes with the violent force that we know as an earthquake.

Scientists describe the movement of the plates in relation to each other in three principal ways. First, when two plates are forced into each other, one plate slides below the other. This is known as a *convergent boundary*. As the lower plate goes down, the upper plate often rises, forming mountains. The Himalayas, for example, were formed by the Indian Plate crashing into the Eurasian Plate. The second type of boundary is where two plates move apart from each other. This is known as a *divergent boundary*. An example of this is the Mid-Atlantic Rift, found at the bottom of the Atlantic Ocean. At this boundary, the North American Plate and the

Eurasian plate are being forced apart, at an average rate of 2.5 centimeters[1] per year. The third type is a *transform boundary*, where the edges of two plates slide in opposite directions parallel to each other. When the pressure between these plates is great enough, they snap violently past each other. This type of interaction between plates is the cause of many of the earthquakes felt in California.

Seismologists, the scientists who study earthquakes, use a device called a seismograph to measure the force of earthquakes and tremors. The most sophisticated of these are capable of measuring even the slightest tremor and locating its origin. The measuring system most commonly used is called the Richter Scale. It was invented in 1935 by a seismologist named Charles F. Richter. Because the difference in power between small and large earthquakes is so great, he developed a logarithmic scale in which an increase of one on the scale represents a tenfold increase in power. This means that an earthquake with a magnitude of 4.0, which would be easily felt at the Earth's surface, is ten times more powerful than a magnitude 3.0 quake and 100 times more powerful than a magnitude 2.0 quake, which often goes unnoticed. The data the scientists collect allow them not only to document past earthquakes, but to learn to predict future events.

While scientists today know much more about earthquakes than ever, there is still much to be learned. Seismologists have helped us understand more about how earthquakes happen and why they occur in some parts of the world but not others. All of this knowledge informs us about our Earth and protects us from some of the potential dangers. There are still, however, many forces in the Earth that we do not understand, with the potential to move, shake, and reshape the world.

Questions 28–33

*Write the correct letter, **A**, **B**, or **C**, on lines 28–33 on your answer sheet.*

28 Modern scientists are

   A uncertain about the cause of earthquakes.
   B able to forecast some earthquakes.
   C more curious about earthquakes than their ancestors were.

29 In ancient times, people explained earthquakes by

   A telling stories.
   B developing scientific theories.
   C watching the reactions of animals.

30 Kashima was a

   A king.
   B catfish.
   C god.

---

[1]British: centimetres

31 The ancient Greeks believed that earthquakes were caused by a god's

    A horses.

    B elephants.

    C frogs.

32 The quantity and diversity of explanations for earthquakes from ancient cultures show that

    A ancient people were not capable of understanding natural forces.

    B people have always been interested in earthquakes.

    C earthquakes were more common in ancient times.

33 The Caribbean Plate

    A sits next to a convergent boundary.

    B forms part of the Mid-Atlantic Rift.

    C lies mostly beneath the ocean.

Questions 34–40

*Complete each sentence with the correct ending from the box. Write the correct letter, **A–J**, on lines 34–40 on your answer sheet.*

A	a transform boundary.
B	a seismograph.
C	an unnoticed tremor.
D	an earthquake measuring 2.0.
E	a logarithmic scale.
F	a divergent boundary.
G	a magnitude 3.0 earthquake.
H	a layer of magma.
I	a collision between two plates.
J	a piece of the Earth's crust.

34 A place where two plates slide in opposite directions is called

35 Tectonic plates lie on

36 An earthquake measuring 4.0 is ten times more powerful than

37 The Himalayas were caused by

38 The Mid-Atlantic Rift is an example of

39 A tectonic plate is

40 The machine used to measure the strength of earthquakes is known as

ANSWER SHEET
General Training
Practice Test 5

Writing Answer Sheet

TASK 1

_____
_____
_____
_____
_____
_____
_____
_____
_____
_____
_____
_____
_____
_____
_____
_____
_____
_____

ANSWER SHEET
General Training
Practice Test 5

-2-

ANSWER SHEET
General Training
Practice Test 5

-3-

TASK 2

ANSWER SHEET
General Training
Practice Test 5

-4-

GENERAL TRAINING MODEL TEST 5

Candidate Name _____

International English Language Testing System

GENERAL TRAINING WRITING

Time: 1 hour

INSTRUCTIONS TO CANDIDATES

Do not open this booklet until you are told to do so.

Write your name in the space at the top of this page.

All answers must be written on the separate answer booklet provided.

Do not remove this booklet from the examination room.

INFORMATION FOR CANDIDATES

There are **2** tasks on this question paper.

You must do **both** tasks.

Underlength answers will be penalized.[1]

---

[1]British: penalised

WRITING TASK 1

You should spend about 20 minutes on this task. You do NOT need to write any addresses. Begin your letter as follows:

Dear _____,

You have decided to leave your current job and look for a new one.

Write a letter to a friend. In your letter

- *explain why you want to leave your current job*
- *describe what kind of job you are looking for*
- *ask for some help or advice*

Write at least 150 words.

WRITING TASK 2

You should spend about 40 minutes on this task.

Write about the following topic:

Even though organic fruits and vegetables are more expensive than conventional fruits and vegetables, they are worth the extra cost.

Do you agree or disagree?

Give reasons for your answer and include any relevant examples from your own knowledge or experience.

Write at least 250 words.

Reading

1. D	15. iii	29. A
2. C	16. vii	30. C
3. A	17. i	31. A
4. D	18. viii	32. B
5. B	19. iv	33. C
6. C	20. vi	34. A
7. D	21. A	35. H
8. G	22. D	36. G
9. B	23. E	37. I
10. J	24. G	38. F
11. E	25. A	39. J
12. H	26. C	40. B
13. K	27. E	
14. F	28. B	

GENERAL TRAINING MODULE—PRACTICE TEST 5

Reading

1. **(D)** The Counseling Office is in Room 109 and has assistance for people searching for employment.

2. **(C)** Tickets for the Friday night lecture series are available in Room 107, the Student Activities Office.

3. **(A)** Students who want to withdraw from a class and get a tuition refund should visit the Registrar's Office in Room 103.

4. **(D)** Class change forms are available in the Counseling Office, Room 109.

5. **(B)** Books are for sale in the Main Office, Room 105.

6. **(C)** The Student Activities Office, Room 107, has information about student social hours and other events.

7. **(D)** The Counseling Office, Room 109, provides assistance with choosing classes.

8. **(G)** Paragraph 1: Friday is the one day of the week that the office is open until 8:30 in the evening.

9. **(B)** Paragraph 2: "If you fail the written test, a thirty-day wait is required before taking the test again."

10. **(J)** Paragraph 2: "If you fail the road test, you must show a certificate of completion of a driver's education course . . . ."

11. **(E)** Paragraph 3: "Citizens of other countries are asked to present a current visa. . . ."

12. **(H)** Paragraph 4: "License renewals can also be made online at the DMV website."

13. **(K)** Paragraph 2: "The fee for a first-time driver's license is $100 . . . ."

14. **(F)** Paragraph 4: "You must renew a license no more than six months after the expiration date to avoid having to retake the written and road tests."

15. *iii.* Section A suggests removing everything from desktop and drawers.

16. *vii.* Section B discusses grouping, or categorizing, desk supplies and paperwork.

17. *i.* Section C discusses creating a place for each group of items.

18. *viii.* Section D discusses a "routine" and "regular practices," that is, habits.

19. *iv.* Section E discusses developing a schedule for reorganizing.

20. *vi.* Section F explains why it is worth the time and effort to keep an organized desk.

21. **(A)** Paragraph 1: "Working from home can mean significant savings in time and money that was formerly spent on daily travel."

22. **(D)** Paragraph 1: There can also be a similar positive effect on the telecommuter's personal life, as there will be more energy and time left to devote to family."

23. **(E)** Paragraph 1: "Not having to deal with traffic, bus schedules, or other logistics of travel also saves the telecommuter a good deal of unnecessary stress."

24. **(G)** Paragraph 1: "As a result, the telecommuter can approach work with more energy and more positive feelings."

25. **(A)** Paragraph 2: "Unfortunately, even the most independent worker can start to feel isolated over time."

26. **(C)** Paragraph 2: "It can be hard to concentrate on work when family members are demanding attention."

27. **(E)** Paragraph 2: "In addition, some telecommuters find that spending their workday at home results in higher costs for electricity and heating. They may also have new expenses, such as paying for an Internet connection . . . ."

28. **(B)** Paragraph 1: "scientists have developed sophisticated equipment to measure, record, and even begin to predict future earthquakes." Choice (A) is contradicted by the discussion of the theory of plate tectonics. Choice (C) is incorrect because there is nothing in the paragraph to suggest that any one group of people is more curious than another.

29. **(A)** Paragraph 1: "ancient peoples used myths to explain earthquakes." *Myths* are *stories*. Choice (B) is how earthquakes are explained in modern times. Choice (C) is not mentioned.

30. **(C)** According to paragraph 2, Kashima is a *deity*, that is, a god. Choice (A) is plausible but is not mentioned. Choice (B) is the animal that appears in the myth of Kashima.

31. **(A)** Paragraph 2: "The Greeks believed that the shaking of the Earth was the rumbling of the god Poseidon's horses . . . ." Choices (B) and (C) are other animals mentioned in the discussion of myths.

32. **(B)** Paragraph 2: "The number and variety of these mythological explanations . . . show how important it has always been to people everywhere to understand what causes the mysterious shakings of the Earth." Choices (A) and (C) are not mentioned.

33. **(C)** Paragraph 3: "the Caribbean Plate, which is mostly underwater in the Caribbean Sea." Choices (A) and (B) refer to other geological features mentioned in the passage.

34. **(A)** Paragraph 4: "The third type is a *transform boundary*, where the edges of two plates slide in opposite directions parallel to each other."

35. **(H)** Paragraph 3: "These plates float on the Earth's mantle, a bed of molten rock called magma."

36. **(G)** Paragraph 5: "an earthquake with a magnitude of 4.0, which would be easily felt at the Earth's surface, is ten times more powerful than a magnitude 3.0 quake . . . ."

37. **(I)** Paragraph 4: "The Himalayas, for example, were formed by the Indian Plate crashing into the Eurasian Plate."

38. **(F)** Paragraph 4: "The second type of boundary is where two plates move apart from each other. This is known as a *divergent boundary*. An example of this is the Mid-Atlantic Rift, found at the bottom of the Atlantic Ocean."

39. **(J)** Paragraph 3: "the surface of the Earth, the crust, is broken into many pieces, called tectonic plates."

40. **(B)** Paragraph 5: "Seismologists, the scientists who study earthquakes, use a device called a seismograph to measure the force of earthquakes and tremors."

Writing

These are models. Your answers will vary. See page 2 in the Introduction to see the criteria for scoring.

WRITING TASK 1

Dear Sam,

I am writing to let you know about my current job situation, hoping that you can give me some advice. I have decided to leave my current position at the Acme Company. I have worked there for several years now, and I think I have advanced as far as possible in this company. I would like to work at a larger company where there are more opportunities for advancement.

As you know, my most recent position at Acme has been as an assistant in the Human Resources Department. I have learned a great deal about this type of work and am very interested in it. I am hoping to find a similar sort of position at a larger company. I do not mind starting at a new company at the same level as I am working at now, as long as I feel there are good opportunities to move up before too long.

Since you have a lot of experience in this field, I was hoping that you could help me identify some companies that might be a good fit for me. I would also appreciate some help with my résumé, if you do not mind my asking. I hope to hear from you soon.

Your friend,
Jane

WRITING TASK 2

Organic fruits and vegetables cost more than conventional fruits and vegetables, but many people are willing to pay the higher price. In my opinion, however, it is not worth paying more for these fruits and vegetables. Often they are not in good condition and they aren't any more nutritious or delicious than conventional fruits and vegetables.

The organic fruits and vegetables I see in the store are usually very sad looking. They have holes and spots and rotten parts. Sometimes they look wrinkled and shriveled. They never look as fresh and tasty as the conventional fruits and vegetables. Why should anyone pay a lot of money for something that looks so bad when you can get much nicer fruits and vegetables at a lower price? It just doesn't make sense.

In addition to their ugly appearance, organic fruits and vegetables don't offer any more nutrition than conventional fruits and vegetables. An organic apple has the same vitamins as a conventional one, for example, so why pay more for the organic one? In addition, the conventional apple tastes just as good, if not better, than the organic one. It seems that the only thing you get by paying more for the organic apple is fruit without chemicals on it. However, all you have to do is wash the apple. Then it is just as clean as the organic one, and just as nutritious, but cheaper to buy.

Organic fruits and vegetables really aren't much better than conventional ones. I don't see any good reason to pay a higher price for them.

General Training Module

Reading and Writing

PRACTICE TEST 6

General Training Module

Reading and Writing

PRACTICE TEST 6

ANSWER SHEET
General Training
Practice Test 6

		✓ 1 ✗
1		
2		2
3		3
4		4
5		5
6		6
7		7
8		8
9		9
10		10
11		11
12		12
13		13
14		14
15		15
16		16
17		17
18		18
19		19
20		20

		✓ 21 ✗
21		
22		22
23		23
24		24
25		25
26		26
27		27
28		28
29		29
30		30
31		31
32		32
33		33
34		34
35		35
36		36
37		37
38		38
39		39
40		40
	Reading Total	

GENERAL TRAINING MODULE TEST 6

GENERAL TRAINING MODEL TEST 6

Candidate Name _____

International English Language Testing System

GENERAL TRAINING READING

Time: 1 hour

INSTRUCTIONS TO CANDIDATES

Do not open this booklet until you are told to do so.

Write your name in the space at the top of this page.

Start at the beginning of the test and work through it.

You should answer all questions.

If you cannot do a particular question, leave it and go on to the next. You can return to it later.

All answers must be written on the Answer Sheet.

Do not remove this booklet from the examination room.

INFORMATION FOR CANDIDATES

There are **40** questions on this question paper.

The test is divided as follows:

Section 1	Questions 1–14
Section 2	Questions 15–27
Section 3	Questions 28–40

SECTION 1

*You are advised to spend 20 minutes on **Questions 1–14**.*

Questions 1–7

*Read the text below and answer **Questions 1–7**.*

A

Good Deal Car Rentals

Have we got a deal for you!

Compact cars only $375/week

We offer:

- The lowest rates in town
- Two convenient locations
- Payment by cash or credit card

To reserve your car, call us at:

432-555-0943 (airport)

432-555-7118 (train station)

Open from 7:30 A.M. to 9:30 P.M.
every day of the week

B

Fast 'n Frugal Car Rental

- Compact and mid-sized cars
- Vans
- Small trucks
- Rent by the day, week, or month

We have the best rates in town. Compact cars start at $350/week.

Special prices for National Car Club members—
10 percent off our usual low prices!

Reserve your vehicle today by calling our
convenient downtown location:
921-555-9642

Open 6:30 A.M. to 10:30 P.M. every day.
Closed Sundays.

All major credit cards accepted. No cash, please.

C

Dollar Dan's Rent-a-Car

- Conveniently located next to the Hilltown Hotel
- Guaranteed lowest prices around. Compact cars only $35/day.

We have hundreds of compact, mid-sized, and luxury cars to choose from, all right on our lot. So come on down and pick out your car. There's no need to reserve a car at Dollar Dan's because we guarantee that we'll always have a car available for you.

- Visit us anytime. We're open twenty-four hours/day, seven days/week.
- Payment by credit card only.

---

*Look at the three advertisements for car rental agencies, **A–C**. Answer the questions by writing the letter of the appropriate car rental agency, **A–C**, on lines 1–7 on your answer sheet.*

Which car rental agency

1   has the lowest price for a compact car?

2   accepts payments in cash?

3   offers a discount?

4   is convenient for people arriving by plane?

5   is always open?

6   does not require a reservation?

7   has vehicles suitable for moving furniture?

Questions 8–11

*Read the text below and answer **Questions 8–11**.*

*The following text has four sections, **A–D**. Choose the correct heading for each section from the list of headings below. Write the appropriate number, **i–vi**, on lines 8–11 on your answer sheet. There are more headings than sections, so you won't need to use them all.*

8   Section A

9   Section B

10 Section C

11 Section D

> **LIST OF HEADINGS**
>
> **i**   Instructor's Teaching Schedule
> **ii**   Assignments
> **iii**   Assistance Outside Class
> **iv**   Using the Language Lab
> **v**   Class Schedule
> **vi**   Grading

Spanish for Health-care Workers
Instructor: Dr. Lucia Mendez

A

Classes are held in Room 203. The class meets twice weekly, Monday and Wednesday evenings from 6:30 to 8:15 P.M. You are expected to attend every class and to arrive on time. Please speak with the instructor about any unavoidable absences.

B

We will use the text *Spanish for Health-care Workers*. Students are required to read one or more chapters before each class (see reading schedule below). In addition, each student will prepare an oral presentation to give to the class before the end of the semester. The Language Laboratory, Room 302, is open Monday–Friday from 9:30 A.M. until 8:30 P.M. In addition to attending class, each student must complete a weekly exercise in the lab.

C

There will be four to five quizzes throughout the semester in addition to a midterm and a final exam. Missed quizzes or exams will count against your grade; there will be no make-ups. The breakdown for calculating each student's final mark is as follows: quizzes and exams—50 percent; oral presentation—30 percent; class participation—20 percent. A grade of B or higher is required to pass this class.

D

If you need extra help or would like to discuss anything with the instructor, my office hours (Room 320) are 5:00–6:30 on Mondays and Wednesdays. The Language Lab staff is also available to help you with your assignments. In addition, individual Spanish tutors are available. Please talk to the staff in the Language Lab for more information about tutors.

Questions 12–14

*Choose the correct answer. Write the correct letter, **A–C**, on lines 12–14 on your answer sheet.*

12 Which of the following people would be most interested in this class?

    A A nurse

    B A tourist

    C A literature student

13 What is located in Room 302?

    A The classroom

    B The language lab

    C The instructor's office

14 How many exams will there be?

    A One

    B Two

    C Four or five

SECTION 2

*You are advised to spend 20 minutes on **Questions 15–27**.*

Questions 15–20

*Read the text below and answer **Questions 15–20**.*

Asking for a Raise

If you are thinking about asking for a raise in salary, there are several things to keep in mind. First, consider whether you deserve a higher salary. You probably do, but you should be able to explain exactly why to your boss. Sit down and make a list of your job accomplishments. Be as specific as possible. For example, think about important projects you have worked on, things you have done to improve the organization[1] of work in your department, or how your efforts have brought more money to the company. Also include any professional development opportunities you have taken advantage of recently and be ready to explain how they have improved your performance on the job. By going through the process of listing your accomplishments, not only will you be better prepared when you meet with your boss, you will also feel more confident that you deserve what you are asking for.

Bear in mind that salary levels are based not only on performance but also on the market for your particular skills. Before you ask for a raise, you will need to do some research. You should investigate the industry standards for salaries for people in similar positions with similar levels of experience. This will help you determine what would be a reasonable amount of money to ask for. Your initial request should actually be slightly higher than the amount you want in order to leave some room for negotiation. Then, if you have to go lower than this amount, you still end up with something close to what you want.

A crucial point is the timing of your request. If you have recently been given new responsibilities, it makes sense to ask for a higher level of compensation. On the other hand, if the company is going through financial difficulties, a request for more money will probably not be met with a favorable[2] response. It would be better to wait until the company is in a better financial position. Finally, there is one thing you should never do: Never give personal reasons for wanting a higher salary. Your need to pay your child's college tuition or buy a bigger house is of no concern to your boss. Your salary level should be based on professional considerations alone, and that is where you need to keep the conversation.

---

[1] British: organisation
[2] British: favourable

Choose the correct answer. Write the correct letter, A–C, on lines 15–20 on your answer sheet.

15 Before asking for a salary increase, you should

    A send your boss a list of your accomplishments.
    B take some professional development courses.
    C write down all the reasons you deserve a raise.

16 Preparing yourself before talking with your boss will help you

    A get the highest raise possible.
    B feel more self-assured.
    C improve your job performance.

17 You should find out

    A salaries of other people in your field.
    B how much money your boss can offer you.
    C what job openings are available in your company.

18 You should ask for

    A slightly more money than you want.
    B the exact amount of money that you want.
    C a little less money than you want.

19 A good time to ask for a salary raise is

    A when your boss is in a favorable mood.
    B before discussing financial records.
    C soon after you have taken on new duties.

20 While negotiating a salary raise, it is a good idea to

    A discuss professional topics only.
    B mention your financial needs.
    C ask your boss about his or her family.

*Read the text below and answer **Questions 21–27**.*

Hanson, Inc.   **Employee Manual**

Chapter V: Employee Benefits

Leave

All full-time employees are entitled to a minimum of two weeks of annual leave time. Employees who have completed five years at Hanson are entitled to three weeks of annual leave. After completing ten years at Hanson, employees may have four weeks of annual leave. In order to take advantage of annual leave time, the employee must complete the Request for Annual Leave Form and submit it to his or her supervisor a minimum of thirty days in advance. The supervisor has the final decision about whether to grant the leave as requested. Any annual leave days not used in a calendar year may be rolled over and added to the leave days for the following year. In addition to annual leave, all full-time employees are entitled to ten personal leave days per year. Personal leave days must be used within the calendar year, or they will be forfeited. Part-time employees are entitled to five personal leave days per year.

Health Insurance

Employees may choose to sign up for a company-sponsored health plan. Complete information on the available plans can be requested from the Human Resources Department. Health benefits are also provided for the employee's spouse and children. The company pays 50 percent of the monthly premiums, with the other 50 percent being deducted from each paycheck. Part-time employees are also eligible for the company-sponsored health plans; the company pays 25 percent of the premiums.

Retirement

Employees may determine how much they wish to contribute to the company retirement fund, up to 5 percent of their salary. Contributions will be deducted from each paycheck. The company will contribute an equal amount to each employee's retirement fund. This benefit is available to both full-time and part-time employees.

Do the following statements agree with the information given in the text about employee benefits? On lines 21–27 on your answer sheet, write:

TRUE   *if the statement agrees with the information*
FALSE   *if the statement contradicts the information*
NOT GIVEN   *if there is no information on this*

21 All full-time employees are entitled to three weeks of annual leave.

22 Annual leave must be requested a month in advance.

23 Annual leave for part-time employees is half that of full-time employees.

24 Personal leave days not used before the end of the year will be lost.

25 The company pays half the monthly insurance charges for full-time employees.

26 Part-time employees do not receive health benefits.

27 Employees must contribute 5 percent of their salary to the retirement fund.

*You are advised to spend 20 minutes on **Questions 28–40**, which are based on the Reading Passage below.*

Green Energy

As energy prices rise and the effects of greenhouse gas emissions become more widespread, people everywhere are becoming increasingly concerned about using fossil fuels. More and more people are turning to so-called "green technologies" as a way to reduce dependence on nonrenewable fossil fuels. The ideal alternative energy source would be sustainable (the supply will not be exhausted), clean (no emissions), and reliable. The three most popular alternative energy sources are geothermal power, solar power, and wind power.

Since geothermal energy taps heat from the earth, its resources range from water found just below the surface of the earth, to hot water and hot rock found a few miles below the surface, to even deeper rock of extremely high temperatures. In a process similar to drilling for oil, wells as deep as a mile or more can be drilled into underground reservoirs. These wells tap steam and hot water that are used to run turbines and create energy. Power companies can then transmit this energy over power lines.

Geothermal power on a smaller scale can be used for heating and cooling houses or commercial buildings. Geothermal heat pumps, also known as ground-source heat pumps, rely on the fact that the earth beneath the surface remains at a relatively constant temperature throughout the year. Like a cave, the ground is warmer than the air above it during the winter and cooler in the summer. The geothermal heat pump transfers the heat stored in the earth into the building during the winter, and transfers it out of the building and into the ground during the summer. The ground, in other words, acts as a heat source in winter and a heat sink in summer. While geothermal heat pumps are an emissions-free and reliable source of energy, the biggest disadvantage is that such systems are expensive to install.

Solar energy has come a long way from the clunky boxes of the 1970s. Today, solar energy is commonly collected by sleek and efficient photovoltaic (PV) panels. The photovoltaic cells convert sunlight directly into electricity and are made of semiconductors such as crystalline silicon or other thin-film materials. The benefits of solar power vary according to how much exposure a given building has to the sun. However, one does not need to live in the desert to take advantage of solar power. Cloudy Germany is the worldwide leader in the use of solar power.

Solar power is not as pricey as geothermal power, but having a panel professionally installed can still be costly. Some enterprising home-owners reduce the initial costs by purchasing inexpensive kits and setting up the system on their own. The biggest disadvantage of a solar power system is its dependence on the amount of sunlight collected, but some cutting-edge panels can generate energy even in the rain.

Wind power is created when wind is used to generate mechanical power or electricity. Most wind turbines convert the wind's kinetic energy into mechanical power. The wind turns the blades, which spin a shaft connected to a generator. A generator then converts this mechanical power into electricity. A group of wind turbines can produce electricity and feed it into the utility grid, where it is sent through transmission lines to homes and businesses. Like solar and geothermal energy, wind is a renewable resource that produces no emissions.

Small wind energy systems can be used by homes, farms, or communities. Such systems can be connected to the larger electrical grid or used for stand-alone energy generation—a particularly attractive option for anyone living far from power company lines. A grid-connected wind turbine can reduce one's reliance on the power company for electricity. If the turbine cannot deliver the needed energy, the power company then makes up the difference. However, in order to take advantage of wind energy, a turbine must be in an area with average wind speed of at least 10 miles an hour, and such systems can be very expensive.

Whether a given home or business uses wind, solar, or geothermal power depends on a variety of economic and environmental factors. However, experts agree that investing in alternative energy now—whether by individuals or power companies—will pay dividends in the future.

Questions 28–30

*Complete the summary below. Choose **NO MORE THAN TWO WORDS** from the passage for each answer. Write your answers on lines 28–30 on your answer sheet.*

These days, people are interested in reducing their consumption of

28 .... They are looking at sources of **29** ....

to supply their power needs. People want sources that are **30** ....,

do not cause pollution, and can be consistently depended on.

Questions 31–33

Which of the following facts about geothermal energy are mentioned in the passage? Choose **THREE** answers from the list below and write the correct letters, **A–E**, on lines 31–33 on your answer sheet.

A   is easiest to use where there is a plentiful supply of groundwater

B   is used to run power plants

C   costs a great deal of money to set up

D   requires electricity to power the heat pump

E   is used for cooling as well as heating buildings

Questions 34–36

Which of the following facts about solar energy are mentioned in the passage? Choose **THREE** answers from the list below and write the correct letters, **A–E**, on lines 34–36 on your answer sheet.

A   can be used even in areas without intense sunlight

B   the panels are usually installed on the roof of the house

C   does not have to be installed by a professional

D   the amount of power generated fluctuates with the amount of exposure to the sun

E   is often used by farmers to power electric fences

Questions 37–40

Which of the following facts about wind energy are mentioned in the passage? Choose **FOUR** answers from the list below and write the correct letters, **A–G**, on lines 37–40 on your answer sheet.

A   wind turbines are considered unsightly by many people

B   is used by individual home-owners as well as by power companies

C   the energy that it generates cannot be stored for later use

D   must be installed in an area that receives a certain amount of wind

E   wind turbines create a lot of noise

F   can be used in conjunction with electricity supplied by a power company

G   is as clean a source of energy as geothermal and solar systems

Writing Answer Sheet

TASK 1

_____

_____

_____

_____

_____

_____

_____

_____

_____

_____

_____

_____

_____

_____

_____

_____

_____

_____

-2-

-3-

TASK 2

-4-

GENERAL TRAINING MODULE TEST 6

GENERAL TRAINING MODEL TEST 6

Candidate Name _____

International English Language Testing System

GENERAL TRAINING WRITING

Time: 1 hour

INSTRUCTIONS TO CANDIDATES

Do not open this booklet until you are told to do so.

Write your name in the space at the top of this page.

All answers must be written on the separate answer booklet provided.

Do not remove this booklet from the examination room.

INFORMATION FOR CANDIDATES

There are **2** tasks on this question paper.

You must do **both** tasks.

Underlength answers will be penalized.[1]

---

[1]British: penalised

WRITING TASK 1

You should spend about 20 minutes on this task. You do NOT need to write any addresses. Begin your letter as follows:

Dear _____,

> You are planning a two-week vacation, and you need someone to take care of your house while you are away.
>
> Write a letter to your neighbor.[1] In your letter
>
> - tell your neighbor that you are going away
> - ask your neighbor to take care of your house for you
> - explain what tasks you would like your neighbor to do

Write at least 150 words.

WRITING TASK 2

You should spend about 40 minutes on this task.

> Write about the following topic:
>
> Some high school students work part-time in addition to going to school. What are the advantages and disadvantages of high school students having part-time jobs?
>
> Give reasons for your answer and include any relevant examples from your own knowledge or experience.

Write at least 250 words.

---

[1]British: neighbour

Reading

1. C	15. C	29. alternative energy
2. A	16. B	30. sustainable
3. B	17. A	31. B
4. A	18. A	32. C
5. C	19. C	33. E
6. C	20. A	34. A
7. B	21. False	35. C
8. v	22. True	36. D
9. ii	23. Not Given	37. B
10. vi	24. True	38. D
11. iii	25. True	39. F
12. A	26. False	40. G
13. B	27. False	
14. B	28. fossil fuels	

GENERAL TRAINING MODULE—PRACTICE TEST 6

Reading

1. **(C)** This agency charges $35 per day, which is $245 per week.

2. **(A)** This agency accepts payment by credit card or cash. The others accept credit cards only.

3. **(B)** This agency offers a 10 percent discount to National Car Club members.

4. **(A)** This agency has a phone number listed for the airport, so we can assume they have an office at the airport.

5. **(C)** This agency is open twenty-four hours a day, seven days a week.

6. **(C)** This agency states: "There's no need to reserve a car . . . ."

7. **(B)** This agency rents vans and small trucks.

8. *v.* Section A explains the days and hours the class meets.

9. *ii.* Section B explains the reading, oral presentation, and language lab assignments.

10. *vi.* Section C explains how the grades are calculated.

11. *iii.* Section D talks about getting help outside of class from the instructor or at the Language Lab.

12. **(A)** The class is for health-care workers, so a nurse would be most interested. Choices (B) and (C) are people who might be interested in a language class, but this class is not intended for them.

13. **(B)** According to section B, the Language Lab is in Room 302. Choice (A) is in Room 203. Choice (C) is in Room 320.

14. **(B)** According to section C, there will be two exams—a midterm and a final. Choice (A) is contradicted by the paragraph. Choice (C) is the number of quizzes, not exams.

15. **(C)** Paragraph 1 mentions listing all your job accomplishments in order to show why you deserve a raise. Choice (A) is confused with the suggestion to make a list of accomplishments, but it is never suggested to share this list with your boss. Choice (B) is confused with the suggestion to include professional development courses taken in the list of accomplishments.

16. **(B)** Paragraph 1 suggests that going over your accomplishments will help you feel more confident. *Confident* means *self-assured*. Choices (A) and (C) use words mentioned in the paragraph, but they are not part of the reason given for preparing ahead of time.

17. **(A)** Paragraph 2: "You should investigate the industry standards for salaries for people in similar positions with similar levels of experience." Choices (B) and (C) are not mentioned.

18. **(A)** Paragraph 2: "Your initial request should actually be slightly higher than the amount you want in order to leave some room for negotiation." Choices (B) and (C) are contradicted by "slightly higher."

19. **(C)** Paragraph 3: "If you have recently been given new responsibilities, it makes sense to ask for a higher level of compensation." Choice (A) repeats the word *favorable*. Choice (B) repeats the word *financial*.

20. **(A)** Paragraph 3: "Your salary level should be based on professional considerations alone, and that is where you need to keep the conversation." Choices (B) and (C) are things that should not be discussed.

21. *False.* Paragraph 1: "All full-time employees are entitled to a minimum of two weeks of annual leave time."

22. *True.* Paragraph 1: "the employee must complete the Request for Annual Leave Form and submit it to his or her supervisor a minimum of thirty days in advance."

23. *Not Given.* There is no information on annual leave for part-time employees.

24. *True.* Paragraph 1: "Personal leave days must be used within the calendar year, or they will be forfeited."

25. *True.* Paragraph 2: "The company pays 50 percent of the monthly premiums . . . ."

26. *False.* Paragraph 2: "Part-time employees are also eligible for the company-sponsored health plans; the company pays 25 percent of the premiums."

27. *False.* Paragraph 3: "Employees may . . . contribute . . . up to 5 percent of their salary." This means they can choose any amount from zero up to 5 percent but no higher.

28. *fossil fuels.* Paragraph 1: "More and more people are turning to so-called 'green technologies' as a way to reduce dependence on nonrenewable fossil fuels."

29. *alternative energy.* Paragraph 1: "The ideal alternative energy source . . . ."

30. *sustainable.* Paragraph 1: "sustainable (the supply will not be exhausted), clean (no emissions), and reliable."

31. **(B)** Paragraph 2: "wells as deep as a mile or more can be drilled into underground reservoirs to tap steam and hot water that are used to run turbines and create energy."

32. **(C)** Paragraph 3: "the biggest disadvantage is that such systems are expensive to install."

33. **(E)** Paragraph 3: "Geothermal power on a smaller scale can be used for heating and cooling houses or commercial buildings."

34. **(A)** Paragraph 4: "However, one does not need to live in the desert to take advantage of solar power. Cloudy Germany is the worldwide leader in the use of solar power."

35. **(C)** Paragraph 5: "Some enterprising home owners reduce the initial costs by purchasing inexpensive kits and setting up the system on their own."

36. **(D)** Paragraph 4: "The benefits of solar power vary according to how much exposure a given building has to the sun."

37. **(B)** Paragraph 6 mentions wind power being used to generate power for the utility grid, and paragraph 7 discusses the use of wind power for individual homes and farms.

38. **(D)** Paragraph 7: "However, in order to take advantage of wind energy, a turbine must be in an area with average wind speed of at least 10 miles an hour . . . ."

39. **(F)** Paragraph 7: "If the turbine cannot deliver the needed energy, the power company then makes up the difference."

40. **(G)** Paragraph 6: "Like solar and geothermal energy, wind is a renewable resource that produces no emissions." This means it is a clean energy source.

Writing

These are models. Your answers will vary. See page 2 in the Introduction to see the criteria for scoring.

WRITING TASK 1

Dear Joe,

I would like to ask you a big favor. Next Saturday I am leaving for vacation. I will be gone for two weeks. That is a long time to leave my house alone, and I was hoping that you would be able to take care of a few things for me.

The tasks I would like you to do are very simple. The most important thing is to keep an eye on the house and make sure no strangers enter it. If you could take the mail out of the box every day and put it inside the house, that would be very helpful. Also, if it is not too much trouble, I would like to ask you to water the garden if it does not rain.

I would be happy to pay you a small amount of money in exchange for your help. Please let me know if you will be able to help me out. Thank you very much.

Your neighbor,
Pat

WRITING TASK 2

Note: Be consistent with your pronoun choice in the essay. Here, the pronoun used consistently is she. The writer could have used he alone or he or she to refer to both males and females, respectively.

Many families encourage their teenage children to get part-time jobs. Other families prefer their children to focus on schoolwork and friends. There are both benefits and drawbacks to teenagers working while they are still in school.

Having a job helps a teenager become an adult. In the first place, it helps her learn a sense of responsibility. She has to be at work at a certain time and do the job she was hired to do. If she does not, she could lose her job. Earning money also brings responsibility. A working teenager may have to pay for her own clothes, school supplies, and entertainment. She may be saving her money for college or even just to buy something fun that she wants for herself. Whatever she does with her money, earning it and learning to use it responsibly help her mature.

On the other hand, having a job can interfere with other important aspects of the teenage years. A job can distract a teenager's energy and attention from her schoolwork. It can leave her with little time to relax and be with friends. In addition, although learning to be responsible is important, teenagers are also still children. Soon enough they will have the responsibilities of college, a career, and a family to care for. The teenage years may be the last time they have the chance for a carefree life. A job could possibly add too much responsibility at too early an age.

Each family has a different situation, and each teenager is a different person. Teenagers and their families have to evaluate their individual circumstances when deciding whether having a job is a good idea.

Audioscripts for Listening Parts 1-4

PRACTICE TEST 1

Narrator:

You will hear a number of different recordings, and you will have to answer questions on what you will hear. There will be time for you to read the instructions and questions, and you will have a chance to check your work. All the recordings will be played once only.

The test is in four sections. Write all of your answers on the test pages. At the end of the test you will be given ten minutes to transfer your answers to an answer sheet.

Now turn to Section 1 [on page 16].

Section 1. You will hear a man asking for information about language classes over the phone.

First you have some time to look at Questions 1 to 4 [on page 16].

You will see that there is an example that has been done for you. On this occasion only, the conversation relating to this will be played first.

Example

Woman: Good morning. Globetrotters Language School. How may I help you?
Man: Yes, I was wondering if you could give me some information on language classes.

Narrator: The woman answers the phone, "Globetrotters Language School," so the word *Globetrotters* has been written at the top of the form. Now we shall begin. You should answer the questions as you listen, because you will not hear the recording a second time. Listen carefully and answer Questions 1 to 4.

Questions 1 to 4

Woman: Good morning. Globetrotters Language School. How may I help you?
Man: Yes, I was wondering if you could give me some information on language classes.
Woman: Certainly. What language are you interested in studying?

Man:	Well, that's the thing. I'm interested in learning Japanese, but I'd also like to improve my Chinese. I don't know which to study right now.
Woman:	Maybe the class schedule will help you decide. Did you want to study in the morning, afternoon, or evening?
Man:	I work in the evenings, so mornings or afternoons would be best.
Woman:	Then that decides it for you. We offer an advanced Chinese class, but it meets on Wednesday and Friday evenings.
Man:	I couldn't do that. When do the Japanese classes meet?
Woman:	We have beginning Japanese on Tuesday and Thursday mornings, no wait, that's intermediate Japanese. Which level do you want? Advanced?
Man:	No, beginning. Definitely. I know some Chinese and some French, but I'm a real beginner with Japanese.
Woman:	Well then, are you free Monday, Wednesday, and Friday mornings? That's when the beginning Japanese classes meet. We also have intermediate French on Friday mornings.
Man:	I could do those mornings, but I'd prefer afternoon. Don't you have anything in the afternoon?
Woman:	We have intermediate Japanese class on Wednesday and Friday afternoons.
Man:	I really need a beginner class. So I'll take the morning Japanese class. Could you give me an idea of the cost? What would be the tuition for the Japanese class?
Narrator:	Before you hear the rest of the conversation, you have some time to look at Questions 5 to 10 [on pages 16 and 17].

Now listen and answer Questions 5 to 10. |

Questions 5 to 10

Woman:	The beginning-level classes meet three times a week, so they cost a bit more than the other levels. For a six-week course, the cost would be $575.
Man:	That's a bit steep.
Woman:	If it's hard for you to pay that much, you could sign up for just four weeks of class and pay $410. Or, you could pay for one week at a time, at $125 a week.
Man:	That comes out to be much more expensive once you add up all the weeks.
Woman:	That's true. You can save money by registering for two levels together. For example, pay for your beginning and intermediate classes now and you'll get twelve weeks of class for just $1,050.
Man:	That's not a bad deal, but I can't come up with that much money at once. I'll just pay for the six-week course.
Woman:	Fine. That class begins next week, so you need to register right away.
Man:	Can't I register over the phone?
Woman:	No, I'm sorry, we don't take phone registrations. What you'll need to do is visit the school office today or tomorrow. Bring a check for the tuition and a photo ID.
Man:	Is that all?

Woman:	Yes, we'll give you a registration form to complete, or you can save time by visiting our website and downloading the form there. Complete it and bring it into the office with your check.
Man:	Great. I'll stop by this afternoon.
Woman:	Fine. When you arrive, ask for Mr. Lindsay. He's in charge of student registration.
Man:	I'm sorry, Mr. who?
Woman:	Mr. Lindsay, spelled L-I-N-D-S-A-Y.
Man:	Thank you for your help.
Woman:	Thank you. We'll look forward to seeing you in class.

Narrator:	That is the end of Section 1. You now have half a minute to check your answers.

Track 3

Now turn to Section 2 [on page 17].

Section 2. You will hear a tour guide giving information about a shopping district.

First, you have some time to look at Questions 11 to 15 [on page 17].

As you listen to the first part of the talk, answer Questions 11 to 15.

Questions 11 to 15

Tour guide:	This afternoon we'll visit the city's shopping district. Several blocks in the area are closed to car traffic, and I know you'll enjoy walking around there. I'd like to give you an overview of the district now since you'll be on your own once we get there.
	You'll see on this map here that the shopping district consists of two streets—Pear Street, which runs north and south, and Cherry Street, which crosses Pear Street right here. Let's start our tour here on Pear Street where the star is. This star marks the Harbor View Bookstore. It's very popular among locals as well as tourists. You can buy a range of books of local interest as well as a variety of magazines and newspapers. It's directly across the street from the City Library, which is also worth a visit. It's in one of the oldest buildings in the city and contains, among other things, an interesting collection of rare books.
	Now, moving up Pear from the bookstore toward Cherry, the next building on the left is the Pear Café. You'll notice it's right on the corner of Pear and Cherry streets. It's a great place to relax while enjoying a delicious cup of coffee or tea. You can talk with friends or read quietly. They have a variety of books and magazines available.
	From the windows of the café, you can look right across Cherry Street for a lovely view of City Gardens. It's a rather small garden, but it contains a variety of exotic plants and flowers.

Let's leave the café and cross Pear Street. On the opposite corner, we're at Caldwell's Clothing Store, which you might also want to visit. They sell both men's and women's fashions from countries around the world.

Continuing down Cherry Street, the next building on the right after Caldwell's is the souvenir shop. Stop in here to get maps and books about the local area, as well as T-shirts and postcards with pictures of the city. Now, we cross Cherry Street and we're at the art gallery, one building down from the corner. Here you can see and, of course, purchase many fine paintings and sculptures by local artists.

Let's keep going down Cherry Street toward the harbor. On the left, right after the gallery, is Harbor Park. It's a lovely place, and it's certainly worth spending some time there.

Narrator: Before you hear the rest of the talk, you have some time to look at Questions 16 to 20 [on page 18].

Now listen and answer Questions 16 to 20.

Questions 16 to 20

Harbor Park was built on land donated to the city by Captain Jones, a life-long resident of this city. Captain Jones designed the park himself, and it was built in 1876. Exactly in the center of the park a statue of Captain Jones was erected, and it's still standing there today. It shows Captain Jones on the bow of his ship.

After viewing the statue, you can follow the path that goes through the woods just behind. It will lead you to a lovely garden, in the middle of which is a fountain. This is a nice place to enjoy a few quiet moments.

If you still feel like walking, continue on to the far end of the garden. There, you'll find a wooden staircase, which will take you down to the harbor. You might enjoy the view of the boats from there. There's also a walking path along the water, which will eventually bring you back up to Cherry Street.

You can see that there's plenty to do in this part of the city. The bus leaves at 1:30.

Narrator: That is the end of Section 2. You now have half a minute to check your answers.

Now turn to Section 3 [on page 18].

Section 3. You will hear a conversation between a university student and a librarian about using the City Archives.

First, you have some time to look at Questions 21 to 24 [on page 18].

As you listen to the first part of the conversation, answer Questions 21 to 24.

Questions 21 to 24

Student:	Hello. I was wondering if you could give me some information about using the archives.
Librarian:	I'd be happy to. Are you a resident of the city?
Student:	Actually, I live just outside the city, but I study at the university downtown.
Librarian:	That's fine. All you need to do is show your university identification card and you can use the archives at no charge, as long as your ID card is current, of course.
Student:	Yes, it's valid. So I don't have to pay anything?
Librarian:	No. City residents pay an annual fee, but students can use the archives for free. Everyone else needs to get special permission from the director, but that doesn't apply to you, of course.
Student:	Oh, good. I was also wondering about the schedule. I have classes every day, Monday through Friday, and I also have a part-time job, so I could really only use the archives on weekends.
Librarian.	That's not a problem at all. We're open all weekend; actually the only day we're closed is Monday. So you can come any day, Tuesday through Sunday.
Student:	Are you open in the evenings?
Librarian:	Yes, we're open from 9:30 in the morning until 8:30 in the evening.
Student:	That will fit my schedule well.
Narrator:	Before you hear the rest of the conversation, you have some time to look at Questions 25 to 30 [on page 19].
	Now listen and answer Questions 25 to 30.

Questions 25 to 30

Librarian:	Is there something else I can help you with?
Student:	Yes. One thing I'll be needing to see for one of my class projects is old photographs. Do you have photographs of the city in the nineteenth century that I could look at?
Librarian:	Yes, we store all the photographs in the basement. Those stairs over there will take you down to the photography collection. Just tell the librarian there what you're interested in, and he'll help you.
Student:	Those would be nineteenth-century photographs?
Librarian:	Yes, the entire collection is there. Now, if you're interested in seeing documents from the nineteenth century, those are right here on the ground floor.
Student:	I would like to see some of those documents. Does that collection include newspapers, too?
Librarian:	No, all the newspapers from the earliest ones, in the eighteenth century, up to the current time, are on the second floor. Here, let me just give you this map of the archives, and you'll be able to find whatever it is you need.
Student:	Thank you. Oh, I see you have a whole room devoted to maps.
Librarian:	Yes, on the third floor.
Student:	That's great because one thing I need to do is look at how the city has developed over time.

Librarian:	I'm sure you'll find a lot of helpful information there. Of course, some of the maps are several centuries old, so generally visitors are only allowed to see photographic reproductions of them.
Student:	That shouldn't be a problem. What's this on the fourth floor—Ogden's Woolen Mill?
Librarian:	As I'm sure you know, Ogden's Woolen Mill was the major entity responsible for the growth of this city in the nineteenth century. The Ogden heirs gave money for the archives to devote an entire floor to information about the history of the mill.
Student:	Will I be able to find information about the Ogden family there—photographs, personal papers, things like that?
Librarian:	Probably the family photographs are stored downstairs in the photography collection. The personal papers would be on the fifth floor, where we keep all the personal papers of famous residents of our city.
Student:	Thank you so much for your help. I'll be able to do a lot of my research here.
Narrator:	That is the end of Section 3. You now have half a minute to check your answers.

Track 5

Now turn to Section 4 [on page 19].

Section 4. You will hear a lecture about wind energy.

First, you have some time to look at Questions 31 to 33 [on page 19].

Now listen carefully and answer Questions 31 to 33.

Questions 31 to 33

Lecturer:	With the rising cost of fossil fuels, there's a great deal of interest these days in developing alternative sources of energy. Today, I'd like to talk about one of these—wind power. In the past couple of decades, there's been an upsurge of interest in using the wind as a source of energy, but the idea isn't new at all. People have been harnessing the power of the wind for centuries, ever since ancient peoples first used sailboats. In ancient China, farmers used a rudimentary sort of windmill to pump water. Wind power was used in other parts of the ancient world, as well. In Persia, for example, farmers used wind-powered mills to grind their grain. During the Middle Ages in the Netherlands, people went back to the ancient idea of using the power of the wind to move water. They used windmills to drain lakes, thereby creating more land for farming.
Narrator:	Before you hear the rest of the talk, you have some time to look at Questions 34 to 40 [on page 20].
	Now listen carefully and answer Questions 34 to 40.

Questions 34 to 40

Lecturer: At present, people around the world are using the wind to generate electricity, some old methods, some new. Is this the solution to our modern energy problems? Well, as with anything, there are both advantages and disadvantages to using wind power. Let's take a look at some of the reasons to use wind power. One of the biggest problems with using fuels such as oil and coal is pollution. Wind power, on the other hand, is clean. It causes no pollution and therefore doesn't contribute to global warming. Another great advantage of wind power is that it's a renewable resource. Oil and coal reserves are limited, but we'll never run out of wind. Economics is another reason to use wind power. Using the wind to generate electricity costs less, much less, than running other types of generators. In addition, since wind turbines don't take up much land, the land around them can be used for other purposes, such as farming.

There are disadvantages, however. Even though generating electricity with wind is relatively inexpensive, the technology isn't cheap. The initial costs of setting up wind turbines can be quite high. Another issue is reliability. Wind doesn't blow at a constant strength. Therefore, at times, a lot of electricity can be produced while at others there may be little or none. Wind turbines usually have to be located in rural areas where the land is open. Their distance from cities, where the most electricity is needed, is another issue. Although wind is considered to be a clean source of energy, wind turbines cause their own sort of pollution. Wind turbines are usually placed in high, open areas, where they're easy to be seen. Rural residents often feel that the beautiful local scenery is spoiled by the sight of the wind turbines. In addition, wind turbines aren't quiet. In fact, one wind turbine can produce as much noise as a car traveling at highway speeds.

Narrator: That is the end of Section 4. You now have half a minute to check your answers.

You will now have ten minutes to transfer your answers to the listening answer sheet.

PRACTICE TEST 2

Narrator: You will hear a number of different recordings, and you will have to answer questions on what you will hear. There will be time for you to read the instructions and questions, and you will have a chance to check your work. All the recordings will be played once only.

The test is in four sections. Write all of your answers on the test pages. At the end of the test you will be given ten minutes to transfer your answers to an answer sheet.

Now turn to Section 1 [on page 58].

Section 1. You will hear a woman asking for information over the phone.

First you have some time to look at questions 1 to 5 [on page 58].

You will see that there is an example that has been done for you. On this occasion only, the conversation relating to this will be played first.

Example

Man: Good afternoon. Plainfield Community Center.

Woman: Yes, hi. I'm new in town, and I was curious about the services the Community Center has to offer.

Narrator: The man answers the phone, "Plainfield Community Center," so the words "Community Center" have been written at the top of the form. Now we shall begin. You should answer the questions as you listen, because you will not hear the recording a second time. Listen carefully and answer Questions 1 to 5.

Questions 1 to 5

Man: Good afternoon. Plainfield Community Center.

Woman: Yes, hi. I'm new in town, and I was curious about the services the Community Center has to offer.

Man: We offer a variety of recreational activities. What were you interested in, in particular?

Woman: Well, everything, I guess. OK, let's start with kids. I have a teenage son. What activities do you have for teens?

Man: Right now, during the school year, we have tutoring sessions for children and teens, in all subjects.

Woman: That would be good. He needs help with algebra.

Man: We can certainly help with that. Just have him come by any Wednesday or Saturday afternoon. That's when the tutoring sessions are scheduled.

Woman: Fantastic. What about sports? Do you have sports activities for teens?

Man: We have tennis lessons on Sunday mornings for teens and Sunday afternoons for adults.

Woman: Hmmm, I don't think my son would like that, but my husband might. For myself, I'd be more interested in yoga. Do you offer yoga classes?

Man: We do. Our yoga classes take place on Tuesday and Thursday evenings. We divide it up into several groups, so there's one class for younger children, one for teens, and one for adults.

Woman: Really? I doubt my husband and son would be interested, but I'd like to sign up for yoga. I also like reading. Do you have any book clubs?

Man:.   We have one just about to start. The first meeting will be next Friday morning. It will focus on early twentieth-century novels.

Woman: Too bad it's Friday morning. I think my son would enjoy it, but of course he's in school at that time.

Man: Well, actually, that book club is for adults only. We may start one up for teens next summer, but we have nothing for that age group right now.

Woman: Oh, well. I suppose he has enough to keep him busy for now. Now, what about fees? Do these classes and activities cost anything?

Before you hear the rest of the conversation, you have some time to look at Questions 6 to 10 [on page 58].

Now listen and answer Questions 6 to 10.

Questions 6 to 10

Man:	There's a small charge for non-members for each class. However, they're all free to members. Would you be interested in becoming a member?
Woman:	How much does the membership cost?
Man:	Not much at all. The yearly fee is $75 for individuals and $225 for families.
Woman:	What do I get with the membership?
Man:	You get free access to all classes and activities, and you can use our facilities, like the tennis court, the exercise room, and the meeting room.
Woman:	It's not a bad deal, really. Could you tell me exactly where the center is located?
Man:	It's at 107 [one-oh-seven] Eliot Street.
Woman:	Is that Eliot with two Ls or one L?
Man:	One L. E-L-I-O-T. It's right downtown.
Woman:	I think I know where it is. Do you have free parking?
Man:	Yes. You can park just across the street. There's a garage there.
Woman:	That sounds easy enough. Maybe I'll come in one day next week and sign up for some classes.
Man:	That would be fine, but don't come on Monday because we're closed that day. We're open Tuesday through Sunday.
Woman:	Oh. Thanks for telling me. Maybe I'll stop in on Tuesday then. Can I pay for the classes with a personal check?
Man:	We accept checks and credit cards.
Woman:	OK. Thank you very much. You've been very helpful.

Narrator: That is the end of Section 1. You now have half a minute to check your answers.

(Track 7)

Now turn to Section 2 [on page 59].

Section 2. You will hear a hike leader giving information about an upcoming hiking trip.

First, you have some time to look at Questions 11 to 15 [on page 59].

As you listen to the first part of the talk, answer Questions 11 to 15.

Questions 11 to 15

Hike leader:	Good evening, everyone. As you know, this is our last meeting before we set off on our annual week-long hiking trip, so tonight I'll be telling you every-thing you'll need to know to be ready for the trip. Let's talk about equipment first. Having the right equipment is essential for your comfort and safety. First, you'll need a warm and comfortable sleeping bag. However, you won't

need to worry about carrying a tent since we'll be sleeping in shelters along the way. Also, part of the fee you've paid for the trip goes toward food, so you won't need to put that on your packing list either. We've found, though, that it's more efficient for each person to bring his or her own dishes, so be sure to pack a plastic bowl, a cup, and a fork, knife, and spoon. That's all you'll need in the way of dishes.

Perhaps the most important item to put on your list is a comfortable pair of hiking boots. Nothing ruins a hike more than getting blisters and sores from ill-fitting boots. So make sure your boots fit you right. Shoes and sneakers aren't adequate for the type of hiking we'll be doing. Of course, a backpack is necessary for carrying your equipment. Make sure you have one that's lightweight and comfortable to carry. Walking poles have become popular among hikers recently, but we don't recommend them. They can get in the way when too many hikers are using them at once, and some serious injuries have been caused, so it's best to leave those at home.

Let's see . . . What else? Oh, yes. Some people have asked me about trail maps. They're available, but you really don't need them, as your hike leaders have scouted out the trail and will be guiding you along the way. And don't forget to bring a warm jacket. You may think you won't need one in this warm summer weather, but remember that evenings in the mountains can get quite cold. Is there anything else I need to tell you? Oh, yes, your guides will each be carrying a first-aid kit, so that's one less thing for you to pack yourself. Remember, you'll be carrying your backpack all day, so keep your load light and don't overpack.

Narrator: Before you hear the rest of the talk, you have some time to look at Questions 16 to 20 [on page 59].

Now listen and answer Questions 16 to 20.

Questions 16 to 20

I know you're all experienced hikers, but it's always worth repeating the rules of the trail since they're so important. These rules are in place for the safety of everyone on the trip. As you know, there'll be a hike leader walking at the head of the line, who will show the group the way. At the end of the line will be the rear leader, or sweep. It's important to always stay ahead of this person while we're on the trail. There are several different trails on the mountain where we'll be hiking, and they cross each other at some points. When you come to any intersection of trails, stop and wait for the rest of the group to catch up. This way we can be sure that no one goes off on the wrong trail. Let me emphasize here how important it is to stay on the trail. We'll be climbing through some steep and rocky areas. Don't be tempted to go off on your own and try to climb some rocks. That can be quite dangerous. Also, it's not likely, but it is possible that we'll encounter some large wild animals along the way. The last thing you want to do is try to feed any of them. That will just encourage them to follow us, which could lead to some dangerous situations. One last thing: Before we set off hiking each morning, be sure to fill up your water bottle. This is perhaps the most important safety rule. Dehydration can be a serious problem when you're out in the wilderness, so you must always be sure to carry an adequate supply of water with you.

I think that covers just about everything. Are there any questions?

Narrator: That is the end of Section 2. You now have half a minute to check your answers.

Now turn to Section 3 [on page 60].

Section 3. You will hear a conversation between a university student and a faculty advisor about the requirements for the student teaching semester.

First, you have some time to look at Questions 21 to 24 [on page 60].

As you listen to the first part of the conversation, answer Questions 21 to 24.

Questions 21 to 24

Advisor: I'd like to go over with you today some of the requirements for your student teaching, which you'll be undertaking next semester.

Student: I'm really looking forward to working in a real classroom and teaching children, but I'm nervous about it, too.

Advisor: One of my roles is to provide you with whatever support you may require. One thing that helps me do that is to know what you're doing in the classroom, so I require all my students to keep a journal about their teaching experience.

Student: That sounds like a lot of work. Will I have to write in it every day?

Advisor: Yes, if you can. You'll give it to me at the end of each week. Another thing I'll want from you is a few sample lesson plans. I'll let you know ahead of time exactly how I want you to do them.

Student: Several of us from the university will be student teaching at the same school. Are we supposed to get together regularly to discuss our work?

Advisor: I'll meet with each student teacher individually, but you aren't required to meet with each other. Of course, you can talk together as much as you want. You will, however, have to observe some of the other teachers in the school, besides the teacher you'll be working with.

Student: Then will I get an evaluation from my supervising teacher at the end of the semester?

Advisor: Actually, no. I'll do your evaluation, and I'll base it on several things. One is your required portfolio, which should contain samples of your class activities and your students' work. Another important thing is your term paper.

Student: Then there won't be a final exam?

Advisor: No, we don't feel that's necessary for student teaching.

Narrator:	Before you hear the rest of the conversation, you have some time to look at Questions 25 to 30 [on page 60].
	Now listen and answer Questions 25 to 30.

Questions 25 to 30

Student:	I know I have to get an agreement form signed. Since you're my advisor, are you the one to do that?
Advisor:	No, that form is for your supervising teacher to sign, to document that he or she agrees to have you in the classroom as a student teacher.
Student:	Oh, I see. I'm concerned about the term paper I'll have to do, and the evaluation process. I'm not sure I understand what I'm supposed to do.
Advisor:	Regarding the term paper, the first thing is to choose a topic. It should be related to your teaching work. You should let me know your term paper topic by the end of the first week of the semester.
Student:	Will you be observing me regularly in the classroom?
Advisor:	Yes, and during the fourth week of the semester, we'll have our first evaluation meeting to discuss my observations.
Student:	One thing I'm really looking forward to is the student teacher conference that the university puts on every year.
Advisor:	I'm glad you're looking forward to it. Of course, everyone in the program is required to attend. The conference takes place, let me check, yes, the seventh week of the semester.
Student:	When will I have to turn in my term paper?
Advisor:	The term paper is due by the end of the fourteenth week of the semester. Then during the fifteenth and final week, we'll get together one last time for a semester review.
Student:	Wow. It looks like I have a busy semester ahead of me.
Narrator:	That is the end of Section 3. You now have half a minute to check your answers.
	Now turn to Section 4 [on page 61].
(Track 9)	Section 4. You will hear a lecture about customer psychology.
	First, you have some time to look at Questions 31 to 35 [on page 61].
	Now listen carefully and answer Questions 31 to 35.

Questions 31 to 35

| Lecturer: | An understanding of customer psychology is an invaluable aid for retailers looking for ways to increase sales. Much can be done to the store environment to encourage shoppers to linger longer and spend more money. The first aspect to consider is the physical organization of the store. Placement of merchandise has a great deal of influence on what customers buy. For example, a common practice among retailers is to place the store's best-selling merchandise near the back of the store. In order to get to these popu- |

lar items from the front entrance, customers have to walk down aisles filled with merchandise that they might not see otherwise. Carpets are also used to direct customers through particular areas of the store. Retailers choose carpets not only for their decorative or comfort value, but also because lines or other types of patterns in the carpets can subtly guide shoppers in certain directions. Besides encouraging shoppers to go to certain areas of the store, retailers also want to keep them in the store longer. One way to do this is to provide comfortable seating throughout the store, but not too close to the doors. This gives customers a chance to rest and then continue shopping.

Retailers can do a number of things to create a pleasant atmosphere in the store, thereby encouraging more purchases. Music is commonly used, not as entertainment, but as a calming influence. It can slow the customers' pace through the store, making them spend more time shopping and, consequentially, making more purchases. Scents are also used in various ways. Everyone has had the experience of being drawn into a bakery by the smell of fresh bread. Experiments have been done with other types of scents, as well. For example, the scent of vanilla has been used to increase sales in clothing stores.

| Narrator: | Before you hear the rest of the talk, you have some time to look at Questions 36 to 40 [on page 62]. |
| | Now listen carefully and answer Questions 36 to 40. |

Questions 36 to 40

| Lecturer: | Use of color is another important aspect of store environment. Certain colors can affect behavior as well as mood. Light purple, for example, has been found to have an interesting effect on customer behavior. People shopping in an environment where light purple is the predominating color seem to spend money more than shoppers in other environments. Orange is a color that's often used in fast-food restaurants. It encourages customers to leave faster, making room for the next group of diners. Blue, on the other hand, is a calming color. It gives customers a sense of security, so it's a good color for any business to use. In addition to using color to create mood and affect customer behavior, color can also be used to attract certain kinds of customers to a business. Stores that cater to a younger clientele should use bold, bright colors, which tend to be attractive to younger people. Stores that are interested in attracting an older clientele will have more success with soft, subtle colors, as older people find these colors more appealing. |

| Narrator: | That is the end of Section 4. You now have half a minute to check your answers. |
| | You will now have ten minutes to transfer your answers to the listening answer sheet. |

PRACTICE TEST 3

Track 10

Narrator: You will hear a number of different recordings, and you will have to answer questions on what you will hear. There will be time for you to read the instructions and questions, and you will have a chance to check your work. All the recordings will be played once only.

The test is in four sections. Write all of your answers on the test pages. At the end of the test you will be given ten minutes to transfer your answers to an answer sheet.

Now turn to Section 1 [on page 98].

Section 1. You will hear a woman making a hotel reservation over the phone. First, you have some time to look at Questions 1 to 4 [on page 98].

You will see that there is an example that has been done for you. On this occasion only, the conversation relating to this will be played first.

Example

Man: Good afternoon. Grandview Hotel.

Woman: Yes, hello. I, uh, I'm planning to spend a few days in your city next week, and I'd like to, uh, make a reservation.

Narrator: The man answers the phone, "Grandview Hotel," so the word "Grandview" has been written at the top of the form. Now we shall begin. You should answer the questions as you listen, because you will not hear the recording a second time. Listen carefully and answer Questions 1 to 4.

Questions 1 to 4

Man: Good afternoon. Grandview Hotel.

Woman: Yes, hello. I, uh, I'm planning to spend a few days in your city next week, and I'd like to, uh, make a reservation.

Man: Of course. When did you want to stay here?

Woman: Next week. Wednesday night and Thursday night.

Man: So, that's February 13th and 14th.

Woman: Yes, that's right.

Man: And how many guests will there be?

Woman: Just me. So, do you have a room available?

Man: Yes, we do. I'll just need to take some of your information. May I have your name, please?

Woman: Oh, right, yes. It's Roxanne Wilson. W-i-l-s-o-n.

Man: Thank you, Ms. Wilson. And may I have your credit card number?

Woman: It's 2336189872.

Man: . . . 9872. Got it. All right, Ms. Wilson, I have your reservation confirmed. Can I help you with anything else?

Before you hear the rest of the conversation, you have some time to look at Questions 5 to 10 [on pages 98 and 99].

Now listen and answer Questions 5 to 10.

Questions 5 to 10

Woman: Well, yes. I was wondering, since I'll have a couple of free hours Friday morning before I leave, is there anything interesting to see close to the hotel?

Man: Do you like museums? The art museum's very close by.

Woman: I love museums, but not art. Can't stand it. I've heard your city has a very interesting science museum, though.

Man: Yes, but unfortunately it's closed in the winter. Are you interested in shopping?

Woman: Sure, I love shopping. Are there any good stores nearby?

Man: Yes. We have a large shopping mall just two bus stops away. You take the bus to Monument Square, and it's just half a block from there. Just look for the post office, and you'll see the mall entrance next to it.

Woman: Fabulous. What about lunch? I hear your city has good restaurants.

Man: Yes. There's a nice restaurant very near. It's just across the street from the park.

Woman: Sounds good. I can have lunch, then walk in the park afterwards. I have one more question. What's the best way to get to the hotel from the airport?

Man: Subway is the fastest, of course. There are buses, but they're quite slow.

Woman: I'll be arriving quite late, after 10 P.M. I thought I might have to take a taxi.

Man: The subway runs until midnight.

Woman: Oh, good. Then I'll do that. Will there be someone at the hotel front desk that late?

Man: Oh, yes. The front desk stays open until two.

Narrator: That is the end of Section 1. You now have half a minute to check your answers.

Now turn to Section 2 [on page 99].

Track 11 Section 2. You will hear a tour leader giving information about a bus tour.

First, you have some time to look at Questions 11 to 15 [on pages 99 and 100].

As you listen to the first part of the talk, answer Questions 11 to 15.

Questions 11 to 15

Tour leader: Thank you for choosing City Tours. The reason so many people choose our tours when visiting this city is because you can design your tour to suit your own interests. Your all-day pass entitles you to board our bus at any stop and stay as long as you like at each place. The all-day bus pass costs $18 for adults. Children between the ages of five and twelve pay half the adult fare, and children under five ride for free. Our buses run every hour on the half hour, starting at 8:30 A.M.

Our most popular tour is the Center City Tour, which goes to all the major attractions in the center of the city. From the starting point here at the tour bus office, the bus goes to the first stop, Hill Park. As you may guess, this park is located at the top of a small hill. The next stop is the fishing docks. Following that, the bus goes on to the third stop, Bay Bridge, located at the foot of the bridge which crosses the bay. The fourth stop is in the shopping district, then the fifth and last stop is at Green Street.

Narrator: Before you hear the rest of the talk, you have some time to look at Questions 16 to 20 [on page 100].

Now listen and answer Questions 16 to 20.

Questions 16 to 20

Tour leader: There are many interesting things to do and see on the Center City Tour. At the first stop, you can enjoy a spectacular view of the bay, the city, and especially of the fishing docks, which are located at the foot of the hill. At the second stop, you can walk around and look at the boats. Fresh fish from the bay is also for sale here, since this is the place where the fishermen bring in their catch. The next stop is where some of the city's finest seafood restaurants are located, so you might want to plan a lunch stop here. You can eat fresh fish here prepared in the traditional local way. The fourth stop is, of course, where you can do your shopping. Don't miss the opportunity to purchase some of our city's famous handmade baskets. You'll want to take several home as souvenirs of your visit to our city. Finally, at the last stop on the tour, you can visit one of the oldest buildings in our city, the theater. This building was built over 400 years ago and is still used today as a place to see plays, musicals, and other performances, as well as our annual film festival.

Narrator: That is the end of Section 2. You now have half a minute to check your answers.

Now turn to Section 3 [on page 101].

Section 3. You will hear a conversation between two students planning a research project.

First, you have some time to look at Questions 21 to 23 [on page 101].

As you listen to the first part of the conversation, answer Questions 21 to 23.

Questions 21 to 23

Student 1:   We'd better start planning our research project, because we don't have much time left before it's due.

Student 2:	I know, only three more weeks.
Student 1:	Is that all? I thought we had more time than that. Well, let's get to work, then.
Student 2:	OK, so we agreed we're going to interview shoppers about their spending habits. Did we decide to conduct our interviews at the department store?
Student 1:	We haven't decided anything definitely yet, but I think the shopping mall would be a better place. We'd get more of a variety of shoppers there.
Student 2:	Yes, that's a good point. So, let's do that. How many interviews did the professor say we had to complete?
Student 1:	She said at least thirty. That sounds like a lot, doesn't it?
Student 2:	Yes, but if we divide it up between the two of us, that's just fifteen each. That's not so bad.
Narrator:	Before you hear the rest of the conversation, you have some time to look at Questions 24 to 30 [on page 101]. Now listen and answer Questions 24 to 30.

Questions 24 to 30

Student 1:	OK, so I guess we'd better start designing our questionnaire.
Student 2:	Well, we have to do some reading first, don't we? Didn't we say we were going to compare our results to the results of a government study?
Student 1:	Right, the government study about how the economic crisis has changed people's spending habits. We want to see if we get similar results.
Student 2:	Yes, so we'd better read that first and then design our questionnaire. Then I guess we'll be ready to go out and interview shoppers.
Student 1:	No. Don't you remember? The professor said she had to approve our questionnaire first, before we actually conducted the interviews.
Student 2:	Oh, right. So we'll get her approval and then conduct the interviews. I think a Saturday would be the best day for the interviews, because everyone's out shopping then.
Student 1:	Right. We'll do it on a Saturday, then.
Student 2:	And let's also plan to get together the next day to analyze the results. It's best to do that while everything's fresh in our minds. Don't you think?
Student 2:	Sure. That sounds like a good idea. OK, so then we're going to have to present our results to the class. Do you have any ideas for that? It's an important part of our grade, so I think we should plan it well.
Student 1:	Well, I think the obvious thing is to prepare some charts showing our results and how they compare with the government study. That will help make the information a lot clearer to the class.
Student 2:	Right. OK, so we'll draw up some charts of the results.
Student 1:	And then that's it. All that will be left to do is give the class presentation. Do you think we can be ready on time?
Student 2:	I sure hope so. Let's get started now.

Narrator:	That is the end of Section 3. You now have half a minute to check your answers.
	Now turn to Section 4 [on page 102].

Track 13

Section 4. You will hear a professor give a lecture on Louisa May Alcott. First, you have some time to look at the questions 31 to 40 [on page 102].

Now listen carefully and complete the timeline in Questions 31 to 40.

Questions 31 to 40

Lecturer:	Good afternoon. Today, I'd like to continue our discussion of the lives of prominent American writers by talking about Louisa May Alcott, one of the best-known nineteenth-century writers. Alcott is known for her moralistic girl's novels, but she was a much more serious individual than those novels might lead one to believe. She was born in 1832, the daughter of Bronson Alcott, who was one of the founders of the Transcendentalist Movement. Bronson Alcott was a philosopher but not a provider, and the family lived close to poverty. From an early age, Louisa was determined to find a way to improve her family's economic situation. As a teenager, she worked to support her family by taking on a variety of low-paying jobs, including teacher, seamstress, and household servant. Alcott also started writing when she was young. She wrote her first novel when she was just seventeen years old; although, it wasn't published until many years after her death. It was called *The Inheritance*.
	In 1861, the Civil War broke out. Alcott worked as a volunteer, sewing uniforms and bandages for soldiers. The following year, she enlisted as an army nurse. She spent the war years in Washington, nursing wounded soldiers at a military hospital. While working at the hospital, she wrote many letters to her family at home in Massachusetts. After the war, she turned the letters into a book, which was published under the title *Hospital Sketches*. She also wrote numerous romantic stories, which she sold to magazines.
	Around this same time, she was offered the opportunity to travel to Europe as the companion to an invalid. When she returned home from Europe in 1866, she found her family still in financial difficulty and in need of money, so she went back to writing. Her big break came in 1868 with the publication of her first novel for girls, *Little Women*. The novel achieved instant success, and the public wanted more. From then on, Alcott supported herself and her family by writing novels for girls. It wasn't the writing she had dreamed of doing, but it earned her a good income.
	Alcott took care of her family for the rest of her life. In 1878, her youngest sister, May, got married. A year later, May died after giving birth to a daughter. Louisa Alcott raised her sister's orphaned child. In 1882, Bronson Alcott suffered a stroke. Soon after that, Louisa Alcott set up a house for him, her

niece, her sister Anna, and Anna's two sons in Boston. Her mother was no longer living by this time. Alcott was still writing novels for girls, including two sequels to *Little Women*: *Little Men* and *Jo's Boys*. The latter was published in 1886.

Louisa Alcott had suffered poor health ever since she contracted typhoid fever while working as a war nurse. She died in March of 1888 at the age of 55. She was buried in Concord, Massachusetts.

Narrator: That is the end of Section 4. You now have half a minute to check your answers.

You will now have ten minutes to transfer your answers to the listening answer sheet.

PRACTICE TEST 4

Narrator:

You will hear a number of different recordings, and you will have to answer questions on what you will hear. There will be time for you to read the instructions and questions, and you will have a chance to check your work. All the recordings will be played once only.

The test is in four sections. Write all of your answers on the test pages. At the end of the test you will be given ten minutes to transfer your answers to an answer sheet.

Now turn to Section 1 [on page 138].

Section 1. You will hear a man arranging to get a telephone connection. First you have some time to look at Questions 1 to 4 [on page 138].

You will see that there is an example that has been done for you. On this occasion only, the conversation relating to this will be played first.

Example

Woman: This is the ClearPoint Telephone Company customer service office. My name is Ms. Jones. How may I help you?

Man: Yes. I'm moving, and I'd like to arrange to have a phone line installed.

Narrator: The woman answers the phone, "This is the ClearPoint Telephone Company customer service office," so the words "Telephone Company" have been written at the top of the form. Now we shall begin. You should answer the questions as you listen, because you will not hear the recording a second time. Listen carefully and answer Questions 1 to 4.

Questions 1 to 4

Woman: This is the ClearPoint Telephone Company customer service office. My name is Ms. Jones. How may I help you?

Man: Yes. I'm moving, and I'd like to arrange to have a phone line installed.

Woman:	Of course. Let me get some information from you first. May I have your name, please?
Man:	It's Kramer. Harold Kramer.
Woman:	And would you spell your last name for me, please?
Man:	K-R-A-M-E-R.
Woman:	M-E-R. Got it. OK, could I have the address where you'd like to have the telephone connected?
Man:	That would be number 58 Fulton Avenue, apartment 12.
Woman:	Is that a business or a residence?
Man:	A residence. It's my new home address.
Woman:	Then the type of phone service you want is residential, not business?
Man:	Yes, yes. It's for my home.
Woman:	All right. Fine. Now let me get your employment information. Who is your current employer?
Man:	I work at the Wrightsville Medical Group.
Woman:	Then your occupation is doctor?
Man:	No, I work for the doctors. I'm the office manager.
Narrator:	Before you hear the rest of the conversation, you have some time to look at Questions 5 to 10 [on page 138].
	Now listen and answer Questions 5 to 10.

Questions 5 to 10

Woman:	OK. And could I have your work phone number?
Man:	It's 637-555-9014.
Woman:	9014. Great. Just one more thing, I need to know how long you've been at your current job.
Man:	I've been working there for quite a while now, let me see, eight, no, nine, that's right, nine years.
Woman:	OK, good. You've been there long enough, so I don't need to ask about any other work history. Now, in addition to our basic phone service, we have several special services available.
Man:	Could you explain them to me?
Woman:	Most customers opt for unlimited long-distance service. It really saves you money if you make a lot of long-distance calls.
Man:	That sounds like a good idea.
Woman:	Then I'll put you down for long-distance service. Another popular service is voicemail. Voicemail takes all your messages electronically, and all it takes is one simple phone call to retrieve them.
Man:	Hmmm, voicemail. No, I don't think so. I have an answering machine to take my messages. It's old, but it still works fine.
Woman:	We also provide Internet service if you're interested in that.
Man:	I am. Please put me down for Internet as well as phone service.
Woman:	Right. OK, I think we're almost finished. I just need to schedule a time for the technician to go to your apartment and do the installation. Let me see . . . . What about next Tuesday? Would that work for you?

Man:	No, not Tuesday. I'll be at a conference all day. Wednesday would work, though.
Woman:	I'm afraid I won't have any technicians in your area on Wednesday. I could send someone on Friday.
Man:	That would be fine.
Woman:	What time of day works best for you? Morning or afternoon?
Man:	Morning would be best.
Woman:	All right then. It's on the schedule. Do you have any questions?
Man:	No, I don't think so.
Woman:	Thank you for calling ClearPoint.
Narrator:	That is the end of Section 1. You now have half a minute to check your answers.
	Now turn to Section 2 [on page 139].
Track 15	Section 2. You will hear a radio interview about an upcoming fair.
	First, you have some time to look at Questions 11 to 14 [on page 139].
	As you listen to the first part of the talk, answer Questions 11 to 14.

Questions 11 to 14

Man:	Good afternoon, and welcome to City Hour, the radio show that brings you all the latest information about events in and around our city. Today we have with us Cynthia Smith, who is heading up this year's City Fair. Cynthia, would you start by giving us some of the basic information about the fair? Where will it take place this year?
Woman:	I'm glad you asked that question, because I know most people will be expecting the fair to be at the fairgrounds as usual, but we've had to change the location this year due to some construction work. You know, they're building the new high school in that neighborhood, and they've been using the fairgrounds as a place to store construction materials. So we've moved the fair to City Park, which I think is a wonderful location.
Man:	Yes, that will be a great place for the fair. I understand that the fair begins on Friday morning with a special opening event.
Woman:	Actually, it won't begin until that evening, but you're right about the special event. Traditionally, we've begun with a parade, but this year our opening event will be a special dance performance, and the most exciting part is that the mayor will be one of the dancers.
Man:	The mayor is a woman of many talents. Cynthia, could you tell our listeners about the price of admission? What will it cost to attend the fair?
Woman:	We're trying to keep the price down as much as possible. A three-day pass is just $25. Or you can buy a Saturday- or Sunday-only pass for $15. The opening event on Friday, the dance performance, doesn't cost anything to attend, and we're hoping a lot of people will come watch that.

Narrator:	Before you hear the rest of the talk, you have some time to look at Questions 15 to 20 [on page 139].
	Now listen and answer Questions 15 to 20.

Questions 15 to 20

Man:	Could you tell us about some of the events planned for Saturday and Sunday, the main days of the fair?
Woman:	We have a lot of exciting things planned. There are a number of events especially for children, including a clown show on Saturday afternoon. On Saturday evening, we've got an event that can be enjoyed by the whole family—a concert by the lake.
Man:	I'm sure that will be a popular event. Is there anything special planned for Sunday?
Woman:	Yes, a really fun event, and we hope a lot of people will participate. There will be a singing contest in the afternoon. It's open to everyone, at no charge. It doesn't matter whether you're an experienced singer or not. If you've always dreamed of singing on stage, this is your chance.
Man:	That sounds like a lot of fun.
Woman:	I think it will be. I'd also like your listeners to know that besides the special events I've mentioned, there will be things taking place all weekend. For example, at the food court, international food will be served. You'll be able to sample dishes from all around the world. There will also be special games for children at different locations around the fair.
Man:	Will there be things people can buy, souvenirs, anything like that?
Woman:	We have a large area set aside where there will be crafts for sale. This will be an opportunity to buy many lovely handmade things, and to get to know some of our local artists and craftspeople, as well.
Man:	It sounds like there will be a lot of fun for everyone at this year's fair. Thank you for sharing the information with us, Cynthia.
Woman:	Thank you for inviting me.
Narrator:	That is the end of Section 2. You now have half a minute to check your answers.
	Now turn to Section 3 [on page 140].
(Track 16)	Section 3. You will hear a conversation between a prospective student and a university advisor about applying to enter the university.
	First, you have some time to look at Questions 21 to 23 [on page 140].
	As you listen to the first part of the conversation, answer Questions 21 to 23.

Questions 21 to 23

Student:	I'm interested in entering your Business Administration program, and I'd like some information on how to apply. I'm a little concerned because I've been out of school for a number of years.

Advisor:	That could actually work to your advantage. It's possible to get academic credit for work experience, if that experience is related to courses in our program.
Student:	I've been working in business for several years. How would I get academic credit for that?
Advisor:	First, you'll need to read the university catalog to see if any of the course descriptions match your specific job experience. For example, if you've worked in accounting, you may be able to get credit for an accounting course.
Student:	So then what would I do?
Advisor:	You would write a summary of your work experience, relating it to specific courses we offer. Submit that to the Admissions Office with a letter from your work supervisor confirming your experience.
Narrator:	Before you hear the rest of the conversation, you have some time to look at Questions 24 to 30 [on pages 140 and 141]. Now listen and answer Questions 24 to 30.

Questions 24 to 30

Student:	Would I submit those things at the same time that I apply for admission?
Advisor:	That would be the best idea. Have you looked at our course catalog yet?
Student:	No, not yet. I guess I should do that soon.
Advisor:	Just go to the university website and you'll find it there.
Student:	OK. Can you tell me how the admissions process works?
Advisor:	Well, first you'll need to fill out an admissions form and submit it. That's on the website, as well. Of course, you'll need to make sure you meet all the admissions requirements.
Student:	How can I know what those are?
Advisor:	The best way to understand them is to come to a special session we're having for prospective students next Wednesday evening. We'll explain the process then and go over the requirements and answer any questions you may have.
Student:	That sounds great. I'd like to attend.
Advisor:	Good. It's at 7:00. Just go to the meeting room in the basement of the library. You know where that is, right?
Student:	Next to the Student Services Center?
Advisor:	Yes, that's it. It'll be a really informative session because it'll also give you a chance to meet several of the professors and get more information about them. By the way, did you come by car today?
Student:	No, bus. But I'll probably drive on Wednesday.
Advisor:	You'll need to get a parking pass, then.
Student:	How do I do that? Can I download one from the website?
Advisor:	No, you have to get it in person from the Student Services Center. Just tell them you're here for the meeting at the library. Now, do you think you'd be interested in applying for a part-time job through the university work-study program?

Student:	I'm considering that. How can I find out what kinds of jobs are offered?
Advisor:	You can access the job listings from the computers in the library. Are you planning to study full time or part time?
Student:	I want to be a full-time student.
Advisor:	Good. Then you'll qualify for the work-study program. Part-time students aren't eligible.
Student:	As a full-time student, would I be eligible for a free bus pass?
Advisor:	No, unfortunately, we don't have those available for any of our students. However, you can apply for financial assistance to help pay for your books or for your tuition.
Student:	I'd like to look into that. Do I apply for that at the Admissions Office?
Advisor:	No, that's through us. You'll need to make an appointment with a counselor.
Narrator:	That is the end of Section 3. You now have half a minute to check your answers.
	Now turn to Section 4 [on page 141].
	Section 4. You will hear a lecture about the black bear.
	First, you have some time to look at Questions 31 to 35 [on page 141].
	Now listen carefully and answer Questions 31 to 35.

Questions 31 to 35

Lecturer:	The black bear, or *Ursus americanus*, has a wide range, inhabiting forested areas of North America, including Canada, the United States, and parts of northern Mexico. Black bears are omnivores, getting their nutrition from a wide variety of plants and animals. The particular foods any one bear eats depends on what's available in the area where that bear lives, as well as on the season of the year. Generally speaking, plant foods make up 90 percent of the bear's diet. The rest of its meals consist of animal foods such as insects and fish.
	Bears have a relatively long gestation period. Mating takes place in the spring or early summer, but bear cubs aren't born until the following winter. Usually, two cubs are born at a time, although some litters may have as many as five cubs. Bear cubs are dependent on their mother and may stay with her for close to two years. Wild black bears can live as long as 25 years. They've lived for as long as 30 years or more in captivity.
Narrator:	Before you hear the rest of the talk, you have some time to look at Questions 36 to 40 [on page 142].
	Now listen carefully and answer Questions 36 to 40.

Questions 36 to 40

Lecturer:	Much of the black bear's range coincides with the range of its close cousin, the grizzly bear. Although these bears are somewhat similar in appearance and habits, it isn't difficult to tell the difference between them. Color isn't necessarily a distinguishing characteristic, as both species of bears occur in a range of colors from almost blonde to dark brown or black. Many black bears, however, have a patch of fur on their chests that's lighter in color than the rest of their fur. Grizzly bears don't have this patch. Size isn't always a distinguishing feature either, although grizzly bears are usually heavier, with an average weight of 225 kilos. Black bears average 140 kilos in weight. Grizzly bears spend time digging in the ground for roots and tubers that make up part of their diet. The large muscles they need for this give them a distinct shoulder hump. This hump is absent in black bears, which don't do the same kind of digging. The shape of the face and ears is also different in each species of bear. Grizzly bears have a depression between the eyes and nose and short, round ears. Black bears, on the other hand, have a straighter profile and longer, more pointed ears. Grizzly bears are known for their fearsome long, sharp claws. Black bears have shorter claws, which are better suited for climbing trees.
Narrator:	That is the end of Section 4. You now have half a minute to check your answers.
	You will now have ten minutes to transfer your answers to the listening answer sheet.

PRACTICE TEST 5

Narrator:	You will hear a number of different recordings, and you will have to answer questions on what you will hear. There will be time for you to read the instructions and questions, and you will have a chance to check your work. All the recordings will be played once only.
	The test is in four sections. Write all of your answers on the test pages. At the end of the test you will be given ten minutes to transfer your answers to an answer sheet.
	Now turn to Section 1 [on page 180].
	Section 1. You will hear a woman booking a bicycle tour over the phone.
	First, you have some time to look at Questions 1 to 4 [on page 180].
	You will see that there is an example that has been done for you. On this occasion only, the conversation relating to this will be played first.

Example

Man:	Global Bicycle Tours. May I help you?
Woman:	Yes, thank you. I'd like to sign up for a bicycle tour.

The man answers the phone, "Global Bicycle Tours," so the word "Global" has been written at the top of the form. Now we shall begin. You should answer the questions as you listen, because you will not hear the recording a second time. Listen carefully and answer Questions 1 to 4.

Questions 1 to 4

Man:	Global Bicycle Tours. May I help you?
Woman:	Yes, thank you. I'd like to sign up for a bicycle tour.
Man:	Which tour were you interested in? We have the River Valley tour coming up in June and the Mountain tour in July.
Woman:	The River Valley tour is in June? I thought it was in May.
Man:	It actually takes place the first week of June.
Woman:	Oh, I see. Well, I can still do that. The River Valley tour is the one I want.
Man:	Splendid. Just let me take your information. May I have your name please?
Woman:	Karla Schmidt. That's Karla with a K, not a C. K-A-R-L-A.
Man:	Thank you, Ms. Schmidt. Address?
Woman:	Do you need a street address, or can I give you my post office box?
Man:	A post office box is fine.
Woman:	It's P. O. Box 257 [two-five-seven], Manchester.
Man:	Thank you. OK, next. Will you be bringing your own bicycle, or do you want to rent one from us?
Woman:	I'll bring my own.
Man:	Excellent. Now, we provide all the meals, so we need to know if you have any dietary restrictions.
Woman:	I don't think so. What do you mean?
Man:	I mean if there's any food you can't eat. Some people have food allergies or are vegetarian or have to avoid dairy products, things like that.
Woman:	Oh, I see. Well, yes, I'm a vegetarian. I never eat meat.
Narrator:	Before you hear the rest of the conversation, you have some time to look at Questions 5 to 10 [on pages 180 and 181].
	Now listen and answer Questions 5 to 10.

Questions 5 to 10

Man:	All right. I'll make a note of that. Now, the total cost of the tour is $750.
Woman:	That much!
Man:	The price includes everything—food, hotel, transportation, everything.
Woman:	Everything?
Man:	Yes, everything. The only other thing is you'll want to tip the tour guide. We usually recommend five percent of the total tour cost.
Woman:	A five-percent tip. I guess that's reasonable.
Man:	In order to reserve your space on the tour I'll need a 30 percent deposit.
Woman:	Do you need that right away?
Man:	We generally ask for the deposit at least four weeks before the tour begins. The River Valley tour begins, let me see, six weeks from now. So you'll need to pay the deposit in two weeks.

Woman:	I think I can do that. I wonder if you could tell me something. How will our luggage be transported? Do we carry it on our bicycles?
Man:	No, you leave that to us. We have a van that carries your luggage from hotel to hotel each day, so you don't have to worry about it.
Woman:	Great! I have a luggage rack for my bike, but I guess I won't have to bring that.
Man:	No, you won't. But there are a few items we recommend that you bring. We can't control the weather, so you should bring a raincoat or rain gear.
Woman:	Yes, that's a good idea. And I should have my own spare tire, too, shouldn't I?
Man:	Actually, you don't need that, as our guide always carries some. And, of course, you won't need maps either, since our guide has the route all planned.
Woman:	What about a water bottle? I'll need that, won't I?
Man:	Yes, you should definitely have a water bottle. A camera would be a good idea, too, since that tour goes through some very scenic areas.
Woman:	I have a guide book of that area. I wonder if I should bring it along.
Man:	We don't recommend guide books. It would just be extra weight, and the tour guide knows a great deal about the area.
Woman:	Yes, I see. Is there anything else I need to know?
Man:	I think we've covered the important points. I'll send you a tour brochure, and you can call again if you have any questions.
Woman:	Thank you very much.
Narrator:	That is the end of Section 1. You now have half a minute to check your answers. Now turn to Section 2 [on page 181]. Section 2. You will hear a tour of a newly renovated health club. First, you have some time to look at Questions 11 to 15 [on page 181]. As you listen to the first part of the talk, answer Questions 11 to 15.

Questions 11 to 15

Guide:	Thank you all for coming to see the new renovations to the Hartford Health Club. I know you'll be as pleased as I am to see the wonderful results of our months of hard work to improve the club and bring you the best facilities ever. We'll begin in here with the swimming pool. You'll notice the new color of the adult pool, a lovely, cool green. Now walk over here and look at the children's pool. It's the same green but, as you see, with brightly colored sea creatures painted everywhere. Both of the pools needed painting, not only for maintenance, but I think the new color greatly improves the atmosphere of this part of the club. Next, let's take a look at the locker rooms. Don't worry, there's no one using them just now. Doesn't it feel roomy in here? We've expanded both the men's and women's locker rooms, so now they'll be much more comfortable to use. There are bigger lockers, a good deal more room in the dressing area, and more places to store extra towels and equipment. Be careful as you walk through here. The floor has just been polished and may be a bit slippery.

Let's go up to the exercise room next. Here you'll notice the new floor. Walk on it. Doesn't that feel comfortable? It's a special material, softer than the old floor, an ideal surface for jogging and exercising. They had to move all the exercise equipment out while they were working on the floor, but don't worry, it will be brought back in before the end of today. Let's step outside now and look at the tennis courts. We haven't done a great deal here except to the equipment. We replaced all the nets and the ball-throwing machine. Otherwise, everything is the same as it was before. Let's walk down this hallway, and here we are at the club store in its new location. We thought here by the entrance was a better place for it than where it used to be by the swimming pool. But it still has all the same items for sale: sports equipment and clothes in the club colors.

Narrator: Before you hear the rest of the talk, you have some time to look at Questions 16 to 20 [on page 182].

Now listen and answer Questions 16 to 20.

Questions 16 to 20

Guide: We're excited about the upcoming activities and events to take place in our newly renovated club. Now that the pools are ready for use again, swimming lessons will begin tomorrow, for both adults and children. If you haven't signed up yet, you can stop by the office before you leave today and put your name on the list. If you're a tennis player, you'll be interested to hear about the tennis competition coming up on Wednesday. Players from different clubs all over the region will be participating. If you'd like to watch the event, tickets are available in the office.

Also, I want to be sure you all know you're invited to our club party, coming up next weekend. We're celebrating the completion of the renovation work, and we have a lot to celebrate. The entire renovation project was finished in just nine months. That's three months less than the twelve months we had originally planned on. We're proud of that and proud that we came in under budget, too. Because we've had such good results with this project, we're already planning the next one. We already have two indoor pools, and next year we plan to install an outdoor pool right next to the tennis courts. Details of these plans will be made available to all club members soon.

All right, I think we've covered just about everything. Are there any questions?

Narrator: That is the end of Section 2. You now have half a minute to check your answers.

Now turn to Section 3 [on page 182].

Section 3. You will hear a museum director talking to several student interns, explaining their internship duties at the museum.

First, you have some time to look at Questions 21 to 25 [on page 182].

As you listen to the first part of the conversation, answer Questions 21 to 25.

Questions 21 to 25

Dr. Johnson:	Welcome to the City Museum of Art. I'm Dr. Shirley Johnson, the director of the museum's internship program. Today I'll be giving you an orientation to the museum and our museum administrator's internship program.
Student 1:	Will we get a chance to tour the museum today?
Dr. Johnson:	Yes. We'll start right now with a tour of the building. We'll skip the basement. Most of that part of the building is devoted to art conservation, which won't be part of your internship. Let's begin here on the ground floor with the museum offices.
Student 2:	I guess this is where we'll be spending most of our time, helping with the office work.
Dr. Johnson:	You'll spend some time working in here so you can learn what the administrative duties involve, but you'll also get a chance to experience all aspects of museum work. This room in here is the Museum Tours Office.
Student 3:	I'm interested in that. I'd really like to help out with the tours.
Dr. Johnson:	That's great because you'll all have a chance to lead some tours and maybe even to develop a tour of your own, too. Let's go up to the second floor now.
Student 1:	This is the board room in here, isn't it? Will we get to go to board meetings?
Dr. Johnson.	Only members of the Board of Directors attend those. Now, back here behind the galleries are the classrooms. You're all welcome to attend any class you want at no charge.
Student 2:	But we won't be teaching any, will we?
Dr. Johnson:	No, the staff of the Education Department is responsible for that. Let's move up to the third floor now and the Research Department. Each of you will spend some time working in here.
Student 3:	Great. I'd like to help with the research.
Dr. Johnson:	We're working on some very interesting research projects right now. Also, as an extension of your research work, you'll probably contribute to some of the museum's brochures.
Student 1:	I'm looking forward to that. I like writing about art. Another thing I've been hoping to be able to do is meet some artists.
Dr. Johnson:	You're in luck, then. We've planned a reception for the first day of your internship, and you'll have the chance to meet several local artists then.
Narrator:	Before you hear the rest of the conversation, you have some time to look at Questions 26 to 30 [on page 183]. Now listen and answer Questions 26 to 30.

Questions 26 to 30

Student 2:	Could you give us a little background of the museum? I mean, when it was built and some information about the collections and things like that?

Dr. Johnson:	Of course. The main part of the museum was built in 1895, with a combination of public and private funds. The new wing was built 60 years later, with a donation from the Rhinebeck family.
Student 3:	That part of the museum was built for the modern art collection, wasn't it?
Dr. Johnson:	Yes, it was. In the main part of the museum, we have a gallery devoted to works by local artists, our sculpture collection, and a small collection of classical European art.
Student 1:	You mentioned classes earlier. What kinds of classes does the museum offer?
Dr. Johnson:	In our Adult Education program, we offer a series of art history classes, and for children we have a program of arts and crafts workshops. You can get a brochure from the office that will give you more information.
Student 2:	I saw a lot of chairs set up in the main hall. What are those for?
Dr. Johnson:	Those are there for tonight's musical performance. We offer a weekly concert series during the fall and winter, and, of course, all of you are welcome to attend. Now, if there are no more questions, let's step into my office and I'll show you your schedules.
Narrator:	That is the end of Section 3. You now have half a minute to check your answers.
	Now turn to Section 4 [on page 183].
Track 21	Section 4. You will hear a lecture about the history of the tomato.
	First, you have some time to look at Questions 31 to 35 [on pages 183 and 184].
	Now listen carefully and answer Questions 31 to 35.

Questions 31 to 35

Lecturer:	The tomato is a popular vegetable, which figures in the cuisine of many countries around the world. It is particularly prominent in Italian cooking, but it was unknown in Europe until Spanish explorers brought it back from the Americas. The tomato originated in the highlands of Peru. From there, it eventually found its way to Mexico, where it was cultivated by the Aztecs. The Aztec tomato wasn't the large red vegetable we know today. Rather, it was small and yellow. When this small, round fruit arrived in Italy, it was named "golden apple" for its bright yellow color. You'll notice I just called it a fruit. That's because a tomato is botanically a fruit, even though most everyone calls it a vegetable. The actual word *tomato* comes from the Aztec name for the vegetable, meaning "plump thing."
	The tomato arrived in Europe in the 1500s and quickly became a popular food in Spain and Italy. In the late 1600s, the Italians began publishing recipes that used tomatoes. The British, however, had a different attitude toward the vegetable. It was grown as an ornamental plant in Britain in the 1600s, but it wasn't eaten because it was thought to be poisonous. It wasn't until the 1700s that tomatoes became part of the daily diet in Britain.

Narrator:	Before you hear the rest of the talk, you have some time to look at Questions 36 to 40 [on page 184].
	Now listen carefully and answer Questions 36 to 40.

Questions 36 to 40

Lecturer:	In the United States, tomatoes were also used as ornamental plants rather than as food for a long time. This attitude began to change in the 1800s. In 1806, a gardener's calendar mentioned that tomatoes could be used to improve the flavor of soups and other foods. Thomas Jefferson did much to enhance the tomato's reputation as a food. He first served tomatoes to visitors at his home in Virginia in 1809. Then, in 1820, a man named Robert Gibbon Johnson decided it was time to discard, once and for all, the idea that tomatoes were poisonous. To prove his point, he ate one kilo of ripe red tomatoes in public. Two thousand people gathered to watch this feat, which took place on the steps of the court house in Salem, Massachusetts. Amazingly enough, Johnson survived this stunt! The popularity of the tomato as a food began growing rapidly. Soon, people all around the country were eating tomatoes. By the 1830s, American newspapers and magazines were publishing thousands of tomato recipes. However, all those recipes involved using tomatoes in some cooked form. Tomato salads and sandwiches were still unknown. It wasn't until a century later, in the 1930s, that it became popular for people to eat raw tomatoes.
Narrator:	That is the end of Section 4. You now have half a minute to check your answers.
	You will now have ten minutes to transfer your answers to the listening answer sheet.

PRACTICE TEST 6

Narrator:	You will hear a number of different recordings, and you will have to answer questions on what you will hear. There will be time for you to read the instructions and questions, and you will have a chance to check your work. All the recordings will be played once only.
	The test is in four sections. Write all of your answers on the test pages. At the end of the test, you will be given ten minutes to transfer your answers to an answer sheet.
	Now turn to Section 1 [on page 220].
	Section 1. You will hear a woman and a man talking about their work at a library.
	First you have some time to look at Questions 1 to 5 [on page 220].
	You will see that there is an example that has been done for you. On this occasion only, the conversation relating to this will be played first.

Example

Woman:	Hello. I'm Mrs. Phillips, the head librarian. You're the new library assistant, aren't you?
Man:	Yes, I'm Robert Haskell, but please call me Bob.
Narrator:	The woman introduces herself as the head librarian, Mrs. Phillips, so the name "Mrs. Phillips" has been written in. Now we shall begin. You should answer the questions as you listen, because you will not hear the recording a second time. Listen carefully and answer Questions 1 to 5.

Questions 1 to 5

Woman:	Hello. I'm Mrs. Phillips, the head librarian. You're the new library assistant, aren't you?
Man:	Yes, I'm Robert Haskell, but please call me Bob.
Woman:	All right, Bob. Let me take a few minutes to explain how the library works and what your duties will be. First, the library opens at 8:30 in the morning, so, naturally, we expect you to be here and ready to work by then.
Man:	Of course.
Woman:	And you can go home at 4:30 when the library closes. Now, let me explain where everything's kept.
Man:	It looks like here on the ground floor is where the reference books are.
Woman:	Yes, that's right. Up on the second floor is where the Adult Collection is, both fiction and nonfiction.
Man:	And the children's books are there, too, aren't they? I thought I saw them in the room by the stairway.
Woman:	No, those are magazines and newspapers for adults. Children's books are up one more flight on the third floor. We'll take a look at them later. Let me show you how we organize our work. Do you see that brown book cart over there?
Man:	The one by the door?
Woman:	Yes, that one. Those books have been checked in and need to go back on the shelves.
Man:	OK, so the brown book cart has books to re-shelve. What about this black cart by the desk?
Woman:	Those books have torn pages or damaged covers. They're all books that need to be repaired.
Man:	OK, I know how to do a lot of that. I'm pretty good at mending torn pages and covers.
Woman:	That's great because we really need help with that.
Man:	And that white cart in the corner? What are those books for?
Woman:	Those are old books that we've taken off the shelves to make room for new ones. We sell them as used books to raise money for the library.
Man:	So they're all ready to sell?
Woman:	Yes, that's right. So, now you know what to do with the books in the carts. Lets talk about our activities schedule.

Before you hear the rest of the conversation, you have some time to look at Questions 6 to 10 [on page 220].

Now listen and answer Questions 6 to 10.

Questions 6 to 10

Man: I understand this library has a number of interesting activities every week.

Woman: Yes, our activities are quite popular. The most popular one is Story Time for the children.

Man: Do a lot of children show up for that?

Woman: Yes, a good many. It takes place in the Children's Room on Thursday mornings at eleven.

Man: Isn't there a family movie night, too?

Woman: Yes, but it's not at night anymore. We used to have Family Movies on Fridays when the library is open until nine, but now we have a different activity at that time, so we had to switch Family Movies to the weekend—Saturday afternoon.

Man: How much do you charge for the movies?

Woman: They're all free. The movie always starts at 2:30 in the Reference Room. But you don't have to worry about that since you don't work on weekends.

Man: And what takes place on Friday evenings?

Woman: We've just started a weekly Lecture Series. We have a different speaker every week, and the lectures cover all different kinds of topics.

Man: That sounds like something I'd be interested in attending.

Woman: Good, because we'll need your help with that. You'll be working Friday evenings, and one of your duties will be to set up the Meeting Room on the first floor for the lecture.

Man: What time will you need that done?

Woman: Let's say by 6:15. The lecture starts at 6:30, and the room needs to be ready well ahead of time. A lot of people arrive early.

Man: Maybe I should have the room ready by six?

Woman: That wouldn't be a bad idea. OK, why don't I take you upstairs and show you the rest of the collection . . . (voice fades out.)

Narrator: That is the end of Section 1. You now have half a minute to check your answers.

Now turn to Section 2 [on page 221].

(Track 23)

Section 2. You will hear a radio interview about a lakeside resort.

First, you have some time to look at Questions 11 to 15 [on page 221].

As you listen to the first part of the talk, answer Questions 11 to 15.

Questions 11 to 15

Woman: Good afternoon, and welcome to today's show. The warm months are with us, and many of you are getting ready to plan vacation trips. To help you with that, we have a special guest today, Robert Sampson, director of the Golden Lake Resort. Robert, I understand Golden Lake is a popular place for families to spend their vacations.

Man: Yes, families enjoy spending time at Golden Lake. Many come back year after year. We have a spectacular location and fun activities for both children and adults.

Woman: Could you describe for us some of the activities available at Golden Lake?

Man: We have a lot of water activities, of course, since we're right on the lake. We have a pleasant sandy beach for swimming. We also have canoes and sailboats available, and many of our guests enjoy boating on the lake.

Woman: I imagine water skiing would be popular among your guests.

Man: Actually, we don't permit waterskiing in the resort area. It can be dangerous for swimmers and for the canoeists, too. We do have a great location for fishing, though, and you'll often see guests fishing from our dock or from the canoes.

Woman: That sounds very relaxing. What about activities on land? Do you have facilities for tennis?

Man: We had tennis in the past, but the courts fell out of repair and since we found that most of our guests weren't interested in the game, we closed the courts down. So that's no longer an option. And, naturally, because of our location in the woods, we don't have an adequate area for a golf course. But I'd like to let your listeners know that we'll be adding a new activity this year. We've made an arrangement with a local stable, so now we're going to have horseback riding available for our guests. We've created several riding trails around the lake.

Woman: That sounds lovely. Now, what about rainy days? What can your guests do when the weather's bad?

Man: We have a games room and a crafts room. When the weather's rainy, some of our very talented staff members offer arts and crafts classes, for all ages.

Woman: What fun. Do you offer any other classes or activities?

Narrator: Before you hear the rest of the talk, you have some time to look at Questions 16 to 20 [on page 221].

Now listen and answer Questions 16 to 20.

Questions 16 to 20

Man: We have a weekly schedule of evening activities, which anyone can attend if they choose. Every Sunday we show a film, always something that's suitable for the whole family. Monday's my favorite night because that's dessert night. Our cook prepares a variety of desserts, and we get to taste them all.

Woman: Mmmmm. I'd like to be there for that.

Man: Yes, it's great. We get more serious toward the middle of the week. Our discussion night is on Tuesday.

Woman: Discussion night?

Man:	Yes, we discuss different current events, depending on what's happening that week in the news. Then on Wednesdays we have lectures. We invite different experts to talk about local history or nature topics. This is actually one of our most popular evening activities. We've found that our guests are really interested in learning about the local area.
Woman:	It sounds quite interesting.
Man:	Yes, we've had some excellent speakers. Thursday nights are totally different because that's when we play games. That's especially fun for the children. The children love Fridays, too, because that's talent show night. Everyone gets in on that, staff, guests, everyone.
Woman:	It looks like you have a lot of fun at Golden Lake Resort.
Man:	We do. And we end every week with big fun, with a dance on Saturday night.
Woman:	Now I understand a little more why Golden Lake is such a popular place for family vacations. With such a variety of activities, there's something for every member of the family there.
Man:	There is, and I hope your listeners will consider spending their next vacation with us.
Narrator:	That is the end of Section 2. You now have half a minute to check your answers.
Track 24	Now turn to Section 3 [on page 222].
Narrator:	Section 3. You will hear two students talking about a class assignment about wild bird rescue and rehabilitation.
	First, you have some time to look at Questions 21 to 25 [on page 222].
	As you listen to the first part of the conversation, answer Questions 21 to 25.

Questions 21 to 25

Student 1:	OK, let's go over the requirements and see what we have left to do.
Student 2:	Well, we've taken lots of notes about our topic, wild bird rescue and rehabilitation. So we'll have to go over those and write up a summary for the professor.
Student 1:	But we only have to hand in the summary, right? The professor didn't say anything about seeing the notes.
Student 2:	Right, but there's the case study, isn't there? We have to do something about that.
Student 1:	I know. We have all the information so it's just a matter of writing it up.
Student 2:	What about charts and graphs? I thought we had to include some.
Student 1:	I don't think so. They aren't really relevant. But we do have to turn in a list of the resources we used.
Student 2:	Naturally. What about videos? I heard some of the other students were doing that.
Student 1:	Well, I guess that must be optional, because I don't see it on the requirements list. OK. We should start planning our class presentation since that counts for half the grade.

Student 2:	We've looked at lots of sources of information, but I think our best source was the interviews we did with the wildlife rehabilitators.
Student 1:	Agreed. That and the journal articles. I think we have enough information from those two sources, for the presentation anyhow. The books we looked at weren't all that helpful.
Student 2:	I wonder if we should try to bring in some live birds for the presentation?
Student 1:	That would be too difficult, don't you think? But we have lots of photos of rehabilitated birds. We can show those.
Narrator:	Before you hear the rest of the conversation, you have some time to look at Questions 26 to 30 [on page 223].

Now listen and answer Questions 26 to 30. |

Questions 26 to 30

Student 2:	Right. OK, I think we should start by talking about how to rescue a bird. Probably first we should help people understand which birds need rescuing.
Student 1:	Yeah, that's really important because a lot of times people see a baby bird that's all alone, or they find a bird sitting on the ground, and they think it needs to be rescued.
Student 2:	And usually those are just baby birds learning to fly, so we should emphasize that people should only attempt to rescue a bird that's clearly injured.
Student 1:	For certain kinds of birds, the rescuer needs to wear protective gloves, because some of those birds have sharp claws and can tear your shirt or, worse, injure your face or some other part of your body.
Student 2:	Yes. that's an important point. OK, next, let's tell people to put the injured bird in a box, a box with good air circulation. We should let them know that a cage isn't necessary and a bag, especially a plastic one, could hurt the bird more.
Student 1:	Another thing we need to say is that the best way to help the bird stay calm is not by petting it or talking to it, but by leaving it completely alone. Then people should take the bird to the bird rescue center as soon as possible.
Student 2:	Right, and we should also point out that when they're driving the bird to the rescue center, it's better not to play music on the radio or talk loudly because those things just stress the bird.
Student 1:	Yes, it's better just to speak quietly while you have the bird in the car. OK, we've got that part covered. Next, we should talk about what happens at the rescue center. . . .
Narrator:	That is the end of Section 3. You now have half a minute to check your answers.

Now turn to Section 4 [on page 223].

Section 4. You will hear a lecture about the Great Barrier Reef.

First, you have some time to look at Questions 31 to 32 [on page 223].

Now listen carefully and answer Questions 31 to 32. |

Track 25

Lecturer:	The Great Barrier Reef, stretching along the east coast of Australia, is the world's largest collection of coral reefs, covering an area of around 300,000 square kilometers. The approximately 3,000 individual reefs that make up the Great Barrier Reef system are composed of over 400 different kinds of coral, the largest variety of corals found anywhere in the world. In addition, around 900 islands, ranging in size from tiny sandy cays to large continental islands covered with vegetation, are scattered throughout the area, particularly at the northern and southern ends.
Narrator:	Before you hear the rest of the talk, you have some time to look at Questions 33 to 40 [on page 224].

Now listen carefully and answer Questions 33 to 40. |

Questions 33 to 40

| Lecturer: | Thousands of species of plants and animals live in the area. Reef habitats make up only about 7 percent of the region's ecosystems. Other types of habitat in the area range from the shallow waters of coastal salt marshes to deep ocean habitat. Plant life in the reef habitat includes 500 different species of seaweed. The islands provide habitat for a wide variety of plant species. Those at the northern end support over 300 plant species, most of which tend to be woody, while the 200 species of plants growing on the islands at the southern end are largely herbaceous.

In addition to the 1,500 species of fish that live in and around the reefs, sea mammals also abound in the area. Among them are whales, certain species of which use the area as a breeding ground. Many types of reptiles can also be found living among and near the reefs, including crocodiles and several species of marine turtles. The former find their home in the saltwater marshes along the coastal areas, while the latter are attracted to sea grass beds. The land as well as the water teems with animal life. At least seven species of frogs, for example, inhabit the reef's islands.

Unfortunately, this wondrous area of the world is threatened by climate change. Rising sea temperatures have led to an effect called coral bleaching, that is, large numbers of corals dying off, especially in the shallower areas of the reef. The Great Barrier Reef Marine Park Authority is attempting to find effective ways to deal with this issue that threatens the reef. One proposed solution involves shading the reef in certain areas to help keep the surrounding water temperatures down. |
|---|---|
| Narrator: | That is the end of Section 4. You now have half a minute to check your answers.

You will now have ten minutes to transfer your answers to the listening answer sheet. |